THE
SHERLOCK
HOLMES
COMPANION

THE
SHERLOCK
HOLMES
COMPANION

AN ELEMENTARY GUIDE

DANIEL SMITH

Aurum
Press

For Rosie and for the Folks

Acknowledgements

I owe thanks to a great many people who have given of their time and expertise during the writing of this book.

Firstly to Melissa Smith, Graham Coster, Natasha Martin, Piers Burnett and Karen Ings at Aurum, my picture researcher Sarah Havelock, and Merlin Cox and Robert Updegraff. I have greatly appreciated the assistance of several people from the wider community of Holmesians, particularly Catherine Cooke at Marylebone Library, Mike Coote (not least for his and his wife's wonderful hospitality!), Mitch Higurashi and Peggy Perdue. Thanks also to David Burke, Caleb Carr, Burt Coules, Philip Franks, Edward Hardwicke, Roger Llewellyn, Douglas Wilmer and Mark Gatiss for their willingness to share their unique insights, and to Richard McCann, Eric Conklin, Nis Jessen, Cherry Liu, Patricia McCracken, Barry Moser, Russell Stutler and George Vanderburgh.

Finally, the biggest thanks to my family, who have provided me with an endless supply of support and encouragement, and to Rosie, who like Irene Adler will always be *the* woman. Alas, despite all this help, any errors in this book remain my sole responsibility.

Picture Credits

Michael Coote: 1, 2, 4, 7, 61, 72, 74, 79, 81, 101, 112, 113 (bottom), 121, 129, 141, 147, 148, 155; **Alamy:** 3, 53, 63, 82, 117, 125, 139, 146, 179, 196–7, 199 (top), 212, 221; **TopFoto:** 8, 16, 24, 53, 89, 106, 166, 180; **Rex Features:** 10, 83, 110, 111, 122, 199 (bottom), 202; **Getty Images:** 12, 18, 21 (bottom), 23, 26, 30 (top), 52, 54, 55, 71, 76, 85, 95, 96, 105, 177, 187; **Westminster Libraries: Sherlock Holmes Collection, Marylebone Library:** 20, 34, 39, 113 (top), 118, 157, 158 (top), 171, 172 (middle and bottom), 184; **The Langham, London:** 21 (top); **Richard McCann:** 22, 51 (all), 50, 51 (left), 91 (courtesy of MC Art), 153 (top), 175; **D. M. Smith:** 15, 23, 29 (top), 30 (bottom), 32, 38 (top right), 40, 43, 45, 56, 62, 67, 73, 77, 80, 104, 119, 120, 124, 127, 130, 136, 140, 144, 152, 154, 158 (bottom), 159, 164, 167, 168 (top row), 170, 172 (top), 173, 178, 185, 189, 194 (bottom), 211, 220; **Punch Cartoon Library:** 27; **Jiangsu People's Publishing House:** 29 (bottom); **Kobal Collection:** 31, 205, 206; **Barry Moser:** 35, 41, 46, 66, 142; **Nis Jessen (www. mr-holmes.com):** 36–7, 57, 222; **Mary Evans Picture Library:** 38 (middle); **Arthur Conan Doyle Collection, Toronto Public Library:** 38 (bottom); **Corbis:** 44, 65, 70, 88, 102, 109, 163, 165, 167, 198, 209, 210, 219; **Roger Llewellyn:** 47; **British Film Institute:** 49, 175, 193 (bottom), 194 (top), 200 (top and bottom); **Russell Stutler:** 50; **Eric L. Conklin USA (www.ericconklin.com):** 58; **The Arthur Conan Doyle Collection Richard Lancelyn Green Bequest, Portsmouth City Council:** 64, 186, 190, 191 (bottom), 193 (top); **Robert Workman:** 69; **John Murray (Publishers):** 75, 145; **Tom Richmond (Richmond Illustration Inc.):** 78; **The Battered Tin Dispatch Box/George McCracken:** 128; **MGM Pictures:** 132–3; **Bantam Books, a division of Random House, Inc,:** 134; **Conway Van Gelder Limited:** 149; **Larry Gosser:** 162, 169; **Tony Davis & Art Meets Matter Ltd:** 168 (bottom left); **Butlers (www.butlers.de):** 168 (bottom right); **Penguin Books:** 183; **The Advertising Archive:** 191 (top); **Hartswood Films:** 207, 208, 213.

CONTENTS

A SOCIAL AND POLITICAL CHRONOLOGY OF 1879-1903

What follows is a selective chronology corresponding to the period from Holmes's first reported professional case – 'The Musgrave Ritual' until he went into official retirement.

1879

11 January
A British-Zulu War begins in South Africa. It ends when British troops defeat Zulu forces at the Battle of Ulundi on 4 July.

26 May
The Treaty of Gandamak sees the Emir of Afghanistan hand significant power to the British.

21 August
Europe's first telephone exchange opens in Paris.

7 October
Germany and Austria-Hungary sign a mutual defence agreement.

21 October
Thomas Edison tests his light bulb.

28 December
The Tay Bridge Rail Disaster kills 75 people.

1880

15 April
Liberal leader William Gladstone replaces the Conservative, Benjamin Disraeli, as British Prime Minister.

6 September
The Oval hosts the first ever Test cricket match in England, against Australia.

2 November
The Republican James Garfield is elected President of the USA.

11 November
The outlaw Ned Kelly is hanged in Melbourne, Australia.

1881

13 March
Czar Alexander II is assassinated in St Petersburg.

23 March
The First Boer War ends after four months with a peace treaty giving Boers self-government in the Transvaal.

18 April
The Natural History Museum opens in London.

19 April
Former Conservative Prime Minister Benjamin Disraeli dies.

14 July
Pat Garrett shoots dead Billy the Kid in Fort Sumner, New Mexico.

19 September
US President James Garfield is assassinated in Washington.

1882

17 January
Aletta Jacobs establishes world's first contraceptive clinic in Amsterdam.

6 May
British Secretary of State for Ireland, Lord Cavendish, is shot dead in Dublin's Phoenix Park by a nationalist organisation.

20 May
Austria-Hungary, Germany and Italy sign the Triple Alliance, promising mutual military support.

6 November
Lillie Langtry makes her debut on the New York stage.

1883

17 March
Karl Marx, co-author of the *Communist Manifesto*, dies in London aged 64.

25 May
The Brooklyn Bridge opens to traffic in New York.

28 August
Krakatoa, a volcano on Java, erupts and claims the lives of over 30,000 people.

1884

24 April
Bismarck, Germany's Chancellor, declares South West Africa as a German possession.

11 July
Cameroon becomes a German colony.

1 August
Belgium's King Leopold declares himself King of the Congo Free State.

1885

26 January
The legendary British General Gordon is killed at Khartoum by the forces of the Mahdi while trying to evacuate the Anglo-Egyptian forces from the Sudan.

30 March
Russian forces crush Afghan troops at Ak Teppe, prompting calls for a settlement between Russia, Afghanistan and Britain.

19 June
The Statue of Liberty arrives in New York from Paris.

November
10,000 British troops head from Lower to Upper Burma to counter French advances in the region. They seize the capital, Mandalay.

28 December
The Indian National Congress is established in Bombay.

1886

8 May
Coca-Cola is put on sale by Dr John Stith Pemberton in Atlanta.

8 June
William Gladstone resigns as Prime Minister over the Irish Question.

3 July
Karl Benz unveils his *Motorwagen*, the world's first commercial automobile, at Mannheim, Germany.

10 July
In London the Royal Niger Company wins a royal charter to colonise Nigeria.

1887

26 May
The Imperial British East Africa Company is given a royal charter to colonise Kenya and Uganda.

22 June
Queen Victoria celebrates her Golden Jubilee

13 November
Hundreds of police and troops clash with thousands of protesters in Trafalgar Square in what becomes known as 'Bloody Sunday'. The protests concerned elements of British rule in Ireland.

December
Sherlock Holmes debuts in *A Study in Scarlet* in *Beeton's Christmas Annual*.

1888

15 June
In Germany Kaiser Wilhelm II takes the throne.

31 August
Mary Ann Nichols becomes the first confirmed victim of Jack the Ripper in London's East End.

8 September
The English Football League is formed.

6 November
Benjamin Harrison, the Republican candidate, wins the US Presidential election.

1889

6 May
The Eiffel Tower opens in Paris.

31 May
The British government passes a Naval Defence Act in response to the growing naval challenge of Russia and France.

22 June
Chancellor Otto von Bismarck passes social welfare legislation in Germany.

19 August
30,000 London dock workers begin a month-long strike.

29 October
The Suez Canal is declared neutral and open to all shipping.

15 November
Brazil becomes a republic after shrugging off Portuguese rule.

1890

18 March
Kaiser Wilhelm demands the resignation of Bismarck.

1 July
Britain and Germany sign an agreement over territorial claims in East Africa. Britain wins Zanzibar and territories north, while Germany takes the southern territory as far as the island of Heligoland.

17 July
Cecil Rhodes becomes Prime Minister of the Cape Colony.

15 November
Charles Parnell, leader of the Irish Home Rule movement, is cited in the divorce case of Kitty O'Shea, precipitating his political downfall.

1891

1 June
Edward, Prince of Wales, is called as a prosecution witness in the Tranby Croft trial concerning a gambling scandal.

31 July
Britain claims control of the region between the Zambezi River and the Congo Basin.

October
The German Social Democratic Party adopts a Marxist manifesto.

1892

15 April
The General Electric Company is founded in the USA.

6 July
In Pittsburgh, USA, detectives from the Pinkerton Agency triumph in a pitched battle with striking steel workers.

18 August
William Gladstone forms his fourth Liberal government in Britain.

8 November
Grover Cleveland, the Democrat candidate, is elected President of the USA.

17 November
France subjects the Dahomey kingdom in West Africa.

1893

13 January
The Independent Labour Party holds its first meeting in Britain.

23 February
Rudolf Diesel registers a patent for the first diesel combustion engine.

10 March
Côte d'Ivoire becomes a French colony.

13 July
The German Army Act paves the way for a significant expansion of the German military.

September
Gladstone sees his Irish Home Rule bill pass through the House of Commons but meets defeat in the House of Lords.

19 September
New Zealand becomes the first country to award women the vote.

1894

3 March
William Gladstone resigns as Britain's Prime Minister after his failure to get his Home Rule bill passed. He is replaced by Lord Rosebery.

24 June
France's President Sadi-Carnot is stabbed to death by an Italian anarchist.

30 June
Tower Bridge opens to traffic in London.

1 August
China and Japan declare war on each other.

1 November
In Russia, Nikolas II becomes czar, following the death of his father, Alexander III.

22 December
Alfred Dreyfus, a Jewish army officer, is sentenced to life imprisonment in France for spying for Germany. His case becomes a notorious miscarriage of justice.

1895

17 April
China and Japan sign a peace treaty at Shimonoskie. China recognises Korea's independence and gives up Formosa (Taiwan) to Japan.

25 May
Oscar Wilde begins a two-year sentence in Reading Gaol for 'sodomy and gross indecency'.

25 June
Lord Salisbury forms a Conservative-Liberal Unionist government.

8 November
Wilhelm Roentgen makes the chance discovery of x-rays.

17 December
A dispute over the British Guiana-Venezuela border threatens British-American relations.

28 December
In Paris, the Lumière Brothers hold the first public movie screening.

1896

1 March
Ethiopian forces under Menelik II rout Italian forces in the province of Tigre.

6 April
The Modern Olympic Games open in Athens, Greece.

15 June
An earthquake in Japan kills over 25,000 people.

6 August
Madagascar becomes a French colony.

12 August
Discovery of gold in a creek off the River Klondike.

26 October
Italy and Ethiopia sign a treaty guaranteeing independence for Ethiopia and awarding Eritrea to Italy.

3 November
The Republican, William McKinley, is elected President of the USA.

1897

14 May
Guglielmo Marconi demonstrates the first wireless telegraphic communication.

12 June
Calcutta sees the opening of the world's first fingerprint bureau.

22 June
Queen Victoria celebrates her Diamond Jubilee.

21 July
The Tate Gallery opens in London.

4 December
Greece signs a peace treaty with the Ottoman Empire to end their conflict over control of Crete.

1898

1 July
Britain obtains control of Hong Kong under a 99-year lease.

2 September
Sir Herbert Kitchener leads British forces to victory over the Mahdists in Sudan at Omdurman, retaking Khartoum.

3 November
French forces leave Fashoda in Sudan, ending a stand-off with the British.

10 December
A peace treaty ends the war between the USA and Spain, declared in May. Spain cedes Cuba, Puerto Rico, Guam and the Philippines to the USA in return for US$20 million.

26 December
Marie and Pierre Curie announce the discovery of radium.

1899

15 June
Germany claims control of the East African kingdom of Rwanda.

29 July
The first Hague Convention is signed, providing a legal framework for the conduct of wars.

19 September
Alfred Dreyfus is granted a pardon in France.

11 October
The Second Boer War begins in South Africa.

1900

1 January
Nigeria becomes a British protectorate.

19 March
Archaeological excavations begin at Knossos on Crete, led by a Briton, Sir Arthur Evans.

2 July
The Zeppelin airship has its maiden flight over Lake Constance.

30 July
In Italy King Umberto is assassinated by an anarchist. Victor Emmanuel III takes the crown.

14 October
Sigmund Freud publishes *The Interpretation of Dreams*.

17 October
Lord Salisbury's Conservative administration wins another term in Britain.

6 November
Republican William McKinley is re-elected President of the USA.

1901

1 January
The Commonwealth of Australia is established.

22 January
Queen Victoria dies, having reigned for 64 years. She is succeeded by her son, Edward VII.

7 September
The Boxer Rebellion in China is brought to a close. The Boxers (the Society of Right and Harmonious Fists) began a campaign of violence in late 1899 against various foreign interests in the country.

14 September
President of the USA, William McKinley, is assassinated by a Polish anarchist. Theodore Roosevelt is sworn in as his replacement.

10 December
The first Nobel Prizes are awarded.

1902

7 April
The Texas Oil Company (widely known as Texaco) is established.

29 May
The London School of Economics and Political Science opens its doors.

31 May
The Treaty of Vereeniging signals the end of the Second Boer War, with British sovereignty fully recognised.

23 June
Austria-Hungary, Germany and Italy sign up to the Triple Alliance for a further 12 years.

12 July
The Conservative, Arthur Balfour, becomes British Prime Minister.

10 December
The Aswan Dam across the Nile in Egypt opens.

1903

22 January
The USA and Colombia reach an agreement on the construction of the Panama Canal.

4 August
Guiseppe Sarto becomes Pope Pius X following the death of Leo XIII, who had reigned for 25 years.

10 October
In Britain, the Women's Social and Political Union is founded by Emmeline Pankhurst.

15 November
With American backing, Panama declares independence from Colombia.

17 November
Vladimir Lenin becomes the leader of the Bolshevik movement.

17 December
The Wright Brothers make a 12-second flight in their heavier-than-air machine in North Carolina.

INTRODUCTION

I first read Holmes when I was about nine years old. I began with 'The Speckled Band' and, having convinced myself that the ghastly goings-on must somehow be the responsibility of the local gypsies, the finale came as a thrilling surprise. I was hooked! At around the same time, the Jeremy Brett series was being shown on television. In common with a great many of the viewing public, I couldn't get enough of this impeccable Holmes and the series' atmospheric evocation of the period. So it was that I came to the character both through the written word of Conan Doyle and via one of myriad second-hand interpretations.

There are few figures so enduring as the Great Detective and there cannot be many people who do not have at least some awareness of him. It is probably true to say that most have never even considered reading one of Conan Doyle's original stories but have picked up their knowledge via other media. As Ian Rankin once observed, 'he's still a great, valid, wonderful fictional character; he's three-dimensional . . . He's bigger than the books.'

I can think of very few other literary characters to have so successfully existed in popular culture virtually independently of the texts that birthed them. That is why I decided to write this book – to look at Holmes as a literary figure and as a cultural phenomenon. Alongside synopses for all four novels and fifty-six short stories that Conan Doyle wrote (though without ever giving away the endings!), there are profiles of Holmes, Watson and a host of other important figures in the Detective's story. A series of essays looks in more detail at specific elements of the literary Holmes, while other pieces aim to put him into his wider cultural context. In addition, a collection of interviews with individuals whose lives have become entwined with the Holmes legend offers up some remarkable insights.

It is my hope that this book will go some way to unpicking the enigma that is Sherlock Holmes. Most of all, I hope it will remind the reader of his magic. In the Detective's immortal words, the game is afoot!

Daniel Smith

SIR ARTHUR CONAN DOYLE

For MANY OBSERVERS, Sir Arthur Conan Doyle epitomised his age. A man of medicine and a man of letters. A knight of the realm. A noted sportsman, who not only faced the bowling of W. G. Grace but served as Portsmouth FC's first goalkeeper and helped popularise skiing. A fighter for social reform and against miscarriages of justice. A man of Empire, prepared to do his duty on the front line at an age when he might reasonably have stayed safely at home.

Yet Conan Doyle was a complex web of contradictions whose life was never far from turmoil. His childhood was overshadowed by the mental and physical breakdown of his father and his own loss of religious faith. In adulthood, his pursuit of economic stability fought against his desire for recognition as a writer of enduring importance, until he fell forever out of love with his greatest creation. In his personal life, he struggled to balance his sense of duty to a wife he loved (but was not in love with) against his wish to be with the woman who had stolen his heart. In later years, as one of the wealthiest and most celebrated men in the country, he risked it all for Spiritualist beliefs that brought widespread derision down upon him. His earnest, upright image captured in portraits so familiar to the public gave little hint of the dramatic, passionate and troubled life that he actually lived.

OPPOSITE: A studio portrait dating to around 1925, by which time Conan Doyle was well-established as a figure of national importance.

Arthur Conan Doyle was born in Edinburgh on 22 May 1859. He was one of nine children (two of whom died in infancy) born to Charles Doyle, a draughtsman who suffered from epilepsy and who had an overfondness for alcohol, and Mary Foley, a strong-willed and intelligent woman from a military family of repute. Arthur was sent off to Lancashire to be schooled at Stonyhurst, a public school run by Jesuits. He did not enjoy the strict routine of Stonyhurst life but did develop a love of literature there, notably Macaulay, Sir Walter Scott and Edgar Allan Poe.

The school played its role in fostering a crisis of religious faith within Arthur. He turned his back on Catholicism while still a teen, a fact that always grieved his mother. However, after Stonyhurst he spent a year in Austria at Feldkirch, another Jesuit school in the area of Vorarlberg. He found the experience far more agreeable, noting that 'I met with far more human kindness than at Stonyhurst, with the immediate result that I ceased to be a resentful young rebel and became a pillar of law and order.'

Having decided on a career in medicine, he returned to Edinburgh to study in 1876. There he became a clerk to Dr Joseph Bell, a man whose startling abilities to deduce facts about a subject's life from the most cursory of examinations were to be immortalised in the figure of Sherlock Holmes. While a student Conan Doyle had his first work published, a story for *Chambers's Edinburgh Journal*. It was during Arthur's undergraduate days that the health of his father went into steep decline. Charles was descended from a notable family of artists and illustrators, and Arthur's uncle Henry was responsible for founding the National Gallery of Ireland. Charles, in the words of Arthur, was a 'great unrecognised genius' but had 'no appreciation of the realities of life'. Increasingly unstable and affected by alcoholism, he spent many years moving from sanatorium to sanatorium, putting the large family under immense financial pressure. Charles did illustrate one of his son's stories, *A Study in Scarlet* in 1888, but the loose drawings expose a talent far from its peak.

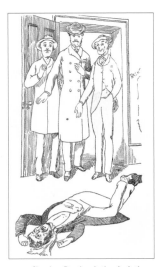

Charles Doyle, Arthur's father, was already in poor health by the time he produced this illustration for an 1888 edition of *A Study in Scarlet*.

Arthur was determined to rise to the challenge of providing for the family. After a friend had to drop out, Arthur took his place as ship's surgeon on an Arctic whaling ship, *Hope*, in 1880. The post was a profitable one and satisfied something of his wanderlust and desire for adventure. A fall overboard took him close to death, despite his underplaying the incident in his letters home. He followed this expedition with a stint on a cargo and passenger ship, the SS *Mayumba*, destined for West Africa. This voyage was in many ways even more dramatic, with the ship almost laid waste by a storm and disease rife, including an epidemic of typhoid that hit Arthur badly. Even as the ship docked in Liverpool in 1882, its hull was on fire.

When an old friend from Edinburgh, George Budd, invited Arthur to partner him in his new medical practice in Plymouth, it was an offer too good to turn down. The arrangement, however, was disastrous. There were plenty of patients but not enough money to support two doctors. Arthur's friendship with Budd, always something of an unscrupulous figure, came under pressure from which it never recovered. The partnership was ended and Arthur set up shop in a suburb of Portsmouth called Southsea. Business was painfully slow. When he filled out his tax return in 1883 to show no liability, it was returned by the Inland Revenue adorned with the comment 'most unsatisfactory'. He returned it with the additional wording 'I entirely agree.' Around the same time he wrote to his mother concerning his writing exploits: 'I want some three figure cheques and shall have them too. Why should I not have a future before me in letters.' These were brave words from a young writer at that time struggling to find a home for his work. It was also indicative of how his literary career would be underpinned by a keen desire to realise his full financial worth.

While his medical practice was not an unreserved success, it did bag him a wife as he married Louise Hawkins, the sister of a patient, in the summer of 1885. He had also started writing the first tale of Sherrinford Holmes and Ormond Sacker, who would evolve into the greatest crime-fighting duo in literature. *A Study in Scarlet*, the first Sherlock Holmes story, was published in *Beeton's Christmas Annual* of 1887. The magazine was owned by the widower of Mrs Beeton, creator of the famous cookbook, and he paid Doyle £25 for all rights. The story was not a great hit and Holmes seemed destined for a short and insignificant existence. But Arthur and Sherlock were given a new lease of life by a dinner at London's grand Langham Hotel on 30 August 1889. Arthur had been invited by J. M. Stoddart, the editor of *Lippincott's Monthly*, an American magazine. Among the other guests was Oscar Wilde. In what must have been a satisfying night's work for Stoddart, he commissioned both authors. Arthur was to write *The Sign of Four* for him while Wilde would produce *The Picture of Dorian Gray*.

Conan Doyle regarded Holmes as a means to an end; a way to kick-start his literary career and bring in much needed funds. But he certainly did not see his future as a purveyor of detective stories, which had yet to shake off a rather tawdry image. Instead he regarded himself as a writer of great historical novels in the vein of Walter Scott. He had already embarked on *Micah Clarke*, based on the seventeenth-century Monmouth Rebellion, which was published in 1889. He followed that up with *The White Company*, an adventure set during the Hundred Years War.

ABOVE: The Langham, London, was the scene of a legendary meeting between Conan Doyle, Oscar Wilde and J. M. Stoddart (the editor of *Lippincott's Monthly*) in 1889.

LEFT: Conan Doyle pictured in 1895 with his first wife, Touie, about to embark on a trip on their tandem tricycle.

Louise (or Touie, as she was known) had given birth to a daughter, Mary Louise, in January 1889. In 1891 Arthur and Touie spent several months in Vienna, where Arthur took the opportunity to further his knowledge of ophthalmics among some of the most respected names in the field. When they returned to England, the Conan Doyles left Southsea for good and moved to London. Arthur had made some little money from his writing, using a share of it to fund a medical surgery on Upper Wimpole Street. But he was soon to recognise that the medical profession held little opportunity of great wealth for him. He claimed to have seen no patients in the six months after setting up practice in the capital. This did hold one advantage though – he was left with plenty of time to write.

The *Strand Magazine* was a new title in a growing magazine market and Arthur saw his chance. He realised the secret lay in having a character who could keep the reader's attention and lure them back for more time after time. Sherlock Holmes, a character for whom he felt no great love, might just fit the bill. So it was that the Great Detective was taken out of the rather overstretched format in which he had found himself in *A Study in Scarlet* and *The Sign of Four* and began a new career in short stories. He was an instant hit and was greatly influential in securing strong circulation for the *Strand*. Arthur was initially paid £35 each for the first six stories, which rose to a princely £50 for the next six. In his letters he refers to knocking four of them out in just a fortnight. In 1892 he signed up to write another dozen tales for £1,000. He had hit the big time.

By the end of 1892 Arthur and Touie had a son, Kingsley, and Arthur had moved the family to the gentrified London suburb of South Norwood. Touie's health, though, was faltering. Arthur took her on a sojourn to Switzerland (where he saw the famed Reichenbach Falls) but to no avail. She was suffering from consumption. Then in October 1893 Charles Doyle died. Arthur, depressed and fearful that Holmes was taking him away from the 'higher' work of historical novels, decided he would kill the Detective off. He would fall to his death at the Reichenbach Falls. There was uproar, both from the owners of the *Strand* and from the public at large, who, it was reported, picketed the *Strand*'s offices.

Arthur, though, was not for turning. He was financially liberated and in a position to pursue his many interests, which included psychic phenomena. Within a month of his father's death in October 1893, or possibly as early as January of that year according to Conan Doyle's biographer Andrew Lycett, he had joined the Society for Psychical Research, a major staging post in his interest in Spiritualism. He also found time to indulge his love of sport (including skiing, which he had picked up in Switzerland) and was a prominent member of literary society, forming friendships with the likes of Jerome K. Jerome and J. M. Barrie

The frontage of No. 2 Upper Wimpole Street, thought to be the location of Conan Doyle's medical practice in 1891, when many of the greatest Holmes adventures were being written.

Hindhead, "Undershaw."

Conan Doyle had Undershaw built near Hindhead in Surrey in 1897, hoping that its airy aspect would improve Touie's declining health. He remained there until 1907, a year after Touie's death.

(with whom he wrote a comic operetta, *Jane Annie; or, The Good-Conduct Prize*). In 1895 work began on a new family home, Undershaw, which he hoped would provide the fresh air to aid Touie's delicate constitution. He turned his hand to straight plays, with *Waterloo* proving a hit, and started a series of light adventures featuring Brigadier Gerard, a cavalry officer in the Napoleonic Wars.

Yet just as Arthur seemed to have defined his role in the world, everything was thrown upside down by a Miss Jean Leckie. Jean, a young beauty living with her parents in Blackheath, met Arthur in March 1897 and they soon fell in love. However, they agreed that the relationship could not become intimate while Touie lived. Though his mother and a good part of Arthur's circle knew of the 'affair', Touie was never told though there is speculation that she might have guessed. As might be imagined, leading this double existence was at times torturous for Arthur.

In 1899 the British army found itself in the midst of the Second Boer War and Arthur, never less than patriotic, was determined to do his bit. Too old to be accepted into the regular army, he was stationed in a field hospital in Bloemfontein for three months in 1900, where he witnessed grave suffering both as the result of wounds and from a typhoid epidemic that claimed 60 lives a day. The experience had a major impact on Arthur, who returned to England and wrote a short work, *The War in South Africa*, in which he defended the British campaign. No longer

A page from Conan Doyle's own manuscript for 'The Adventure of the Missing Three-Quarter', showing his neat and precise script.

simply a famed writer, he had become a national figure. In 1902 he was knighted, an honour he wished to reject (much to his mam's annoyance) but which he ultimately accepted to save any embarrassment in future meetings with Edward VII. It should be noted that Arthur's apprehension had less to do with an aversion to honours per se but rather how his acceptance might be seen by his peers. 'Fancy Rhodes or Chamberlain or Kipling doing such a thing!' he wrote. 'And why should my standards be lower than theirs?'

1902 marked eight years since 'The Final Problem' when Holmes had fallen to his death, apparently concluding his uneasy relationship with Arthur. To Arthur, the Detective was always more appealing for the financial benefits he brought rather than his literary potential. As early as 1891 he had threatened to kill Holmes off, relenting only when his mother protested. 'He takes my mind from better things,' he argued. In an interview with *The Bookman* in May 1892 he declared that 'Sherlock is utterly inhuman, no heart, but with a beautifully logical intellect.' A year later he spoke of being 'weary of his name' and suggested after the Reichenbach Falls incident that 'If I had not killed Sherlock Holmes I verily believe that he would have killed me.'

By no means the first nor the last, Arthur was a man with a talent he didn't fully understand. His greatest strengths lay not where he desired them; the image he had of himself did not fit with the popular appetites of the day. While he wanted to write historical epics, his plotting was tightest and most efficient in the short story format. And where the tone of his other novels can often stray into pomposity and self-conscious literariness, his disregard for Holmes freed up his prose style to make the stories impeccably readable. Over the course of sixty stories, Arthur added layer upon layer to Holmes's character, with every careless discrepancy and inconsistency that flowed from his pen providing greater nuance.

Try as he might to leave Holmes behind, the economic motive was never far from Conan Doyle's mind. In 1899 he explained how he made his choice of publishers. 'It's entirely a question of money what I write for. I try to make my stuff as good as I can. Whether what it appears in is good is nothing to me if they make it worth my while.' So it was not too shocking when in 1902 a new story appeared. Set before Holmes's 'death', it remains the most famous of all the Holmes stories: *The Hound of the Baskervilles*. The project was initially to be a joint venture with his journalist friend Fletcher Robinson, who had introduced him to the legend of a spectral hound (and whose coach driver was apparently called Harry Baskerville). In March 1901 Conan Doyle talked of the collaboration as 'a small book . . . a real Creeper'. Holmes was to have no place in it until Norman Hapgood at *Collier's Weekly*, an American magazine, started pressing for some more Holmes stories. With Holmes and Watson rather shoehorned into proceedings, Arthur commented that 'it is not as good as I should have wished'.

The following year Holmes miraculously returned from what aficionados have come to call his 'Great Hiatus'. With the publication of 'The Empty House', Arthur explained away the Detective's apparent death in 1891 and his three subsequent years of wanderings. *Collier's* offered him an unheard-of $45,000 for thirteen stories, irrespective of length. In 1899 Arthur had written that 'Even an attempt and a failure at quite a new thing is better than an unambitious repetition of old successes.' But clearly there were limits. The public lapped up the new tales, though there was in certain circles the feeling that they lacked the sharpness of the older stories. Arthur himself admitted that it was 'impossible to prevent a certain sameness and want of freshness'. Indeed, he positively delighted in relating an incident where a Cornish boatman told him: 'When Mr. Holmes had that fall, he may not have been killed, but he was certainly injured, for he was never the same man afterwards.'

In 1906 Touie died after thirteen years of ill health. Arthur married Jean Leckie in September of the following year and moved into a new estate, Windlesham, at Crowborough in Sussex. The couple would have three children – Denis, Adrian and Jean, born between 1909 and 1912. Always a committed and passionate man (he twice stood unsuccessfully for parliament), Arthur found himself in a deep malaise following Touie's death. Seemingly in an attempt to extricate himself from this dark place, he took on a host of causes, sometimes winning acclaim for his advocacy, other times only derision. He fought to clear the name of George Edalji, a solicitor of Indian extraction who was convicted of maiming horses despite the want of any solid evidence. The case was evocatively imagined in Julian Barnes's

Conan Doyle pictured in April 1922 with his second wife, Jean, and their three children, Denis (then thirteen years old), Adrian (twelve) and Jean (ten).

2005 novel *Arthur and George*. He also fought for the cause of Oscar Slater, wrongly convicted of murder, though Slater's dubious past made him a less sympathetic character for the public at large. A third campaign, for a pardon for Sir Roger Casement, an Irish Nationalist accused of treason for his support of Germany, ended without success. Casement was executed in 1916.

On the political stage, Arthur wrote a pamphlet denouncing the activities of the colonial Belgian authorities in the Congo. In addition, he was a leading advocate for closer union with the USA, suggesting the formation of an Anglo-American Society, and wrote much to alert the British public to the threat of Germany. The First World War was to exact a heavy toll on Arthur, who was too old to serve but did visit the front line. With several family members having lost their lives, he wrote in 1916 that 'We have paid our full share in our family.' Yet the most devastating loss of all was still to come when his beloved Kingsley died in 1917 during the Spanish flu epidemic (an illness that had also claimed Conan Doyle's younger brother, Innes).

It was around this stage that Arthur became a leading public face for the Spiritualist movement. However, it was surrounded by much public scepticism, in part inflamed by the high numbers of frauds and cranks associated with it. Arthur himself had lost some public credibility when he argued the authenticity of the Cottingley Fairies, a series of photos in 1917 ostensibly showing real fairies but which turned out to be a hoax by two young girls. Nonetheless, Arthur continued to expend vast amounts of money and time for the Spiritualist cause and in September 1919 claimed he had been contacted by Kingsley. In a country ravaged by war and where everyone had lost someone, there was an element of sympathy for Arthur. But his stance won considerable criticism and, retrospectively, was an extraordinary twist in a remarkable life.

'The Adventure of Shoscombe Old Place', the last Sherlock Holmes story, appeared in 1927. Arthur noted: 'I fear that Mr Sherlock Holmes may become like one of those popular tenors who, having outlived their time, are still tempted to make repeated farewell bows to their indulgent audiences. This must cease and he must go the way of all flesh, material or imaginary.' Arthur himself died on 7 July 1930. The epitaph on his Spiritualist grave read 'Steel True, Blade Straight'.

Arthur left behind an admirable literary legacy: *Micah Clarke*, *The White Company*, *Rodney Stone*, *Sir Nigel* and *The Lost World*, to name but a few. However, perhaps the great tragedy of his life is that he could not bring himself to love and recognise his most perfectly realised creation. As Dorothy L. Sayers, the crime writer and affirmed Holmes enthusiast, wrote:

'For all the world, and probably for all time, the fame of Conan Doyle must stand coupled with the name of Sherlock Holmes.'

Shackled: This cartoon by Bernard Partridge appeared in *Punch* on 12 May 1926, capturing the troubled relationship between the author and his most famous creation.

THE CANON

ARTHUR CONAN DOYLE wrote a total of four Sherlock Holmes novels and fifty-six short stories. These texts are referred to as 'the canon'. The short stories were first published in magazines (the *Strand Magazine* in the UK and a number of titles in the USA) and then collected in book form in five volumes. Below is a table showing the publishing history of the canon:

The vast majority of the stories are narrated by Holmes's companion, Dr Watson. However, there are some exceptions where Holmes himself narrates or, on one occasion, a third-person narrator is employed.

Conan Doyle did not write the stories in any sort of chronological order. Some specify the date at which they are set in their narratives, while others may be accurately dated by specific references to historical events or other stories. A number, however, can only be guessed at. The issue of chronology has long fascinated certain Holmesians, who cross-reference stories in a way that the Great Detective himself might have admired. Nonetheless, the field of Holmes's chronology is full of pitfalls, not least because Watson was a somewhat unreliable narrator and the stories are littered with contradictions and temporal impossibilities.

In the synopses in this book I have included a 'setting date' for each of the stories and have turned to the chronology in *The New Annotated Sherlock Holmes* (Arthur Conan Doyle, edited by Leslie S. Klinger; W. W. Norton & Co., 2004–5) whenever there is debate. Other much respected Holmes scholars have disagreed with some of that edition's conclusions but the choices are always well reasoned and sensible. This book is not the arena for a debate on specific chronological questions but readers should be aware that such debates do exist and can be fiercely contested.

A Study in Scarlet	1887
The Sign of Four (originally called *The Sign of the Four*)	1890
The Adventures of Sherlock Holmes	1892 (comprising stories published 1891–2)
The Memoirs of Sherlock Holmes	1894 (comprising stories published 1892–3)
The Hound of the Baskervilles	1902
The Return of Sherlock Holmes	1905 (comprising stories published 1903–4)
The Valley of Fear	1915
His Last Bow	1917 (comprising stories published 1908–13 and 1917)
The Case-Book of Sherlock Holmes	1927 (comprising stories published 1921–7)

NB 'The Adventure of the Cardboard Box' is included in the UK in *The Memoirs* but American collections tend to group it in *His Last Bow*.

A STUDY IN SCARLET

FIRST PUBLISHED: *Beeton's Christmas Annual*, November 1887

SETTING DATE: 1881

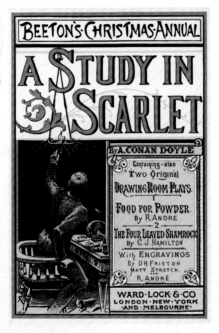

THE NOVELLA-LENGTH STORY that marked the meeting of the most famous crime-fighting duo in history. Dr John Watson has returned to London from the Second Afghan War, having suffered a bullet wound to the shoulder (or is it leg?). He meets up with Stamford, a former colleague from St Bartholomew's Hospital, and tells him he is in search of rooms. Stamford thinks he may have just the answer and introduces Watson to Sherlock Holmes, a consulting detective who makes his first appearance straight from perfecting an infallible test for bloodstains (which he is sure will revolutionise the criminal justice system). Within minutes Holmes had discerned much of Watson's

The cover of the 1887 *Beeton's Christmas Annual* in which Holmes and Watson first appeared. Original copies are extremely rare and represent the holy grail for Holmesians the world over.

life history as if by magic, and so the world's greatest deductive mind has its first public airing.

Before long Holmes is engaged in some detection work by two Scotland Yard inspectors, Messrs Gregson and Lestrade. Holmes is quick to bring in Watson as his assistant. The corpse of an American called Enoch Drebber has been discovered in a deserted house in Lauriston Gardens, Brixton. The victim is well dressed but his face speaks of a terrifying end. On the wall of the room where he is found are scrawled the letters 'Rache' in blood red. A woman's wedding ring is found close to the corpse. Was Drebber trying to communicate the name of his killer while in his death throes? Is this a classic case of *cherchez la femme*?

Holmes quickly works out that all is not as it seems and employs his loyal Baker Street Irregulars to help solve the puzzle. He makes use of the wedding ring found at the crime scene and looks on as Scotland Yard bungles its way through the investigation. It is not long before Holmes hits upon the solution but it comes too late for Drebber's secretary, Joseph Stangerson, as the narrative sweeps across continents (and specifically to Utah) before offering up its answers.

A comic book version of the story published by the Jiangsu People's Publishing House of China in 1981.

SHERLOCK HOLMES

ABOVE: An 1839 portrait of Horace Vernet (1789–1863), the great French painter and director of the French Academy in Rome, from whom Holmes claimed descent.

RIGHT: The Carlton Club on Pall Mall opened in 1832 to provide a refuge for members of the Conservative Party. It was located 'some little distance' from the Diogenes Club of Sherlock's brother, Mycroft.

HAD HOLMES THE Man one day wandered into 221B Baker Street, no doubt Holmes the Detective would have given him a quick look up and down and figured out his life story. For the rest of us, though, biographical information about Holmes is thin on the ground.

A reference in *His Last Bow*, which is set in 1914, suggested that Holmes was then sixty, so we can assume the year of his birth was 1853 or 1854. 'The Greek Interpreter' yields more information about his early life. Here we learn that one family line were country squires and that his grandmother was the sister of Vernet, the French artist. Whether this was Claude Joseph Vernet (1714–89) or his son, Antoine Charles Horace (1758–1835), is not clear, though the younger man seems a more likely candidate. We also meet Mycroft Holmes, Sherlock's elder brother by seven years who goes on to feature in 'The Bruce-Partington Plans'. Grossly obese but even more intellectually brilliant than Sherlock, Mycroft's spiritual home was the Diogenes Club ('full of the most unsociable and unclubbable men in town') on Pall Mall. It will emerge that Mycroft is exceedingly close to the heart of government and that 'again and again, his word has decided the national policy'.

For a while Sherlock Holmes was destined to have a quite different name. In early drafts of *A Study in Scarlet*, Conan Doyle had marked him down as Sherrinford Holmes. How or why he eventually decided on Sherlock Holmes is not completely clear. It seems most likely that Conan Doyle's interest in the American doctor, writer and philosopher Oliver Wendell Holmes influenced the

AN ELEMENTARY GUIDE

choice of surname, while Andrew Lycett wrote in *Conan Doyle: The Man Who Created Sherlock Holmes* (Weidenfeld & Nicolson, 2007) that Sherlock (which has its origins as an Old English first name meaning 'fair-haired') came from Patrick Sherlock, an old Stonyhurst classmate. However, Eille Norwood, the star of a series of silent Holmes films and much admired by Conan Doyle, related how the author had told him that Holmes was named after two cricketers.

It is possible to piece together a rather incomplete and rough chronology of the major milestones in his life. Holmes certainly went to university (though where can only be guessed at). Over two years he made but one true friend, Victor Trevor – a relationship that would precipitate Holmes's involvement in the *Gloria Scott* case (sometime around 1874) and thus propel him towards the life of the consulting detective. This trend of failing to establish friendships continued, as when in 'The Five Orange Pips' Holmes replies to Watson's 'Some friend of yours, perhaps?': 'Except yourself I have none.'

After college Holmes moved to London, taking up lodgings in Montague Street near the British Museum. His first documented case as a professional consulting detective was 'the Musgrave Ritual' in 1879. While not a student of St Bart's, he clearly had some agreement that allowed him to carry out his rather unorthodox scientific research there, where, of course, he would be introduced to Watson in 1881. It was then on to the glory days at 221B Baker Street, before Watson rather thoughtlessly got married and moved into a new home around 1889.

The 4th of May 1891 seemed to have marked the end of the Holmes legend, the Detective going out in a blaze of glory over the Reichenbach

MYCROFT HOLMES
~

Sherlock's older (by seven years), fatter and brighter brother, Mycroft appeared in two stories, 'The Greek Interpreter' and 'The Bruce-Partington Plans'. Despite a stated lack of energy and ambition that made him unsuitable for detective work, he nonetheless emerged as one of the pivotal figures in British society, no doubt the result of his particular specialism: 'omniscience'.

Mycroft comes across as something of a slob, with a 'gross body' and 'a suggestion of uncouth physical inertia'. But intellectually he was brilliant and Holmes even said of him: 'He has the tidiest and most orderly brain, with the greatest capacity for storing facts, of any man living.'

Mycroft's spiritual home was the Diogenes Club on Pall Mall, 'the queerest club in Britain' full of 'the most unsociable and unclubbable men in town' for whom silent contemplation was the order of the day. He worked in Whitehall and had rooms there too, just opposite the club which he attended every evening from quarter to five until twenty to eight. This triangle of locations formed practically all the points in his orbit from one year to the next. 'Mycroft has his rails,' Holmes explained, 'and he runs on them.'

When he is introduced in 'The Greek Interpreter', he is a man good with figures and responsible for auditing the books of various government departments. Yet Watson has dispensed with such underplaying by the time of 'The Bruce-Partington Plans', when it emerges that 'occasionally he is the British government'. Despite taking the modest annual salary of £450, he was 'the most indispensable man in the country'. 'Again and again,' it transpires, 'his word has decided the national policy.'

Mycroft's brilliance was undeniable; he just preferred to express it from the comfort of an arm chair. One suspects that he felt running around in a paddy was better left to little brothers.

The Henry VIII Gate at St Bartholomew's Hospital. It was in the chemical laboratory at St Bart's that Stamford instigated the first meeting between Holmes and Watson.

Falls. However, to the utter astonishment of both Watson and Mrs Hudson, he returned to action on the streets of London in 1894. There has been much speculation as to what might have occupied Holmes in the three years when he was missing and presumed dead. His own explanation to Watson in 'The Empty House' is regarded by many enthusiasts as but a cover story. However, it is all that the canonical reader has to go on and offers up the possibilities of myriad gripping adventures. Employing his devilish skills of disguise, he took on the persona of Sigerson, a Norwegian explorer, news of whose 'remarkable explorations' made it into the public arena. After two years in Tibet with a spell in Lhasa (where he became reasonably acquainted with the head lama), he passed on through Persia, visited Mecca and made a 'short but interesting visit to the Khalifa at Khartoum'. Then for good measure he returned to Europe, spending some time carrying out experiments at a laboratory in Montpellier.

With Watson widowed by then, the old partnership was re-established at 221B for several more case-packed years until Watson again went in search of independence around 1902. That same year Holmes turned down a 'knighthood for services which may perhaps some day be described' and went into official retirement the following year. He moved to the Sussex coast, not far from Eastbourne, and indulged his passion for bee-keeping (although he was rather a martyr to rheumatism in his later years). However, he was unable to leave detection behind entirely, solving the case of 'The Lion's Mane' in 1907 and then carrying out vital work for the Foreign Office from 1912 to 1914 ('His Last Bow'). The end of his life was not documented by Conan Doyle.

In terms of physical appearance, Conan Doyle depicts an imposing, well-presented fellow, though lacking the fussiness of, say, an Hercule Poirot. Holmes is variously described as a 'tall spare figure' and 'austere' with a 'dark, athletic outline' and an 'iron constitution'. He was undoubtedly a physically fine specimen, as the poker-bending scene in 'The Speckled Band' or his impressive feat of running in *The Hound* attest. Nor is Holmes a slouch sartorially. He could cut quite a figure, whether it be in a natty peajacket and cravat combo, the classic tweed suit and cloth cap look or, for those more intimate times, one of an array of dressing gowns.

We learn much about Holmes's apparent intellectual leanings from Watson's early impressions in *A Study in Scarlet*, where he noted that Holmes's 'ignorance was as remarkable as his knowledge'. He then gave the most thorough list of the Detective's strengths and weaknesses in the canon:

Sherlock Holmes – his limits

1. Knowledge of Literature. – Nil.
2.   "   " Philosophy. – Nil.
3.   "   " Astronomy. – Nil.
4.   "   " Politics. – Feeble.
5.   "   " Botany. – Variable.

Well up in belladonna, opium, and poisons generally.
Knows nothing of practical gardening.

6. Knowledge of Geology. – Practical, but limited.
Tells at a glance different soils from each other. After walks has
shown me splashes upon his trousers, and told me by their colour
and consistence in what part of London he had received them.

7. Knowledge of Chemistry. – Profound.
8.   "   " Anatomy. – Accurate, but unsystematic.
9.   "   " Sensational Literature. – Immense.

He appears to know every detail of every horror perpetrated in the century.

10. Plays the violin well.
11. Is an expert singlestick player, boxer, and swordsman.
12. Has a good practical knowledge of British law.

Yet we should be careful of giving this list too much credence. Take the alleged ignorance of literature. In 1948, E. V. Knox, editor of *Punch*, wrote that we see Holmes 'quote Goethe twice, discuss miracle plays, comment on Richter, Hafiz and Horace, and remark of Athelney Jones: "He has occasional glimmerings of reason. Il n'y a pas des sots si incommodes que ceux qui ont de l'esprit!"' To that can be added references to Tacitus, Jean Paul, Flaubert, Thoreau and Petrarch. Clearly not quite the slouch that Watson in his youth assumed. Similarly, the man with no idea about astronomy is able to hold forth with remarkable confidence on the 'causes of the changes of the obliquity of the ecliptic' in 'The Greek Interpreter'.

Holmes himself seems to have enjoyed playing a game around the apparent gaps in his knowledge. In 'The Noble Bachelor', he proudly declared, 'I read nothing except the criminal news and the agony column' while in *A Study in Scarlet* he defended his ignorance of the solar system with a defiant 'What the deuce is it to me?' Yet deep down Holmes was confident in the breadth and range of his intellect. He pretended not to care but nothing else was more important. 'I am a brain, Watson,' he said in 'The Mazarin Stone'. 'The rest of me is a mere appendix.'

OPPOSITE: An introspective Holmes, drawn by American illustrator Barry Moser for HarperCollins' *Books of Wonder* edition of the *Adventures*, published in 1992.

This last observation is among the Detective's saddest for in it he revealed that he regarded himself as something less than a whole person. It seems quite probable that such a sense of inadequacy might have been responsible for any number of his flaws, from his inability to form lasting relationships to his reliance on drugs and his susceptibility to the black dog of depression. What is certain is that Holmes turned to work to define himself. 'Holmes had the impersonal joy of the true artist in his better work, even as he mourned darkly when it fell below the high level to which he aspired,' wrote Watson in *The Valley of Fear*.

At times, he appeared utterly tortured (as perhaps all great artists are) in an inevitably doomed pursuit of perfection. Take the following observation from 'The Man with the Twisted Lip': 'when he had an unsolved problem upon his mind, [he] would go for days, and even for a week, without rest, turning it over, rearranging his facts, looking at it from every point of view until he had either fathomed it or convinced himself that his data were insufficient'.

Certainly Holmes was not one to downplay his gifts, as when in *A Study in Scarlet* he asserted that he had brought more 'study' and 'natural talent' to detective work than any other person. Vainglorious he may have been but such self-belief no doubt brought with it considerable burdens of pressure. When in the same story he claimed that if others knew the secrets behind his abilities they would consider him 'a very ordinary individual after all', we may assume that he didn't really believe that for a moment. In his heart he felt a heavy duty to let his gifts benefit the world.

Ward, Lock & Company chose D. H. Friston to be the first Holmes illustrator, providing drawings to accompany *A Study in Scarlet* in the 1887 *Beeton's Christmas Annual*.

"He examined with his glass the word upon the wall, going over every letter of it with the most minute exactness." (Page 29.)

Despite his tendency to collapse into black moods, it would be wrong to think that Holmes did not garner any pleasure from life beyond the intellectual challenge of solving crime. He is described as having an 'impish habit of practical joking' and as harbouring a sense of humour that was 'strange and occasionally offensive'. He also loved a touch of the dramatic. While generally restraining himself from the Poirotesque habit of assembling rooms full of suspects to heighten the sense of theatre at the denouement of a case, he would occasionally milk a scene. In *The Valley of Fear* he conceded that 'Some touch of the artist wells up within me, and calls insistently for a well-staged performance.' And of course, he was never one to let slip the chance to slap on a disguise. It is in some of these moments that we see him most enjoying life.

For, despite it all, Holmes did have a great propensity for pleasure. He was a far more complex and layered character than the deerstalker-wearing, pipe-smoking detecting machine of popular perception. His interests, ideas and personality are dealt with in more detail elsewhere in this book.

This remarkable rendering of Holmes and Watson was produced by the Danish artist, Nis Jessen, for a fully illustrated edition of *A Study in Scarlet*, published by Hakon Holm Publishing in 2005.

THE SIGN OF FOUR

FIRST PUBLISHED: *Lippincott's Monthly Magazine*, February 1890
SETTING DATE: 1888

THE SECOND HOLMES story, again of novella length. The book opens with Holmes in downbeat mood, professionally unchallenged and taking refuge in cocaine. Fortunately, a suitably complicated problem is soon at hand to focus his mind. The first part of the story is concerned with the mystery of the charming Miss Mary Morstan, whose

father was an Indian Army captain who disappeared in London ten years earlier. For several years she has annually received an anonymous gift of a pearl. This year the gift has come along with a note inviting her and, conveniently, two friends to meet her benefactor at the Lyceum Theatre. The invitation informs that she is 'a wronged woman, and shall have justice'. Miss Morstan invites Holmes and Watson to accompany her.

The intrepid three are taken to the house of Thaddeus Sholto, an eccentric orientalist with a twin brother named Bartholomew. They are the sons of a Major Sholto, an old friend of Captain Morstan. Sholto Senior died within seven days of Mary receiving her first pearl. With death close upon him, the Major had revealed that Mary was rightful

heir to the valuable Agra Treasure. It was an argument between the Major and Captain Morstan over the treasure that prompted the apoplectic fit that claimed the Captain's life. Thaddeus, Mary, Holmes and Watson proceed to Bartholomew's residence (Pondicherry Lodge in Upper Norwood) to unite Mary with her inheritance, only to find Bartholomew dead and the treasure gone. At the root of the story is the tragic tale of Jonathan Small and his loyal companion, Tonga, a native of the Andaman Islands. As in the previous story, the Baker Street Irregulars prove to be invaluable.

On a happier note, Watson and Miss Morstan discover an enduring love for each other.

TOP: The fort at Agra, a focal point for Europeans caught up in the Indian Mutiny.

FAR LEFT: An 1892 edition of *The Sign of Four*, published by George Newnes, owner of the *Strand Magazine*.

LEFT: The story debuted in 1890 in *Lippincott's Monthly Magazine*, based in Philadelphia.

DR JOHN H. WATSON

I F HOLMES IS the great genius whose remarkable skills provide the narrative drive of each tale, Watson is the everyman who gives the stories their heart and humanity.

Watson was initially going to be called Ormond Sacker until Conan Doyle realised that the rather less fussy 'John Watson' suited the character far better. As with Holmes, canonical information about Watson's early life is patchy. An episode displaying Holmes's deductive powers in *The Sign of Four* tells us that Watson's father had been dead for many years and that Watson had an 'unhappy brother' who 'was left with good prospects, but he threw away his chances, lived for some time in poverty with occasional short intervals of prosperity, and finally, taking to drink, he died'. The exact nature of this rather sad existence remains elusive.

In 1878 Watson qualified as a doctor at the University of London. It was while working at St Bart's during this period that he met Stamford, who would later engineer the fateful meeting with Holmes. After qualifying Watson went to Netley to train as an army surgeon. Signing up with the Fifth Northumberland Fusiliers as an assistant surgeon, he was posted to India just as the Second Afghan War began. Having arrived at Bombay, he was sent straight on to Candahar and endured a thoroughly rough time.

Removed from his brigade for unspecified reasons, he was assigned to the Berkshires and served at the battle of Maiwand. Here he was shot with a jezail bullet, though whereabouts is not clear. In *A Study in Scarlet* it was in the shoulder, while by the time of *The Sign of Four* the wound had descended to his leg. In 'The Noble Bachelor' he offers the rather vaguer 'one of my limbs'. Regardless, he faced certain death had he not been thrown over a packhorse and sent to safety by his orderly, Murray.

After Maiwand, Watson recuperated at Peshawar, only to be struck down by enteric fever. When strong enough, he returned to England but with his health 'irretrievably ruined', no family to turn to and a meagre pension of eleven shillings and sixpence a day. Living at digs on the Strand, he frittered his money away (not least on a love of gambling) before deciding that a change of lifestyle was required.

W. H. Hyde illustrated several of the Holmes stories for *Harper's Weekly* in the USA. This drawing appeared with 'The Adventure of the Yellow Face' in February 1893.

Perhaps thinking he would treat himself to one last blow-out at the Criterion Bar, destiny stepped in and reacquainted him with Stamford.

'The Adventure of Charles Augustus Milverton' provides us with the biggest clue as to Watson's physical appearance. In it Lestrade described his suspect as 'a middle-sized, strongly-built man – square jaw, thick neck, moustache', to which Holmes responded: 'Why, it might be a description of Watson!' (Which, of course, it was.)

The canon offers a handful of other 'by-the-by' facts that nonetheless give an insight into his character. For instance, we learn that he smoked Ships tobacco, was partial to a drop of Beaune wine, was a handy rugby player for Blackheath and was not by nature an early riser.

Watson took on his role as Holmes's companion and recorder with gusto and not inconsiderable skill. As Holmes himself admitted, 'I am lost without my Boswell.' However, in 'The Copper Beeches', Holmes chided him for degrading 'what should have been a course of lectures into a series of tales'. Harsh as this may be, Watson was never one to let the facts get in the way of a good story and was thus distinctly unreliable – just as the jezail question suggests. The chronology of the stories is, frankly, all over the shop and his writing is littered with apparent impossibilities and inconsistencies, leading to a string of unanswered questions.

Take the episode of the disappearing dog in *A Study in Scarlet*. Here Watson described himself as the owner of a bull pup, a creature never again to appear in the canon. The famed Sherlockian Jack Tracey speculated that this particular pup was of the type commonly used in Victorian Britain to refer to a fiery temper. A canine to represent the emotions along the lines of Winston Churchill's black dog of depression. Holmes himself is evidently partial to dogs, as epitomised by his use of Toby in *The Sign of Four* and Pompey in 'The Missing Three-Quarter'. But it should not be forgotten that he was happy enough to dispatch a hound if the situation demanded, most notably the beast of Dartmoor. This being the case, it does not seem beyond the realms of possibility that Watson's pup, decidedly of this earth and with its canine instincts thrown quite off balance on meeting Holmes, scampered to safety and out of the tales altogether. Yet Watson failed to mention the fate of this poor dog at all.

More intriguing still is the question of Watson's marriages. We know that he married Mary Morstan, the damsel in distress in *The Sign of Four*. By the time of Holmes's emergence from the Great Hiatus around 1894, Mary had died. Yet Watson's wife was mentioned again in 'The Illustrious Client' (set in 1902) and 'The Blanched Soldier' (1903). Surely this could not be another case of Watson simply getting his dates mixed up. Who was this wife? Indeed, was there more than one other? Holmesian scholars have devoted whole works to the

Mary Morstan, featured here on a 1923 Alexander Boguslavsky cigarette card, consulted Holmes in *The Sign of Four* and went on to become Dr Watson's wife.

Barry Moser captures the steadfastness of Watson in an illustration that echoes some of the later photographic portraits of Conan Doyle himself.

question, particularly in light of Watson's assertion in *The Sign of Four* that he had 'experience of women which extends over many nations and three separate continents'.

In too many dramatised versions of Holmes and Watson, the Doctor has been depicted as trailing round after the Detective like a slightly stupid puppy. Indeed, in a televised interview Conan Doyle himself called him Holmes's 'rather stupid friend'. Yet their relationship was considerably more nuanced – even changeable – than that. Certainly Holmes at times verged on unkindness, especially concerning Watson's writing, yet elsewhere he conceded that Watson was not without gifts.

This is no more evident than in this comment from 'The Abbey Grange', where the insult and compliment nestle together in the same line: 'I must admit, Watson, that you have some power of selection, which atones for much which I deplore in your narratives.'

Holmes's compliments were often backhanded, as when in 'The Blanched Soldier' he described how 'one to whom each development comes as a perpetual surprise, and to whom the future is always a closed book, is indeed an ideal helpmate'. Elsewhere, in admittedly exceptional circumstances during 'The Dying Detective', he rather brutally described Watson as 'only a general practitioner with very limited experience and mediocre qualifications'.

Sometimes Watson adopted a subservient role too easily, referring to Holmes as 'my master' in *The Hound* and alluding to 'my own insignificant personality' in *The Valley of Fear*. Yet he was quite capable of passing acerbic comment on Holmes, whether for his 'vanity', 'egotism', deficiency 'in human sympathy' or his 'offensive' humour. Nor was Watson the archetypal lapdog, at several stages breaking away from Holmes to concentrate on marriage and medicine (his practice at times busy though 'never very absorbing'). In 'The Stockbroker's Clerk' he talked of a three-month period when the two men saw little of each other. In 'The Final Problem' he said their joint investigations grew 'more and more seldom' and in 'The Creeping Man' he bemoaned the fact that their relationship had become 'peculiar', with Watson feeling like only a 'habit' of Holmes. By the time of 'The Lion's Mane', 'an occasional week-end visit' was all that existed between them.

In the final reckoning though, both men harboured a deep affection and respect for one another. To Holmes, Watson was 'my friend and partner' and 'a conductor of light'. At the crucial times he would turn to no one else because 'there is no man who is better worth having at your side when you are in a tight place'. In 'The Dying Detective', there is a sense not only of companionship but indeed of reliance when he told Watson: 'You won't fail me. You never did fail me.' Watson for his part realised that he had much to offer Holmes. 'I was a whetstone for his mind,' he wrote in 'The Creeping Man'. 'I stimulated him.'

Watson might have had many more wonderful tales to tell had he mined the notes he kept in his battered tin dispatch box in the vaults of Cox & Co. of Charing Cross. Despite the occasional memory lapse or mistake in his writing, he emerges from the stories as a rock, an utterly dependable man of decency who provides a bridge between the reader and Holmes. The Detective summed it up entirely when, in 'His Last Bow', he told his companion: 'You are the one fixed point in a changing age.'

A SCANDAL IN BOHEMIA

FIRST PUBLISHED: The *Strand Magazine*, July 1891, UK; published one month later in the US edition of the *Strand*

SETTING DATE: 1889

"What honour to be born on Fortune's hill? The merit is to climb it"

Lillie Langtry, famed actress and lover of Bertie, the Prince of Wales, is sometimes cited as a model for Irene Adler.

THE FIRST STORY to appear in the *Strand* and so arguably the one that set Holmes on the path to immortality. Watson has seen little of his old friend, having been distracted somewhat by married life. Mrs Hudson also seems to have given way as landlady to a certain Mrs Turner.

Having rather waspishly pointed out Watson's matrimonial weight gain, Holmes is soon engaged by the King of Bohemia (who proves rather less adept at disguise than our hero) three days before the king's wedding to the daughter of a Scandinavian monarch. In order to avert any potential scandal, the king wants Holmes to retrieve a tell-tale photo from a former lover, the renowned beauty and celebrated opera singer Irene Adler.

The king has instigated a handful of previous attempts to get back the item but all to no avail. The stage is set for Holmes to take on the characters of a sozzled groom and a rather bewildered clergyman. Throw in some admirable assistance from Watson and a few pyrotechnics, and Holmes looks to have succeeded in his mission. However, has he met his match in the clever, determined and alluring Miss Adler? Suffice to say, to Holmes she will always be known by the honourable title of '*the* woman'. His attitude to her is in stark contrast to his low opinion of the king that he barely tries to conceal.

Also includes a touching arm-in-arm walk by Holmes and 'my Boswell', which has been identified by certain critics over the years as suggestive of a love that dare not speak its name.

THE RED-HEADED LEAGUE

FIRST PUBLISHED: The *Strand Magazine*, August 1891, UK; published one month later in the US edition of the *Strand*

SETTING DATE: 1890

A<small>N OUTLANDISH AND</small> utterly compelling mystery. The wonderfully named Jabez Wilson, a pawnbroker by trade, comes to Holmes to relate the extraordinary events to which he has been a party. He reports being directed by his assistant, a keen amateur photographer called Vincent Spaulding, towards a newspaper advertisement calling for applicants to join the League of Red-Headed Men. The League, it emerges, was founded on the bequest of a fabulously rich American philanthropist, Ezekiah Hopkins. The impeccably qualified Wilson, having fought off strong competition for the post, is then set to work by a Mr Duncan Ross on copying out the *Encyclopaedia Britannica*. Being paid a generous fee (£4 a week for four hours' labour a day), all seemed to be going well (he was powering through the As) until he appeared at the office one day to discover a sign reading 'THE RED-HEADED LEAGUE IS DISSOLVED'. On consulting the landlord of the building in which the office was housed, Wilson learned that nothing was known of the mysterious Ross.

Holmes and Watson (who is living in digs south of Hyde Park) subsequently sound out the locale of the pawnbrokers and also investigate the assistant, Spaulding, who, it is noted, has dirty knees. An energetic bout of paving-stone tapping focuses Holmes's mind on a likely solution. He calls in Jones from Scotland Yard and a certain Mr Merryweather to join him and Watson in the denouement.

Holmes designates the case a 'three pipe problem' – that is to say, one that needs some considerable thought. Conan Doyle himself named it his second-favourite tale in the canon.

Pawn shops played an important role in London's nineteenth-century economy despite a reputation for dealing in stolen goods.

A CASE OF IDENTITY

FIRST PUBLISHED: The *Strand Magazine*, September 1891, UK; published one month later in the US edition of the *Strand*

SETTING DATE: 1889

HOLMES IS BUSY with 'some ten or twelve' cases at the start of the story, and this one is clearly little more than a brief and trivial distraction to him. Mary Sutherland visits Holmes with a sorry tale of the disappearance of her fiancé, Hosmer Angel, from the carriage taking him to their wedding. Mary lives with her mother and her stepfather, the unsympathetic James Windibank. She is well provided for by a generous bequest from her Uncle Ned in New Zealand, although her mother and Windibank have use of Mary's money while she lives with them. She further supplements her income by typing.

Windibank revels in his role as head of the house and has done all he can to keep Mary within the family unit and away from the wider world. However, when he was away on business she took up an invitation to the Gasfitters' Ball (gasfitting having been her deceased father's business), where she met the mysterious Angel. He is a shy man with a preference for evening trysts and typewritten love letters, who speaks with a gentle voice – the result of childhood illness – and wears tinted sunglasses. Mary knows little of his background, other than that he works in an office on Leadenhall Street.

Their affair was conducted in the gaps when Windibank was away from home and Hosmer soon suggested they seize the opportunity of his absence to get married one Friday. What should have been a joyous day for Mary turned into a tragedy when Hosmer disappeared (having seemingly had a premonition that something was afoot and extracted a promise of fidelity from Mary should anything happen to him).

Holmes effortlessly reads what has really happened but, sensitive to Mary's frail disposition, fears that she will be devastated by the truth. So it is that our almost incomprehensibly unobservant heroine (complete with 'vacuous face' and 'preposterous hat') is denied a satisfactory conclusion while Holmes concludes that the culprits are beyond the reach of the law.

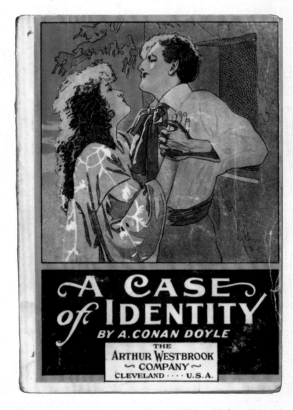

The somewhat melodramatic cover of a pirated edition of 'A Case of Identity', published by the Arthur Westbrook Company in Cleveland, Ohio in 1900.

THE BOSCOMBE VALLEY MYSTERY

FIRST PUBLISHED: The *Strand Magazine*, October 1891, UK; published one month later in the US edition of the *Strand*

SETTING DATE: 1889

THE FIRST OF the tales in which our heroes investigate a crime committed outside of London. Watson is summoned to meet Holmes at Paddington to head for Boscombe Valley in Herefordshire. One Charles McCarthy has been found dead near a secluded pond, shortly after he had been spotted arguing with his son, James, at the scene. James was also witnessed stalking his father to the pond. The case seems an open-and-shut one, and Inspector Lestrade of the Yard is certainly convinced that James is the murderer.

Holmes, however, is of the opinion that 'there is nothing more deceptive than an obvious fact'. For starters, why won't James reveal the subject matter of their dispute? With capital punishment his likely destiny, he seems to have little to lose. Then there is the strange call of 'Cooee!' used by both father and son, and the dead man's strange last words, ostensibly concerning a rat. Nor is Holmes alone in doubting that the case is quite as simple as Lestrade believes. Alice Turner, daughter of a local landowner and deeply in love with James, is convinced that her sweetheart is a wronged man.

With James languishing in prison, Holmes unravels the mystery. In accordance with the suspect's wishes, the whole truth is kept secret from the world at large but Holmes does enough to ensure that James will emerge a free man.

Holmes is described as donning a 'long grey travelling cloak and close-fitting cloth cap', providing illustrator Sidney Paget with the opportunity to depict Holmes in deerstalker and cape for the first time. Holmes also reads both Petrarch and George Meredith, suggesting that Watson's rating (in *A Study in Scarlet*) of Holmes's knowledge of literature as 'nil' may be wide of the mark.

Charles McCarthy lying dead under a tree near Boscombe Pool. But is his son, James, responsible? (Illustration by Barry Moser)

HOLMES AND ME  ROGER LLEWELLYN

Roger Llewellyn has worked extensively on stage and screen for over thirty-five years. Since 1999 he has toured his one-man Holmes show, The Last Act, *throughout the world. In 2008 he premiered a new show,* Sherlock Holmes . . . the Death and Life. *The BBC has described his performance as 'faultless and of the highest pedigree'. He is fast approaching 500 performances as the Great Detective.*

THE ROLE OF Holmes has completely changed my life. I was quite a successful actor but I wasn't famous and I wasn't rich. I had been offered a scholarship to RADA, where I won the Shakespeare prize. I had done lots of television and two or three films but didn't really enjoy any of them. I was about fifty-five. I could have declined into an out-of-work sixty-year-old actor. But playing Holmes has changed everything. It's tripled my income, taken me around the world, given me fans who will come and see the play repeatedly.

The first time I played Holmes was in a production of *The Ruling Class* in Manchester in 1977. I was playing the role of the schizophrenic Jack Gurney, which Peter O'Toole had made famous, and Holmes is one of the characters that he becomes. I thought, 'I know this fellow' but never gave it another thought. Then I was working for Exeter Rep and was asked to play Lestrade alongside Ron Moody in *Sherlock Holmes: The Musical*, which transferred to the Cambridge Theatre in London. A little later I got an invitation to play Holmes in Stoke-on-Trent, which turned out to be very successful.

Roger Llewellyn has played a captivating Sherlock Holmes for over a decade. As well as Holmes, he plays a host of other characters from the canon in each of his one-man shows.

Various members of the Sherlock Holmes Society came to watch, and when I met them afterwards they were very complimentary. Speaking to one of them, he said it was a shame I couldn't do a one-man show. At the time a very good friend of mine, Gareth Armstrong – now my director – had been touring the world with a show he had written himself, *Shylock*. So the idea of a one-man show was in my mind. But I thought, 'You couldn't, could you?!'

A fortnight later, my agent said a man from the Holmes Society had been in touch and wanted to speak to me. It was David Stuart Davies. He outlined to me what would become *The Last Act* and said, 'What if I wrote it as a one-man show?' About three weeks later he sent this super first act and Gareth said to me, 'We could do this!'

The play did need some work. Originally the second half had a huge section on *The Hound*. I was already playing fourteen characters and that would have been another eight. There are only so many regional accents you can do. So I said to David that I wanted something truly startling to happen in Act 2 and he duly came up with a brilliant idea. So we took it from there.

We premiered it at Salisbury and then I took it to Edinburgh where it got a five-star review. I met an American producer who took me to New York and we started touring in America and then did eight weeks in Canada. I have been all over with it, to the Middle East, the Far East, all round Europe. On the *QE2*. One of the highlights was performing at the British embassy in Riyadh and being treated like a royal guest, staying in the suite they had given to Prince Charles and then Tony Blair.

After nearly 450 performances it felt like things were coming to a gentle end. Then Mark Makin – now my tour booker – asked if I'd thought about doing a new Holmes play. If it was something that interested me, he said he'd like to be in at the beginning. So I asked David if he'd like to write another show for me and he said, 'Oh yes.' Another Holmes? 'Oh my God!' To come up with one Holmes solo show idea is difficult. Two is nigh on impossible but he's done it in spades.

I frequently get asked if I base the performance on Jeremy Brett. I think he was incomparable, quite superb, but I can't base it on something like that. I can't work from the outside in. I need to perform it from the inside out. It's taken me six months, working every day, to rehearse the new show. I consider every single word that David writes. I try to deal with every thought and development and go all the way through the character. It's like cutting your way through an overgrown forest, cutting every problem out of the way until eventually you get to the top of the hill and look back and then you see the shape of the path. Then you recognise the character.

I say to people, 'I don't play Sherlock Holmes, I play a rather sad, lonely and dysfunctional old man.' You can't play the myth as an actor. You can't play an icon. You have to play the man. The wonderful thing is his contradictions. You can go so far to make him unpleasant and the more unpleasant you make him the more the audiences like it. He is so consummately arrogant. He is an extraordinary character for an actor to play. It's a privileged existence and it doesn't fall to many people.

MRS HUDSON

~

Considering that Mrs Hudson has become one of the iconic figures of Sherlock Holmes's world, there is very little to be found in the stories themselves about London's most patient landlady. We are never told her first name or given any physical description (though she did apparently have a 'stately tread'), nor do we know anything of her family background. In fact, her very position as landlady to the world's greatest detective is thrown into some doubt when one Mrs Turner turns up with a tray in 'A Scandal in Bohemia'. Who was this interloper? Could she have been Holmes's actual landlady, or was she perhaps the holiday cover or even a lowly assistant to the great woman? It seems this same Mrs Turner also held sway in an early draft of the 'Empty House', so perhaps it is safest to assume that it was simply a case of Conan Doyle's mind, not for the first time, wandering to higher things as he wrote the Holmes tales.

Clearly Holmes was a testing tenant for even the most long-suffering of landladies but Mrs Hudson endured 'the very worst tenant in London' and his visiting 'throngs of singular and often undesirable characters' with great fortitude throughout. We can only wonder whether Holmes's 'incredible untidiness, his addiction to music at strange hours, his occasional revolver practice within doors, his weird and often malodorous scientific experiments, and the atmosphere of violence and danger which hung around him' would have imperilled any rental deposit she might have asked him to pay when taking him on.

However, Mrs Hudson did not merely endure Holmes's presence but eventually discovered a fondness for him and particularly, as Watson told us in the 'Dying Detective', his 'remarkable gentleness and courtesy in his dealings with women'. There are few warmer moments in the canon than when Watson in the 'Empty House' described the scene as he and Holmes entered 221B after Holmes's apparent return from the dead. Mrs Hudson, he reported, 'beamed upon us both as we entered'.

While Holmes's affection for her could never be described as filial, and he certainly never curbed his own eccentricities to make her life easier, he did at least make an effort to praise her cooking. Not wishing to overstate the case in the 'Naval

ABOVE: Irene Handl as an endearing Mrs Hudson in *The Private Life of Sherlock Holmes.* Mary Gordon in the Rathbone films and Rosalie Williams in the Granada TV series did much to form the popular image of the landlady.

Treaty', he points out that 'her cuisine is a little limited' but does then concede that 'she has as good an idea of breakfast as a Scotchwoman'. Her breakfasts again come in for special mention in 'Black Peter', and no wonder when we consider the comparative efforts of a 'new cook' who crops up in 'Thor Bridge' proffering two boiled eggs rendered somewhat unappealing as a result of her being distracted by the romantic contents of the *Family Herald*.

But given only scant recognition in Conan Doyle's narrative, it has in the end fallen to TV and film to cement Mrs Hudson's place in the public consciousness. She has been well served here with such admired character actresses as Mary Gordon, Irene Handl, Rosalie Williams and – most recently – Una Stubbs providing us with memorable portrayals of the occasionally tetchy but ultimately sympathetic stalwart of 221B.

221B BAKER STREET

Without doubt the most famous residential address that never existed, 221B was home to Holmes for the years 1881–1903. Despite a few periods of absence, Watson shared lodgings with him for most of this time.

Holmes and Watson rented their digs, set in a Georgian terrace, from the venerable Mrs Hudson. Their rooms were sited up a flight of seventeen steps and consisted of 'a couple of comfortable bedrooms, and a single airy sitting-room, cheerfully furnished and illuminated by two broad windows'. Though how airy the sitting-room was once it had been filled with Holmes's mass of books and papers and his noxious chemical experiments is not clear.

The contents of 221B included several chairs (including a sofa, basket chair and arm chair), a coal scuttle for the storage of smoking paraphernalia, a Persian slipper filled with tobacco, a bear skin rug, a mantelpiece to which Holmes attached post with a jack knife and, at least latterly, a gramophone. Among the pictures that Holmes and Watson possessed were portraits of General Gordon (popular hero of the Siege of Khartoum) and Henry Ward Beecher, the American anti-slavery campaigner, as well as a photo of Irene Adler. One wall was pockmarked with the bullet holes that Holmes had patterned into a 'VR' in recognition of Queen Victoria. The two men thus made the place very much their own.

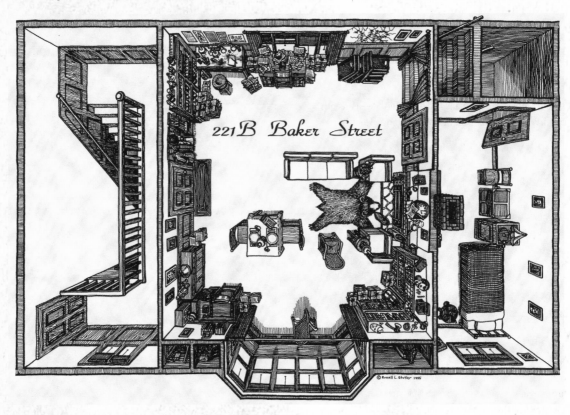

This plan of Holmes and Watson's rooms was made by Russell Stutler after a close reading of all the canonical stories.

The plaque on the wall of the Sherlock Holmes Museum on Baker Street.

221b
SHERLOCK HOLMES
CONSULTING DETECTIVE
1881-1904

In a dubious demonstration of devotion to his sovereign, Holmes adorned a wall of 221B with this insignia picked out with bullets.

Baker Street was originally laid out in the late eighteenth century by Edward Berkeley Portman. During Holmes's tenancy, it was a relatively respectable address but certainly not the best to be found in London. Nor was it devoid of some of the more disreputable amusements available to Victorian society. Conan Doyle's intended location of 221B is not clear and has been a source of endless speculation among aficionados of the Detective.

During the period in question, properties on the real Baker Street were numbered only up to 85. Some argue that canonical hints point to 221B's location at the northerly end of modern Baker Street (which was then designated Upper Baker Street). Others who believe the best clues are to be found in 'The Empty House' place it much further south. When Baker Street was renumbered in the 1930s, the stretch that included No. 221 was taken by Abbey House, the headquarters of the Abbey National Building Society. So it was that the Abbey found itself inundated with post for the Great Detective. The issue was further muddied when the Sherlock Holmes Museum opened a few doors further north in 1990 and claimed '221B' for itself. Ultimately, though, the real 221B is only to be found in the imagination of the reader.

While Baker Street today has little of its Holmesian character, the nearby Manchester Street has retained much of its original appearance.

THE BAKER STREET IRREGULARS

Sherlock Holmes was waging a war on crime and, like any great leader, needed an army to fight with him. Unconvinced by an official police force too often sluggish and slow-witted, he established his own private battalion; the Irregulars. This motley crew of street urchins was called on to run errands and track down information for Holmes, on a basic pay scale of a shilling a day each with rewards (typically a guinea) for the first Irregular to successfully complete a task.

In *A Study in Scarlet*, Watson described 'half a dozen of the dirtiest and most ragged street Arabs that ever I clapped eyes on' but Holmes instead called them 'the Baker Street division of the detective police force'. He was very clear in his motives for choosing this rag-tag band rather than going through the official channels at Scotland Yard, saying 'There's more work to be got out of one of those little beggars than out of a dozen of the force.'

Indeed, the troops worked with admirable efficiency across a variety of stories, assisted by their ability to 'go everywhere and hear everything'. 'They are as sharp as needles, too; all they want is organization,' said Holmes, and that is precisely what he gave them, with the assistance of the Irregulars' 'dirty little lieutenant', a lad named Wiggins.

Holmes was skilled at developing a network of talents to assist him in any given situation, and the canon makes reference to several other notable 'outsider' figures in his employ. In *The Hound* he called upon Cartwright, a 14-year-old boy working at a district messenger office in London, to rummage through the rubbish of 23 hotels in the Charing Cross area. And in 'The Illustrious Client' there is the shadowy figure of Shinwell Johnson 'a valuable assistant' who 'made his name first as a very dangerous villain and served two terms at Parkhurst'. A reassuringly repentant criminal, he served as Holmes's conduit into the darkest corners of the London underworld.

Then there is Billy, a pageboy at 221B who crops up in *The Valley of Fear*, 'The Mazarin Stone' and 'Thor Bridge'. 'Wise and tactful', at the time of The Mazarin Stone he seems almost to have taken over Watson's role, being described as filling 'the gap of loneliness and isolation which surrounded the saturnine figure of the great detective'. For all Holmes's apparent arrogance, he realised the value of reliable assistants and was humble enough to look for them in those places where others of his status might never have deigned to tread.

Holmes relied on his own troop of street urchins, the Irregulars, to seek out information and carry out errands for him.

THE FIVE ORANGE PIPS

FIRST PUBLISHED: The *Strand Magazine*, November 1891, UK; published one month later in the US edition of the *Strand*

SETTING DATE: 1889

WHEN JOHN OPENSHAW rushes from Sussex to 221B on the wildest of nights, it is obvious that danger is in the air. His tale begins in 1869 when his uncle Elias gave up his life in Florida (where he had served with the Confederate army) to begin a new life in Horsham. John had resided with his uncle, though there was a room in the house permanently off-bounds to him.

In 1883 Elias received a letter from India, inscribed with three letter Ks and containing five orange pips. Receipt of the strange missive prompted a change in Elias, who made a will bequeathing his estate to John. He also turned to alcohol and his behaviour grew erratic, culminating in his drowning in the garden pond three months after the letter arrived. Two years later Joseph – Elias's brother and John's father – received a similar 'triple-K'-inscribed note, this time sent from Dundee. With it were instructions to leave some papers on a sundial. John wanted to go to the police but his father refused and three days later he was found dead.

John possesses a page from Elias's journal of 1869 which relates how three men have been sent orange pips. Furnished with this clue, Holmes dismisses John into the night with the advice that he should put the diary scrap into a box and leave it at the sundial with a note explaining that the rest of his uncle's papers had been destroyed.

Holmes is able to put together the true train of events but the next morning he receives upsetting news about Openshaw. Holmes sets the wheels of justice in motion but circumstances conspire against him. So ends a rare instance of Holmes failing both to protect a client and to see that the wrong-doers face their just punishment. For all its atmospheric slow-burning tension, the story fails to grab the modern reader, who, with a cursory knowledge of twentieth-century politics, will be able to see what has been going on long before even the Great Detective.

Waterloo Bridge, linking Westminster and Lambeth, was opened in 1817. It appeared in several canonical tales and it was near here that a terrible crime was committed in this story.

THE MAN WITH THE TWISTED LIP

FIRST PUBLISHED: The *Strand Magazine*, December 1891, UK; published one month later in the US edition of the *Strand*
SETTING DATE: 1889

THE STORY OPENS with Watson braving an East End opium den to extricate a friend's husband. To his surprise he discovers Holmes there too, disguised as an old man and on the quest for information. There is perhaps no better start to a story in the canon.

A Mrs St. Clair has reported the strange disappearance of her husband, a businessman called Neville. While on a shopping expedition in town, Mrs St. Clair had to enter a far from salubrious area to pick up a parcel she was expecting from a shipping office. What she did not expect to see was her husband waving at her from a window above an opium den.

She attempted to access the building but her path was blocked by a Lascar (a sailor of East Indian origin). Returning with some local police, she entered the premises and rushed upstairs but found only a decrepit old beggar, Hugh Boone, 'the man with the twisted lip'. However, she soon spied her husband's clothing and a box of bricks he had bought as a present for their son. The outlook seemed bleak when bloodstains were detected on the sill of a window that opened on to the river. When Boone's coat was found in the water, weighed down with his beggar's earnings, he was arrested for murder.

Holmes is convinced that St. Clair has been murdered until, several days after his disappearance, Mrs St. Clair receives a letter in her husband's script. Re-evaluating the evidence, Holmes concludes that he is 'one of the most absolute fools in Europe' and decides to pay Boone a visit in prison. Armed with a common-or-garden sponge, the solution is soon at hand.

Rather disconcertingly, Watson's wife calls him James instead of John in this story. The reader can only hope this is an unfortunate lapse of memory on her part or perhaps a ploy to make sure he is paying attention, rather than anything more sinister.

An illustration of an East End opium den that appeared in the periodical, *The Graphic*, in 1880. Holmes himself did not favour the drug.

THE ADVENTURE OF
THE BLUE CARBUNCLE

First Published: The *Strand Magazine*, January 1892, UK; published one month later in the US edition of the *Strand*

Setting Date: 1889

It is Christmas time and Watson looks in at 221B Baker Street on his old companion, who is nattily attired in a purple dressing gown. Holmes is studying a tatty old hat, skilfully deducing the circumstances of its owner. The hat was brought to him by a commissionaire named Peterson, who had retrieved the item in the aftermath of a street attack on a man by a gang of rogues. As well as his hat, the unlucky victim fled without the goose which he had presumably been taking home for his Christmas table.

Holmes sends Peterson off with the goose so that he may enjoy his good fortune with his wife. However, the commissionaire soon returns, this time bringing a large blue stone that his wife has discovered in the bird's crop. Just such a gem has recently been stolen from the Countess of Morcar while she was staying in a London hotel. John Horner, a plumber with a history of thieving and access to the Countess's rooms, is already in custody for the offence.

So how did the carbuncle end up in the neck of a goose? Holmes and Watson are spurred into action by such a delicious conundrum. They quickly track down the owner of both hat and goose, who turns out to be wholly innocent of any involvement in the crime. However, his information sets the duo off on a race across London. They question a trader in Covent Garden Market, who expresses his annoyance at the number of people pestering him about his produce and so alerts Holmes to the existence of others on the trail of the stone. Holmes is about to wrap the case up with a visit to a goose breeder in Brixton when the real culprit – a rather pathetic specimen – reveals himself.

Assured that an innocent man will not be wronged, and convinced that he should not cover for the errors of Scotland Yard, Holmes shows the criminal extravagant seasonal generosity and allows him to flee the country.

The festive London setting, light humour and Christian charity all hark back to the Christmas stories of Charles Dickens.

W. H. C. Groome, who illustrated many of Charles Dickens's stories, produced this painting of Covent Garden Market. Despite its reputation for fruit, vegetables and flowers, it featured in this story as the scene of poultry trading.

THE ADVENTURE OF THE SPECKLED BAND

FIRST PUBLISHED: The *Strand Magazine*, February 1892, UK; published one month later in the US edition of the *Strand*

SETTING DATE: 1883

ONE OF HOLMES'S classic cases that brilliantly 'tends towards the unusual, and even the fantastic', blessed with an ingenious plot and one of the most dastardly villains in the canon.

The clearly frightened Helen Stoner brings the case to Holmes. She describes finding herself in similar circumstances to those experienced by her sister Julia before her death two years earlier. The sisters lived on a large estate with their violent and unpleasant stepfather, Dr Grimesby Roylott. Descended from the once-rich Roylotts of Stoke Moran, he was left to make his own way in the world. He married the girls' mother, a wealthy widow, while practising medicine in Calcutta. The family returned to England but shortly afterwards the mother died in a rail accident.

Roylott's increasingly erratic temper ensured the girls had few companions, but in a brief visit away Julia found a suitor and was soon engaged to be married. With her bedroom lying between Helen's and Roylott's, Julia complained of being able to smell the doctor's cigar smoke and of hearing whistling in the dead of night. One evening before the wedding, Helen heard her sister screaming and discovered her collapsed and near death. Her elusive final words were 'It was the band! The speckled band!', spoken as she pointed to Roylott's room.

After an extensive investigation, the coroner decided there were no suspicious circumstances. Helen believes her sister died from terror. The reference to the speckled band, however, points to the possible involvement of local gypsies who wear just such items around their necks. Now Helen is also engaged and finds Roylott has moved her into a new room (ostensibly because of building works) and that she is hearing the same whistle (followed by a metallic clang) that her sister described.

Holmes dismisses the woman, promising his help. Soon afterwards Roylott, who has followed her into town, bursts into 221B. He makes unwise threats to Holmes and attempts to intimidate by bending a metal poker, though Holmes proves his equal. With Roylott gone, Holmes makes a study of the girls' mother's will before setting off for Stoke Moran. After surveying Helen's room, he primes Watson for his role in an exciting night-time denouement.

Conan Doyle himself nominated this story as his favourite.

A theatrical bill from 1911 advertising the dramatised version of 'The Speckled Band'. It had opened the previous year with H. A. Saintsbury in the lead.

HOLMES AS THE DETECTIVE-SCIENTIST

. . . the rapid deductions, as swift as intuitions,
and yet always founded on a logical basis.
'The Adventure of the Speckled Band'

IT IS TO his abilities as a logician and his unrivalled deductive powers that Holmes owed his fame and career. Without them, it is quite possible that he might have become but another Neville St. Clair of 'Man with the Twisted Lip' fame. A figure oscillating between Victorian respectability and the lowest depravity the age had to offer, spurred on by a love of the dramatic and a penchant for dressing up. Instead, he set about elevating detection to 'an exact science'.

In *A Study in Scarlet* we can read Holmes's own thoughts on deductive power as outlined in his article 'The Book of Life'. In it he says that:

From a drop of water, a logician could infer the possibility of an Atlantic or a Niagara without having seen or heard of one or the other. So all life is a great chain, the nature of which is known whenever we are shown a single link of it. Like all other arts, the Science of Deduction and Analysis is one which can only be acquired by long and patient study . . .

Nis Jessen depicted Holmes's analytical approach towards evidence in his 2005 illustrated edition of *A Study in Scarlet.*

It is interesting that his method is here encapsulated as both a science and an art, that empirical fact must collide with creative imagination to make the leap from water droplet to ocean and waterfall. Indeed, in *The Valley of Fear* Holmes pondered 'how often is imagination the mother of truth?' However, the imagination can only be employed constructively after the gathering of facts, a natural order that he outlined in *The Hound*: '. . . we balance probabilities and choose the most likely. It is the scientific use of the imagination, but we have always some material basis on which to start our speculation.'

So at the very core of Holmes's method is information. 'Data! data! data!' he said in 'The Copper Beeches'. 'I can't make bricks without clay.' Then in 'The Boscombe Valley Mystery': 'You know my method. It is founded upon the observation of trifles.' Having satisfied himself that he had extracted all the information to be offered up in any given scenario, he turned to his remarkable creative faculties to dexterously spin the available facts into a likely narrative. By analysing each possible narrative to see which best incorporated all the known facts, he fulfilled the criteria of his famous test: when you have excluded the impossible, whatever remains, however improbable, must be the truth.

Eric Conklin, a trompe l'oeil artist, produced this Mystery Painting. The viewer should be able to identify the story depicted from clues within the picture.

Holmes's assimilation of detailed information was quite remarkable, as can be illustrated by just a partial roll-call of his referenced knowledge. He was, we are told, able to distinguish between forty-two different impressions left by tyres ('The Priory School'), one hundred and sixty separate ciphers ('The Dancing Men'), a hundred and forty forms of cigar, cigarette, and pipe tobacco, the hands of slaters, sailors, cork-cutters, compositors, weavers, and diamond-polishers (*The Sign of Four*) as well as seventy-five perfumes (*The Hound of the Baskervilles*). Not to mention his close study of tattoo marks ('The Red-Headed League').

He was a man forever cross-indexing his huge book of references and summarising his knowledge in countless monographs. Furthermore, he was happy to take his theories and expose them to the most exhaustive practical tests, whether that involved sitting hunched for hours over foul-smelling potions or, more quixotically in 'Black Peter', satisfying himself that with 'no exertion of my strength can I transfix the pig with a single blow'.

However, Holmes's knowledge, for all its breadth and impressiveness, was not without its limitations. As we might expect, Conan Doyle was among the most vociferous doubters of Holmes's abilities. While he acknowledged that his reasoning had a 'real practical application to life' he also described his methods as 'semi-scientific . . . occasionally laboured and slow as compared with the results of the rough-and-ready practical man'.

In a sense Conan Doyle was wrong to suggest that his creation was not a 'rough-and-ready practical man' for virtually Holmes's whole life was geared towards knowing that which needed to be known to solve crimes. Holmes was no Renaissance Man mastering countless intellectual spheres but instead equipped himself with just what was needed to achieve his aim of being the best in his chosen field. As he conceded in 'The Lion's Mane': 'My mind is like a crowded box-room with packets of all sorts stowed away therein – so many that I may well have but a vague perception of what was there.' This seems to tally with Watson's initial impressions of him in *A Study in Scarlet*, when he noted that 'His ignorance was as remarkable as his knowledge' and made special mention of Holmes's apparent ignorance of the Earth's rotation round the Sun (which, it must be conceded, would have assisted him little in solving any of his cases).

Holmes has come to be seen as something of a pioneer in the field of criminal forensics, which was blossoming only slowly in the late nineteenth century. There can be no denying that he readily understood that careful examination of even the seemingly most unpromising crime scene could offer up vital clues. This at a time when the official police were only just beginning to realise the value of trace evidence. Images of Holmes whipping 'a tape measure and a large round magnifying glass from his pocket' or sitting huddled in 221B conducting a malodorous experiment are some of literature's most enduring. His use of forensic methods is extensive throughout the canon. He may be seen tracking footprints ('There is no branch of detective science which is so important and so much neglected'), discerning the height of a suspect from the length of his stride, studying finger-prints, checking for the differences in ears, noting the peculiarities of individual typewriters, and so the list goes on.

Conan Doyle's sons, Denis and Adrian, were considerably kinder about Holmes than their father ever was. They were quoted in *The People* in July 1953 as saying: 'The police systems of the modern world are founded on the new ideas in crimin-ology, expressed by our father in his detective stories . . . Father invented the use of plaster of paris for preserving footprints, the minute examination of dust on a man's clothes to discover his occupation or where he had been, and the precise dif-ferentiation among various tobacco ashes.'

It is indeed true that Conan Doyle would himself employ some of his creation's methods during his involvement with real-life cases. In the George Edalji case, he was particularly insistent that the suspect's poor vision should have ruled him out as a realistic culprit for a series of horse mutilations. And Holmes was not without admirers within the ranks of professional investigators. For instance, Dr Edmond Locard, the godfather of French forensic science, regularly urged his students to study the methods of Holmes.

Holmes adopted several investigative methods that were at the very least cut-ting-edge. In 'The Naval Treaty' he expressed his admiration for Alphonse Bertillon, who in the 1880s had developed a system to identify individuals by eleven body measurements that did not change after twenty years of age. In *The Hound* James Mortimer even described Holmes as 'the second highest expert in Europe', Bertillon having the greater appeal 'to the man of precisely scientific mind'.

Elsewhere, Holmes's use of typewriter evidence in 'A Case of Identity' was cer-tainly very high-tech, and the references to thumbprint evidence in 'The Norwood Builder' came in a story set seven years before Scotland Yard opened its own fingerprint bureau. His ballistic knowledge, too, in 'The Dancing Men', 'Thor Bridge' and 'The Reigate Squires', was most impressive.

Holmes was also an early proponent of employing dogs to assist an inquiry, including Toby in *The Sign of Four* and Pompey in 'The Missing Three-Quarter'. His effective use of these canines was in sharp contrast to the doomed use of two bloodhounds, Burgo and Barnaby, in the Jack the Ripper investigation. Not only did they fail to track down the Ripper but they brought further embarrassment on the police when they themselves went missing for several days. It was not until the turn of the century that the Belgian police force started to make serious progress in the use of dogs.

Holmes's reputation as something of a cold fish was not greatly alleviated by his scientific approach to life. Stamford warned Watson in *A Study in Scarlet* that 'Holmes is a little too scientific for my tastes – it approaches to cold-bloodedness,' before suggesting he would not be averse to poisoning a chum if it furthered his investigations. In the same story, we cannot fail to be a little shocked on hearing that Holmes has been seen beating corpses with a stick to verify how far bruises may be produced after death. But always his motives were pure, and science would have progressed little over the years if it sought to avoid offending the squeamish.

However, Holmes was not always the icon of innovation that he appeared to be. Take his debut appearance in *A Study in Scarlet*,

Mike Coote hand-coloured Sidney Paget's original drawing of Pompey the Dog, who had a key role to play in 'The Missing Three-Quarter'.

when he patted himself on the back for inventing 'an infallible test for blood stains'. His criticisms of the existing Guaiacum test may all be justified but he gave no nod to the fact that there had been an effective spectral analysis test for blood that had been in use in criminal trials since the mid-1860s. Nor was he quite so ahead of his time in the tracking of footprints, which had been a decisive investigative strand in the murder of one Jessie M'pherson in Glasgow in 1862.

Unsurprisingly, Holmes had little time for superstition to intrude into his investigations. In 'The Devil's Foot' he utterly refused 'to admit diabolical intrusions into the affairs of men', and he famously declared in 'The Sussex Vampire': 'This world is big enough for us. No ghosts need apply.' But he was not above becoming caught up in some of the more pseudoscientific theories of his era. This is no better epitomised than by his dabbling in the now discredited field of phrenology (the study of the skull to identify character traits) in 'The Blue Carbuncle'. Watson told us how 'Holmes clapped the hat upon his head. It came right over the forehead and settled upon the bridge of his nose. "It is a question of cubic capacity," said he; "a man with so large a brain must have something in it."' Phrenology, or cranioscopy as it was originally known, was principally the creation

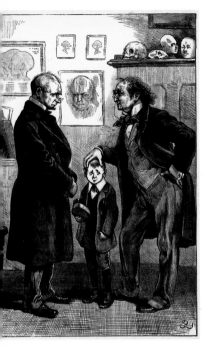

An 1889 newspaper illustration of a rather nervous-looking child being taken for a visit to a phrenologist. Phrenology linked skull shape with character.

of the physiologist Franz Joseph Gall in the late eighteenth century. Not only were his theories largely debunked owing to the lack of empirical proof but they came to be reviled when they were adopted as 'evidence' by advocates of theories of racial superiority.

A rather more significant failing of Holmes as a scientist–detective was his inability to engage with the psychopathological and sociopathological. It has often been noted that no mention was ever made in the canon of perhaps the most notorious murderer in British criminal history, Jack the Ripper. Other writers subsequently engineered numerous engagements between Holmes and the man responsible for the deaths and mutilations of anywhere between five and eleven prostitutes in London's Whitechapel between 1888 and 1891. But there was simply no place in Conan Doyle's tales for the kind of criminal whose crimes seem born from a hateful madness that is beyond rationality or easily identifiable motive. Holmes's opponents are driven by broadly understandable urges of passion, or to secure wealth, or to avenge a wrong. It may be difficult to unlock the mysteries they leave behind, but it is not difficult to get inside their minds and, on many occasions, even to sympathise with their crimes.

Holmes's underlying method of detection may be characterised as imposing a pattern of normality on the world, then searching for where that pattern had become warped or broken. It was in these distortions and gaps that the story of a crime could be read – the bell-rope that did not ring, the dog that did not bark, the building with outer dimensions that didn't correspond to its interior. 'What is out of the common is usually a guide rather than a hindrance,' he said in *A Study in Scarlet.* For all Holmes's eccentricities and general lack of personal engagement, he was a master at reading the world as it should be in 'normal' circumstances and brilliant at spotting the lapses in normality.

It may be argued that in building such a world view of 'normality', Holmes necessarily fell upon stereotypes and archetypes. There is evidence that Holmes was happiest when dealing with simple, shorthand psychological insights. Take his exclamation in 'Shoscombe Old Place': 'Capital, Watson! A thumb-nail sketch. I seem to know the man.' In *The Sign of Four* he expressed his agreement with the philosopher Winwood Reade's assertion that while 'the individual man is an insoluble puzzle, in the aggregate he becomes a mathematical certainty'.

It is very difficult to imagine where he would have started had he been presented with, say, the disembowelled body of Mary Kelly – the fifth victim of Jack the Ripper – discovered in a room in Spitalfields in November 1888. A murder committed with utterly unnecessary brutality against a woman who formed just one link in a chain of victims united only by their geography, profession and poverty. All the plentiful forensic evidence that (Scotland Yard's clumsiness aside) might have been available would have surely counted for little in a crime that did not simply distort the 'natural' pattern but tore it up entirely and left only chaos.

So while there remain those who believe that had Holmes's methods been employed, the identity of Jack the Ripper would be known today, many others recognise that Holmes's analytical skills were best suited to uncovering the cunning of others, not their madness. As he himself said in 'The Naval Treaty', 'the most difficult crime to track is the one which is purposeless'.

Holmes was undoubtedly skilled at employing his powers of analysis and his scientific knowledge but it may be argued that he over-relied on the empirical. Certainly there must be a place for emotional intuition in the solving of crime, yet this was where Holmes was at his most lacking. In the words of Watson, he was as 'deficient in human sympathy as he was preeminent in intelligence'. However, if Conan Doyle had chosen to right this imbalance, we would have been reading about a superhero and not a human being, and that would have been much less fun.

Media coverage of the Ripper Murders was sensationalist. Here the slaying of Annie Chapman in Whitechapel in September 1888 is ghoulishly reported.

THE ADVENTURE OF
THE ENGINEER'S THUMB

FIRST PUBLISHED: The *Strand Magazine*, March 1892, UK; published one month later in the US edition of the *Strand*

SETTING DATE: 1889

WATSON, CURRENTLY LIVING with his wife and running a practice in Paddington, engages Holmes on a case, one of only two such instances. Watson has been stirred from his slumbers some hours earlier by the arrival of Victor Hatherley, a hydraulic engineer brought to the doctor by a guard at the railway station. Hatherley's thumb has been severed.

Hatherley relates how the previous day he had received a visit from a man going by the name of Colonel Lysander Stark. He requested that Hatherley accompany him to a location in the country to inspect a hydraulic press used to make bricks from fuller's earth. Stark emphasised that discretion was essential but managed to overcome the engineer's misgivings with the promise of a fifty-guinea fee.

Hatherley took a train which arrived at the designated station at the prearranged hour of 11.15 p.m. Stark's coach, complete with frosted glass, then took him on an hour-long journey to the country house. Despite Hatherley's attempts to make conversation, Stark had taken on a rather unfriendly air. On arriving at the house, a woman pressed Hatherley to take the opportunity to escape but he failed to heed her warnings.

He then inspected the press and suggested the necessary repairs to restore it to working order. Sure that its stated use of brick-making was a cover story, the engineer challenged Stark. The Colonel promptly turned the machine on and Hatherley only narrowly escaped being crushed within its workings. With the help of the mysterious woman, Hatherley made his escape, but was pursued by two men. As he hung from a window sill, one of the pursuers swung a weapon at him, separating the engineer from his thumb. Nonetheless, he made it to the station and got on an early morning train bound for London.

Holmes immediately works out what the owners of the machine have been up to. Having alerted the police, he, Watson and Hatherley head back to the country house. However, they discover it ablaze and find the criminals have fled. The case is a rare failure for Holmes, who somewhat frivolously suggests the engineer put it down to experience.

A poster from 1923 advertising the imminent release of a film version of 'The Engineer's Thumb'. It starred Eille Norwood, the first screen Holmes superstar.

THE ADVENTURE OF THE NOBLE BACHELOR

FIRST PUBLISHED: The *Strand Magazine*, April 1892, UK; published one month later in the US edition of the *Strand*
SETTING DATE: 1888

LORD ST. SIMON, a rather petulant example of British aristocracy, enlists Holmes's help to investigate the disappearance of his bride, Hatty Doran, on their wedding day. Doran, a wealthy mining heiress from San Francisco, had seemed excited about embarking on married life with her fiancé. All had gone well during the wedding service, save for an insignificant moment of clumsiness when Hatty dropped her bouquet and it was returned to her by a man in the front pew.

However, immediately after the ceremony she snapped at St. Simon in a most uncharacteristic manner and the day went from bad to worse. A former sweetheart, one Flora Millar, made a scene on the doorstep of St. Simon's house during the reception, before she was forcibly packed on her way. Then Hatty went missing, last seen entering Hyde Park with an unknown male. Later her wedding garb was discovered on the shore of the Serpentine.

Holmes and Lestrade embark on a characteristically competitive pursuit of the truth. When a note to Hatty is found, signed 'F. H. M.', Lestrade is sure that culpability rests with Millar. Holmes, though, is less convinced and sets about finding the solution without leaving the confines of 221B. He soon discovers the fate of Hatty and realises that the answer to this knotty problem rests in her past back in the United States. St. Simon is ultimately granted a full explanation of events, but not enough to appease his deep sense of injustice.

A classic view of the streets of San Francisco, the former home of Hatty Doran. Conan Doyle had a fascination with the USA.

A keen Americophile, Conan Doyle used this story to voice his hope of one day seeing 'the same world-wide community under a flag which shall be the quartering of the Union Jack with the Stars and Stripes'. However, the reliance on a giant red herring leaves the reader feeling a little cheated. In Conan Doyle's own opinion, the story rated 'about bottom of the list'.

THE ADVENTURE OF THE BERYL CORONET

FIRST PUBLISHED: The *Strand Magazine*, May 1892, UK; published one month later in the US edition of the *Strand*
SETTING DATE: 1886

THE HIGHLY AGITATED Alexander Holder, a prominent banker from Streatham, calls on Holmes in a bid to save his reputation. Holder has been approached by a renowned private client for a loan of £50,000. The client offered the Beryl Coronet, a greatly valuable diadem under public ownership, as a guarantee. Holder, unwilling to keep such an item in the bank's vaults, instead took it home so as to keep it under his personal guard.

He awoke during the night to discover his son, Arthur (a man with a penchant for gambling), in his dressing room manhandling the crown. Then Mary, the banker's niece, stumbled upon the scene and immediately fainted. On closer inspection three beryls were discovered missing from the crown. Yet under his father's questioning, Arthur refused to provide any explanation of what had gone on. Holder then turned to Holmes as the man to avert a scandal.

Watson feels the evidence of Arthur's silence is compelling but Holmes's contrasting interpretation is that it is a potential sign of innocence. He takes an inventory of people associated with the house, including Arthur's rather raffish friend Sir George Burnwell, a maid, Lucy Parr, and her one-legged boyfriend, Francis Prosper. He then undertakes a close study of the house and inspects various tracks evident in the recently fallen snow, as well as assuming the guise of a 'common loafer'.

When Holmes reveals the truth of the apparent theft to Holder, his initial joy soon turns to shock and disappointment.

An atmospheric depiction of Alexander Holder wandering through a London snowstorm. (Illustration by Barry Moser)

THE ADVENTURE OF
THE COPPER BEECHES

FIRST PUBLISHED: The *Strand Magazine*, June 1892, UK; published one month later in the US edition of the *Strand*
SETTING DATE: 1890

THE FEISTY AND elegant Violet Hunter approaches Holmes with a most unusual conundrum. She has been offered a job as a governess by one Jephro Rucastle, who is offering an extremely generous £120 per year (up from the £48 she had previously earned) as long as Miss Hunter fulfils certain strange conditions. One of these is that she must cut her thick head of chestnut hair. She ultimately accepts the job at the Copper Beeches, an estate in Hampshire, but both she and Holmes have some reservations and the Detective reassures her that, should it be needed, a telegram will guarantee his help.

Sure enough, barely two weeks pass before he is called to a tryst in Winchester with Miss Hunter. Her story has become no less strange. Her six-year-old charge has a streak of cruelty that sees him torturing animals, while the household servants, Mr and Mrs Toller, are an unfriendly pair. He is a drunkard responsible for looking after Rucastle's mastiff, which is kept deliberately underfed and allowed to prowl the estate. On introducing Violet to the beast, Rucastle gave an ominous warning that she had best not cross the threshold at night.

The Rucastles have made yet more odd requests, including that Violet should wear a dress of electric blue and sit with her back to a window in the front room. Mr Rucastle on occasions entertains her

The fragrant Violet Hunter, as depicted on an Alexander Boguslavsky cigarette card of 1923. A wronged heroine, she appealed to Holmes's more tender side.

with uproarious stories while his wife sits utterly unmoved. She is Rucastle's second wife and he had a daughter, Alice, from his first marriage though he says the girl has moved to Philadelphia. Suspicious that there was something going on behind her back through the window, Violet one day smuggled a shard of mirror glass inside a handkerchief and spotted a young man looking up from the road below.

She then discovered a lock of what she thought was her hair locked up in a drawer before realising her tress was still packed in with her belongings. The house has an unused wing where Violet strayed one evening and believed she saw someone. Terrified, she fled, only to be confronted by a very angry Rucastle, who eventually claimed he used the wing to indulge his passion for photography.

Holmes quickly surmises the nature of the dastardly plot into which Miss Hunter has been unwittingly dragged. With the crime solved, Miss Hunter begins a new life running a school for girls. Meanwhile, Watson's hopes that Holmes's heart might be melted by the governess are disappointed. The tale was developed by Conan Doyle from a plot devised by his mother.

HOLMES AND ME  PHILIP FRANKS

Philip Franks is a familiar face on TV and the stage, playing roles as varied as Hamlet for the RSC, Charlie in The Darling Buds of May *and Sergeant Craddock in* Heartbeat *(both for ITV). He has also had a distinguished career on radio and has won much acclaim as a theatre director. He played Dr Watson to Peter Egan's Sherlock Holmes on stage in* The Hound of the Baskervilles.

Was Watson a character you had always wanted to play?

Yes, I had wanted to have a crack at Watson for some time. I inherited a love of the stories from my father, and a love of the Basil Rathbone/Nigel Bruce films, though it's a complicated love affair, given how very far away they are from Doyle. It's one of the great double acts of literature, isn't it? They are funny with each other, supportive, argumentative, and entirely complementary. When the offer came through to do *The Hound* I jumped at it, and luckily got on extremely well with Peter Egan. I can imagine how painful it would be for a Watson who didn't like his Holmes, and vice versa.

The Spectator *described your performance as 'the perfect Watson – tweedy, loyal and far from thick'. What for you are the key aspects of Watson?*

Well, 'tweedy, loyal and far from thick' sounds pretty accurate to me. I never read reviews – I think they can only harm your work, be they good or bad, but it's nice to know someone liked it. He is tweedy, in that tweed, a hard-working, modest and durable material, is both made to high-quality traditional designs but is also made up of many varied colours, though the final effect is muted. So, if he were a cloth, tweed is what he would be. Loyal certainly, as loyal as a dog, but not uncritical by any means – Holmes's instability and lack of social grace are a constant worry to Watson and he spends a lot of time making up for his friend's almost autistic inability to interact with fellow human beings. Far from thick, indeed – he is, after all, the author of the stories, an intelligent, sensitive man and a qualified doctor. What he is not, and Holmes *is*, is a genius, and he is quite clever enough to realise this, and modest enough not to mind.

Did you look back at the original stories or other actors' performances ahead of performing the role?

The script that Clive Francis put together is very faithful. I did watch a lot of other screen versions, but the script, the story and the other stories are all you really need.

Philip Franks imbued his Watson with a sense of dependability and strength.

My favourite Watson of all is Edward Hardwicke, but I do have a sneaking affection for dear old Nigel Bruce, because he is just so funny and sweet. Hardwicke is dead-on perfect, though. Modest and intelligent, a perfect foil to the brilliant Jeremy Brett's tortured genius of a Holmes.

I loathe any version that tries to send them up, though – shame on Peter Cook and Dudley Moore! I'm not mad keen either on versions that try to be cleverer than Doyle (Billy Wilder, Ben Kingsley). The actor I thought was going to be perfect, Ian Richardson, was let down by clunky direction. I thought John Wood was marvellous on stage but he didn't really have a Watson at all in the Gillette play. Nicol Williamson is interesting and Peter Cushing is fine but without the terrifying edge that makes Brett so special, or the laser precision of Basil Rathbone.

But were there ever to be another TV version of a tranche of the stories I would be beating a path to the door of whoever produces it with my tweeds brushed and my moustache neatly trimmed . . .

What is it that makes Holmes still popular for a modern audience?

I think the relationship is true and the stories are exciting, and that means they will continue to hook audiences.

SCOTLAND YARD AND THE POLICE

HOLMES HAD A healthy disrespect for most official forms of authority and, as a private consulting detective, he set himself apart from the regular police. While always quick to have a little dig at whichever Bobby decided to disregard his hints and advice, his relationship with the police was largely one of playful competition. As a *consulting* detective, it was often the police that were doing the consulting – if they did not have faith in his abilities or he in their basic worth, the relationship could never have worked.

The lot of a nineteenth-century officer of the law was not, on the whole, a very happy one. The Glasgow Police were established in 1800, becoming the world's first organised force. London's Metropolitan Police Force was formed in 1829 and the City of London Police came into being ten years later. In part, this was a response to a period of particularly intense lawlessness that accompanied Britain's post-Napoleonic Wars economic depression. The police, known as Peelers after their founder Robert Peel, did not receive a warm welcome from the public at

Great Scotland Yard in Westminster was the original home of the Metropolitan Police. The Force moved to New Scotland Yard, pictured here, in 1890.

large. For many proud Englishmen who valued their civil liberties above all else, there was a fear that the police would restrict these freedoms as had happened in several countries on the Continent. The sense of animosity towards the police was such that there were over 2,000 recorded assaults against officers in 1887.

Officers customarily worked seven days a week and got paid roughly the same as an unskilled labourer. In the early days, policing was a fairly rudimentary business and it was not until 1842 that anything as sophisticated as a detective force was established, and then only comprising an inspector and six officers. It would be another 36 years until the CID came into being.

With the relative affluence that marked the second half of the nineteenth century, crime levels fell significantly and consistently. Yet with the middle class navel-gazing over issues of personal morality and a spiralling number of newspapers in search of a good story, there was a sense that Britain had never been a more dangerous place. This panic reached its nadir with the Jack the Ripper murders in 1888. Public faith in the ability of the police to protect them collapsed, and not entirely without reason. For instance, it would come to light that at the murder scene of victim number 4, Catherine Eddowes, there was a slogan chalked on a nearby wall, presumably by the Ripper. It read 'THE JUWES ARE THE MEN THAT WILL NOT BE BLAMED FOR NOTHING'. Terrified that there would be an anti-Semitic riot if news of the graffiti leaked out, Scotland Yard's Commissioner, Sir Charles Warren, had it wiped away before it could be photographed. While his motives in taking this action may have been noble, it would certainly have horrified Holmes, who was ahead of his time in realising the value of thorough crime scene analysis.

Holmes enjoyed nothing more than ruffling Scotland Yard feathers. He famously employed the Irregulars, a posse of ragamuffins known as 'the Baker Street division of the detective police force' and led by their 'dirty little lieutenant' Wiggins. Holmes believed there was 'more work to be got out of one of those little beggars than out of a dozen of the force'. In *The Sign of Four* he went still further by claiming to value the assistance of a dog, Toby, more 'than that of the whole detective force of London'. In 'The Blue Carbuncle' Holmes said that he was 'not retained by the police to supply their deficiencies' but all too often he found himself solving cases in spite of their efforts. In 'The Boscombe Valley Mystery' the police had ravaged the crime scene 'like a herd of buffalo' and he would regularly decry the 'imbecility' of individual officers.

Yet in gentler moments Holmes found some admirable qualities among his professional colleagues, particularly their courage. For instance Jones, the official police agent in 'The Red-Headed League', was condemned as one of the imbeciles but then praised for being 'as brave as a bulldog and as tenacious as a lobster'. Then in 'The Red Circle' Holmes said: 'Our official detectives may blunder in the matter of intelligence, but never in that of courage.' Of all the policemen he worked with, he had highest hopes for the young, alert and eager Stanley Hopkins (active in 'Black Peter', 'The Abbey Grange' and 'The Golden Pince-Nez'), who in turn had much respect for Holmes's methods. Perhaps the greatest evidence of Holmes's grudging affinity with the professional force was his willingness to allow them to take the praise for his successes. In 'The Naval Treaty' he revealed that of fifty-three cases he had solved, a full forty-nine had been credited to the police. So it may even have been with a tinge of sadness that in *The Valley of Fear* he said: 'I go into a case to help the ends of justice and the work of the police. If I have ever separated myself from the official force, it is because they have first separated themselves from me.'

If Holmes was critical of the police, they were highly suspicious of his deductive methods. Holmes made a virtue of keeping very close to his chest any progress he was making. He was reluctant to share theories until he had convinced himself of their correctitude, and then, with a flourish, he would reveal all. As if by magic. Indeed, in 'The Second Stain' he was described as 'a wizard, a sorcerer'. Such unpredictability was disquieting for the average plod of the stories. Inspector Athelney Jones voiced the concern of no doubt countless colleagues when, in *The Sign of Four*, he said of Holmes: 'He is irregular in his methods and a little quick perhaps in jumping at theories.' Lestrade went so far as to suggest that he was 'too much inclined to be cocksure' in 'The Norwood Builder'.

And yet these apparent sceptics turned to Holmes time and time again. Scratch away at the criticism they threw in his direction and a rather more sympathetic attitude towards the Detective is evident. Jones, for all his doubts, conceded that Holmes 'would have made a most promising officer'. Similarly, Gregson said in 'The Red Circle' that 'I was never in a case yet that I didn't feel stronger for having you on my side.' *The Valley of Fear* even alludes to a relationship approaching friendship between Holmes and one Alec MacDonald, a superstar among the police force whose own excellence allowed him to recognise that of Holmes.

The most famous of all Conan Doyle's policemen was Inspector Lestrade, who appeared in thirteen of the stories. The jousting between him and Holmes amus-

Despite a tendency to bait each other, Holmes and Lestrade possessed a grudging mutual respect. Sidney Paget drew this illustration for 'The Norwood Builder'.

ingly symbolised the undulating relations between police and consulting detective. Appearing first in *A Study in Scarlet*, he and his colleague Inspector Gregson were described as 'the pick of a bad lot' – hard-working but uninspired with a 'want of imaginative intuition'.

Conan Doyle depicted Lestrade as sallow and rat-faced (somewhat at odds with a description of him in 'The Second Stain' as having 'bulldog features'), ferret-like, furtive and sly-looking, with beady eyes. At times Holmes was openly rude about him. In 'The Boscombe Valley Mystery' he told him 'demurely' that he was poorly equipped to handle facts and referred to him as an 'imbecile'. And in *The Sign of Four* he suggested that being out of his depth was Lestrade's normal state. Nor was Lestrade insensitive to Holmes's barbs, and in *A Study in Scarlet* there is the rather pathetic sight of Lestrade speaking with 'the injured tone of one who suspects that he is being laughed at'.

Yet elsewhere Holmes is distinctly more charitable. In *The Hound* Holmes called him 'the best of the professionals' and in 'The Cardboard Box' suggested that his tenacity 'has brought him to the top at Scotland Yard'. By the time of 'The Six Napoleons', Watson reported that Lestrade was a regular evening visitor to 221B and that 'his visits were welcome to Sherlock Holmes'. Progress indeed. In the same story, Lestrade revealed the now high regard in which Holmes was held by the average Peeler:

'We're not jealous of you at Scotland Yard. No, sir, we are very proud of you, and if you come down to-morrow, there's not a man, from the oldest inspector to the youngest constable, who wouldn't be glad to shake you by the hand.'

And quite right too, for even the best that the Yard had to offer paled against the Great Detective. E. W. Hornung summed it up best of all: 'There's no police like Holmes.'

A rather stern-looking Inspector Lestrade as depicted in Alexander Boguslavsky's cigarette card series of Conan Doyle's creations.

THE ADVENTURE OF
SILVER BLAZE

FIRST PUBLISHED: The *Strand Magazine*, December 1892, UK; published in the US edition of the *Strand Magazine* one month after UK publication and in *Harper's Weekly*, 25 February 1893, USA

SETTING DATE: 1888

WITH THE FAMOUS Wessex Cup approaching, the 3–1 favourite for the race, Silver Blaze, is reported missing from the stables of Colonel Ross, at King's Pyland on Dartmoor. In addition, the body of the horse's trainer, John Straker, has been found on the moor, his head caved in. Holmes's presence was requested by both Ross and one Inspector Gregory, but Holmes tarried in the belief that such a prominent horse cannot possibly be hidden for long. This, he admits, was 'a blunder'.

By the time he and Watson arrive at King's Pyland, Gregory has a man in custody. The suspect is a London turf accountant, Fitzroy Simpson, who had paid a visit to the estate on the night of the disappearance, ostensibly in search of tips from the stable lad, Hunter. Simpson carried a heavy walking stick. The stable lad saw him off and sent word back to Straker, who set out to check all was well at the stables. It was after daybreak that the horse was discovered missing and then Straker's body found (along with a small knife). It is assumed he died in a struggle with the horsenapper. Yet Holmes is unconvinced that Simpson is the guilty party. Where could he possibly have hidden Silver Blaze? And if he had wanted to kill the horse, why not simply do so at the stables?

Holmes traces prints, both human and equine, across the moor and soon ascertains the location of Silver Blaze. To uncover the murderer, he assimilates a host of clues including a sizeable milliner's bill found in the victim's coat, a wax vesta match, an opium-laced dish of curried mutton, some lame sheep and, of course, 'the curious incident of the dog in the night-time'. The final question is, will Silver Blaze turn up in time to race for the Cup?

A classic tale, exhibiting some of Holmes's most imaginative deductions, it also marked the beginning of a fruitful relationship between Detective and Dartmoor (later used as the setting for *The Hound of the Baskervilles*).

While betting was not among Holmes's multitude of vices, Watson was rather partial to placing a wager on the horses.

THE ADVENTURE OF
THE CARDBOARD BOX

FIRST PUBLISHED: The *Strand Magazine*, January 1893, UK; published in the US edition of the *Strand Magazine* one month after UK publication and in *Harper's Weekly*, 14 January 1893, USA

SETTING DATE: 1888

THIS STORY WAS initially included in *Memoirs* but at the behest of Conan Doyle, unhappy with its gory and sensationalist content, it was removed from subsequent editions. Some twenty-four years after initial publication it appeared in American editions of *His Last Bow*, but in British editions it has traditionally been kept with the *Memoirs*.

The story opens with a set piece in which Holmes explains the train of thought that allows him to seemingly read Watson's mind. Owing to the story's disjointed publishing history, the opening scene was repeated wholesale in 'The Resident Patient'.

Inspector Lestrade has invited Holmes to help solve a much publicised incident in Croydon, in the London suburbs. Susan Cushing, an unassuming spinster aged fifty, has received a parcel from Belfast containing two severed human ears preserved in salt. Holmes, it emerges, has made some study of the human ear and instantly recognises that these examples come from two individuals. The image of the severed ears would have had particular

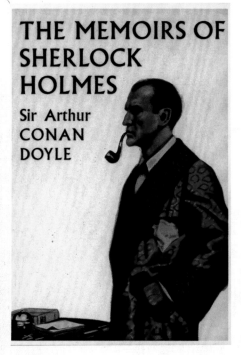

THE MEMOIRS OF SHERLOCK HOLMES

Sir Arthur CONAN DOYLE

John Murray published the canon in an iconic series of 'White' covers in the 1920s and '30s.

resonance given that Jack the Ripper had hacked off the ear of one of his victims, Catherine Eddowes, at around the same time as this story is set.

Lestrade suspects that this is a distasteful prank perpetrated by three medical students who had previously lodged with Miss Cushing until she evicted them for unruly behaviour. However, Holmes considers that the roughly hacked ears and the absence of preserving fluid point to a non-medical perpetrator. His view is affirmed when he considers the facts of the Belfast posting location, the rough handwriting of the address label (including the initial misspelling of Croydon) and the knot used to tie string around the parcel. He continues his investigations by visiting Susan's sister Sarah in nearby Wallington and remains undeterred when she is unable to see him on account of suffering 'brain fever'. A telegraph to Liverpool concludes his investigations.

THE ADVENTURE OF THE YELLOW FACE

FIRST PUBLISHED: The *Strand Magazine*, February 1893, UK; published in the US edition of the *Strand Magazine* one month after UK publication and in *Harper's Weekly*, 11 February 1893, USA

SETTING DATE: 1888

HOLMES IS SUFFERING yet another period of insufficient professional stimulation. After an amble in the park with Watson, he arrives back at 221B to discover a caller has come and gone, leaving behind a pipe. From this evidence, Holmes characteristically impresses with an analysis of the potential client.

This client turns out to be one Grant Munro, nervously restless, who tells a story of matrimonial deceit. He recounts how his wife Effie, for three years the perfect loving spouse, has for the last few days seemed distant, as if there is a barrier between them. He tells Holmes and Watson of Effie's past as a settler in America, where she married a lawyer and became Mrs Hebron. The couple had a child but when both father and daughter died of yellow fever, Effie returned to England and lived comfortably from her personal fortune.

Grant had then married her and the Munros set up home at Norbury, set amid the countryside outside London. All had been well until one day Effie asked Grant for one hundred pounds. She would not divulge the reason she needed such a sum. He then discovered her paying visits at all hours to a nearby cottage, where he had seen at the window 'an unnatural and inhuman' yellow face. Naturally, his suspicions were roused and, unable to extract an explanation from Effie, he broke into the house to find it empty, save for a portrait of his wife.

Holmes packs Grant off with instructions to make contact again should the cottage be reoccupied. Holmes divulges to Watson that 'this is a bad business' and speculates that Effie's husband may never have died at all. Grant soon enough summons Holmes and Watson to Norbury, where a showdown takes place. It is apparent that Holmes has for once been barking up quite the wrong tree and he beseeches Watson to whisper the word 'Norbury' to him should he ever get overconfident.

The story has split subsequent generations of readers over whether it conveys a message of admirable social liberalism or rather underscores the ingrained prejudices of the Victorian period.

It is likely that Holmes and Watson took their walk at the beginning of the story in Hyde Park, one of London's most popular destinations for a promenade. Pictured here is the Park's famous Rotten Row.

THE ADVENTURE OF
THE STOCKBROKER'S CLERK

FIRST PUBLISHED: The *Strand Magazine*, March 1893, UK; published in the US edition of the *Strand Magazine* one month after UK publication and in *Harper's Weekly*, 11 March 1893, USA

SETTING DATE: 1889

HOLMES PAYS A visit to his old friend Watson, who has established a thriving practice in Paddington following his marriage. He is nonetheless happy to drop everything and take up Holmes's invitation of a trip to Birmingham in the company of his new client, Hall Pycroft, the eponymous stockbroker's clerk.

Pycroft, a young, honest-faced cockney fellow, relates how he had previously worked for the firm Coxon and Woodhouse's until they had fallen on hard times. After a spell out of work, he secured a new position (without even the formality of an interview) with Mawson & Williams, one of the most respected stockbroking firms in the City, for £200 per year. However, he immediately received a counteroffer from a gentleman called Arthur Pinner, who claimed he had heard great things of Pycroft and was offering a mouth-watering £500 a year basic to come and work for the Franco-Midland Hardware Company in Birmingham. The company ran a chain of hardware stores in France and had further bases in Belgium and Italy, Pycroft was told. The opportunity seemed too good to turn down.

Pinner explained that he had rowed with Mawson & Williams over the prospective employee and persuaded Pycroft that he should not even bother with a letter of resignation to them. Pinner advanced him £100 and got Pycroft to sign a declaration that he was willing to act as the company's business manager for the agreed salary. He then gave him instructions to travel to Birmingham the

Corporation Street in Birmingham, pictured here as it was around the turn of the twentieth century, was constructed in the 1870s and '80s after a slum clearance.

following day to receive further instructions from Arthur's brother, Harry.

The interview did not go as Pycroft expected. The company's unmarked office was shabby, and rather than being sent to Paris to oversee business, Pycroft found he was to remain in Birmingham extracting information from French business directories. Pycroft was also unnerved by the astounding physical resemblance between the two brothers, even down to the presence of a gold tooth. He concluded that Arthur and Harry were one and the same man. It was then that Pycroft decided on returning to London to consult the Great Detective. On arriving in Birmingham, Holmes, Watson and Pycroft head straight for the company's office at 126b Corporation Street and discover Pinner, anxiously studying the newspapers. The scene is set for a dramatic conclusion to the tale.

HOLMES AND HIS PLEASURES

'Which is it to-day,' I asked, 'morphine or cocaine?'
The Sign of Four

A light-hearted take on the Holmes legend, created by Tom Richmond, whose work is featured in numerous publications including *Mad Magazine*.

WATSON'S DESCRIPTION OF Holmes as 'a brain without a heart' ensured that the Detective would be dogged by a reputation for coldness and austerity. Indeed, when he was engrossed in his work he would live a frugal existence devoid of any distractions. But at other times Holmes, described as a 'Bohemian soul' in 'A Scandal in Bohemia', drank from the cup of *fin de siècle* hedonism with the best of them. Watson's assertion in 'The Yellow Face' that 'save for the occasional use of cocaine, he [Holmes] had no vices' simply does not stand up against the evidence. More accurate are his words in 'The Devil's Foot' that Holmes 'showed some symptoms of giving way in the face of constant hard work of a most exacting kind, aggravated, perhaps, by occasional indiscretions of his own'.

The vice most readily associated with the Detective is, of course, tobacco. Cigarette, cigar and pipe were all much loved friends, his tobacco stuffed indelicately into a Persian slipper at 221B. Only four stories fail to mention smoking and some of his finest work was undertaken amid a 'dense tobacco haze'. In 'The Golden Pince-Nez' Holmes presented himself as a 'connoisseur' of cigarettes, while an old and oily clay pipe was described as 'a counsellor' in 'A Case of Identity'. Cigars tended to be smoked in company and cigarettes on the go but his real passion was for pipes. It is one of life's oddities that the canon makes mention of assorted pipes – clays, briers and long cherry-woods – but never the calabash (or bent), the long and curved pipe that has become a virtual Holmes trademark. It would seem that we owe thanks to a long list of illustrators and actors for its dominant place in the public perception.

As for tobacco, Holmes favoured the strongest shag (rough-cut) tobacco he could find. Watson was an ally in this particular hobby and went for ship's tobacco, itself not for the faint-hearted. In many ways smoking was the stuff of life for Holmes, though Watson appears to have been something of a hypocrite for in 'The Devil's Foot' Holmes promised to 'resume that course of tobacco-poisoning which you have so often and so justly condemned'. In 'The Dying Detective' Holmes fasted for three days but it was not food or water he missed most. Instead 'it is the tobacco which I find most irksome'. The sign of a really good case was the amount of smoking required to work through the problem. There is something rather touching in the image of Holmes 'sitting upon five pillows and consuming an ounce of shag' as he unknotted the case of 'The Man with the Twisted Lip'. 'The

Red-Headed League' even contributed a new phrase to the English language when that particular mystery was described as 'a three pipe problem'. Such a passion was tobacco that Holmes produced a monograph on the subject of identifying 140 different types of ash.

He also enjoyed the occasional drink, presumably finding a willing partner once more in Watson, who we know favoured the Burgundy wines of Beaune. While he happily enjoyed a good claret, Holmes seems to have gone more for a whisky and soda, a tipple he enjoyed in both 'The Red-Headed League' and 'The Noble Bachelor'. However, he did not restrict his drug intake to the relative innocence of tobacco and alcohol, dabbling with rather graver substances too. It is a common misconception that Holmes partook of opium, probably arising from his appearance in an opium den for professional reasons at the start of 'The Man with the Twisted Lip'. His actual drugs of choice were cocaine and, to a lesser extent, morphine.

Cocaine had been presented to the world in 1884 as a wonder anaesthetic by Karl Koller and it was some decades before its effects and addictiveness were understood. Nonetheless, Watson was a strong advocate against its use and Holmes could have been under no illusion as to its detrimental impact. 'I suppose that its influence is physically a bad one,' he admitted in *The Sign of Four*, somewhat coyly underplaying the dangers. A habitual injector who favoured a 7-percent solution in water, his usage was most prolific in the early part of his career and had virtually ended by the later stories. For a modern reader, the description in *The Sign of Four* of Holmes self-administering remains graphic and shocking. This was Conan Doyle as a Victorian Irvine Welsh:

Sidney Paget expertly captured Holmes's sense of serenity as he spent time on possibly his second favourite activity (after catching criminals).

Sherlock Holmes took his bottle from the corner of the mantelpiece, and his hypodermic syringe from its neat morocco case. With his long, white, nervous fingers he adjusted the delicate needle and rolled back his left shirtcuff. For some little time his eyes rested thoughtfully upon the sinewy forearm and wrist, all dotted and scarred with innumerable puncture-marks. Finally, he thrust the sharp point home, pressed down the tiny piston, and sank back into the velvet-lined armchair with a long sigh of satisfaction.

His drug taking was directly linked to his workload (or absence thereof). The art of detecting provided him with the mental stimulus he craved, but when he lacked a case to get his teeth into he would turn to drugs. Again in *The Sign*

of Four he explained: 'Give me problems, give me work, give me the most abstruse cryptogram, or the most intricate analysis, and I am in my own proper atmosphere. I can dispense then with artificial stimulants. But I abhor the dull routine of existence. I crave for mental exaltation.'

Fortunately, the ever faithful Watson stuck doggedly to his task and by the time of 'The Missing Three-Quarter' he reported that Holmes had been gradually weaned from 'that drug mania which had threatened once to check his remarkable career'.

Music, and specifically the violin, was a more constructive passion for the Detective. In *A Study in Scarlet* he pondered: 'Do you remember what Darwin says about music? He claims that the power of producing and appreciating it existed among the human race long before the power of speech was arrived at.' His tastes were reasonably eclectic. Mendelssohn, Watson related in *A Study in Scarlet*, was a particular favourite and there were honourable mentions for Chopin (*A Study in Scarlet*), Wagner ('The Red Circle'), Jacques Offenbach ('The Mazarin Stone') and Paganini ('The Cardboard Box'). Additionally, he made special efforts to see the famed violinists Wilhelmina Norman-Neruda and Pablo de Sarasate and wrote a treatise on the little-known Motets of Lassus.

Holmes played himself and according to Watson had some gift, his skills 'remarkable, but as eccentric as all his other accomplishments'. Alas for Watson, Holmes tended towards idle scraping that might or might not be melodious at any given moment. However, when he set his mind to it Holmes could play classical pieces in a most accomplished way and would compensate Watson for the odd droning session 'by playing in quick succession a whole series of my favourite

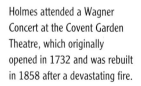

Holmes attended a Wagner Concert at the Covent Garden Theatre, which originally opened in 1732 and was rebuilt in 1858 after a devastating fire.

airs'. Holmes owned his own Stradivarius, the greatest of all violins, which 'was worth at least five hundred guineas' but which he had bought for fifty-five shillings on the Tottenham Court Road. This purchase, detailed in 'The Cardboard Box', suggests Holmes was an extraordinary wheeler-dealer or else rather naive not to doubt the provenance of his instrument. Incidentally, in 'The Illustrious Client' Holmes intriguingly made reference to 'my old friend Charlie Peace', a real-life robber and killer of the period who had won some early fame on stage as 'The Modern Paganini'.

As a descendant of the famed Vernet painters, we might have expected Holmes to have had some considerable interest in the visual arts too. However, this seems somewhat wide of the mark. In *The Hound* he did spend two hours 'entirely absorbed in the pictures of the modern Belgian masters' at a gallery on Bond Street but would not talk of art, of which, Watson held, 'he had the crudest ideas'.

A master of fisticuffs, Holmes is pictured preparing to send his adversary 'home in a cart'.

More to his taste, somewhat surprisingly, was old-fashioned fighting. In 'The "Gloria Scott"' he admitted that 'bar fencing and boxing I had few athletic tastes'. His claim in 'The Solitary Cyclist' that 'I have some proficiency in the good old British sport of boxing' was seemingly borne out in *The Sign of Four*, where he encountered a prizefighter called McMurdo. It emerged that Holmes had fought three rounds against him in a match several years earlier. McMurdo recalled the contest and suggested Holmes had wasted his talent and that he might have gone far. Later, in 'The Yellow Face', Watson would confirm that he was 'one of the finest boxers of his weight that I have ever seen'. We see Holmes fighting first-hand in 'The Solitary Cyclist', taking on the disreputable Woodley in a bar-room brawl. Holmes emerged the winner and recalled the fight to Watson: 'The next few minutes were delicious. It was a straight left against a slogging ruffian. I emerged as you see me. Mr. Woodley went home in a cart.' Rarely is Holmes seen so pumped up with adrenalin anywhere in the canon. In *A Study in Scarlet*, Watson also alluded to Holmes's skills in armed combat, relating that he was an expert in singlestick and sword fighting.

Then there is the Detective's proficiency in 'baritsu', a fighting style that seems never to have existed and was almost certainly an authorial error. It is probable that Holmes actually excelled at Bartitsu, a hybrid English martial art that he employed to overcome Moriarty at the Reichenbach Falls. It is ironic that when push literally came to shove, the great cerebral detective should have owed his life to his passion for physical combat.

DR JOSEPH BELL

ADRIAN CONAN DOYLE famously noted: 'Sherlock Holmes was Sir Arthur Conan Doyle. A man, he once wrote, cannot spin a character out of his own inner consciousness and make it really life-like unless he has the possibilities of that character within himself.'

Arthur, though, acknowledged that Holmes sprang from other sources, most notably Joseph Bell, under whom he studied during his medical training at Edinburgh University. In 1892 Conan Doyle wrote to his old mentor to tell him: 'It is certainly to you that I owe Sherlock Holmes . . . I do not think that his analytical work is in the least an exaggeration of some effects which I have seen you produce in the out-patient ward.'

Bell was born in 1837 and became a professor of clinical surgery. He first taught Conan Doyle in 1877 and two years later Conan Doyle became his outpatient clerk at the Edinburgh Royal Infirmary (a relationship dramatised, and fictionalised, many years later in the BBC's *Murder Rooms* series). Endowed with a remarkable power to notice and deduce, Bell's show-stopping trick was to diagnose a patient and provide details of his background without being given a word of history. He was reputedly able to discern a sailor by a rolling gait, a traveller's route by the tattoos he bore, and any number of occupations from a glimpse at a subject's hands. Bell was to write:

From close observation and deduction you can make a correct diagnosis of any and every case. However never neglect to ratify your deductions.

One could quite imagine Holmes asking for these words on his gravestone. Indeed, in 'The Book of Life', an article referenced in *A Study in Scarlet*, Holmes wrote:

Let him, on meeting a fellow-mortal, learn at a glance to distinguish the history of the man, and the trade or profession to which he belongs. Puerile as such an exercise may seem, it sharpens the faculties of observation, and teaches one where to look and what to look for. By a man's finger nails, by his coat-sleeve, by his boot, by his trouser knees, by the callosities of his forefinger and thumb, by his expression, by his shirt cuffs – by each of these things a man's calling is plainly revealed.

On one occasion Conan Doyle witnessed Bell accurately describe a patient as a non-commissioned officer, recently discharged from the Highland Regiment

A rare portrait of Dr Joseph Bell, Conan Doyle's inspirational mentor during his studies in Edinburgh who served as a blueprint for the Great Detective.

posted in Barbados. Holmes was to echo this incident very closely when he deduced Watson's history on first meeting him in *A Study in Scarlet*. Physically, too, Bell had similarities to the Great Detective, being tall and lean and possessing a rather hawkish nose and piercing eyes. He was also friends with a Dr Watson, who had served with distinction in the Crimean War.

There is a growing theory among some scholars that Bell secretly took part in the investigation of several Edinburgh murders. Most notable was the case of Eugene Marie Chantrelle, a French immigrant accused of poisoning his wife Elizabeth and attempting to make it look like she had been gassed accidentally. (See section on Dr Henry Littlejohn.) Most certainly Bell was a man of considerable accomplishment. A Fellow of the Royal College of Surgeons, his medical text books were widely published and he also found time to be a Justice of the Peace and Queen Victoria's personal surgeon. He died in 1911.

Sir Ian Richardson played both Bell and Holmes on television. Also pictured here are Charles Dance as Sir Henry Carlyle and Robin Laing as Conan Doyle.

DR HENRY LITTLEJOHN

If Joseph Bell was the principal real-life inspiration for Holmes, there is a good case to say that Edinburgh's Dr Henry Littlejohn played his part too.

Henry Duncan Littlejohn was born in the Scottish capital in 1826, the son of a master baker. Having graduated in Medicine from Edinburgh University, he moved to Paris to study at the Sorbonne before returning to his hometown in 1854 to become a Fellow of the Royal College of Surgeons.

In a remarkable career he was, inter alia, Edinburgh's Police Surgeon and Medical Officer of Health as well as Chair of Forensic Medicine at his alma mater. He wrote an influential report on hygiene standards in the city and co-founded the Royal Hospital for Sick Children but was best known for his role in some one hundred capital trials. With an interest in toxicology and the latest forensic developments, he cut a dashing figure in his frock coat and top hat and was a formidable presence in the courtroom. Conan Doyle was aware of his work not only through reports in the press but as an attendee at his university lectures.

In 1893 Littlejohn appeared for the prosecution in the infamous Ardlamont Case. Three companions – a young tutor called Alfred Monson, his pupil Cecil Hambrough and another friend of Monson – had gone hunting on the Ardlamont Estate in Argyll but Hambrough never returned, having supposedly shot himself. Monson subsequently attempted to cash in two life insurance policies taken out a few weeks previously, with Monson's wife as the main beneficiary. He was duly charged with murder. Littlejohn gave evidence showing how Hambrough's wounds could not have been self-inflicted but the jury sensationally returned a verdict of 'not proven' (an option available in Scottish courts alongside 'guilty' and 'not guilty'). The case was also notable because Littlejohn's testimony was supported by that of his colleague and friend, Joseph Bell.

Fifteen years earlier the two almost certainly cooperated in the conviction of Eugene Marie Chantrelle, with Littlejohn attending the subsequent execution. As Chantrelle went to the gallows, he is said to have addressed Littlejohn with the words: 'Give my compliments to Joe Bell. He did a good job in bringing me to the scaffold.'

THE ADVENTURE OF THE 'GLORIA SCOTT'

FIRST PUBLISHED: The *Strand Magazine*, April 1893, UK; published in the US edition of the *Strand Magazine* one month after UK publication and in *Harper's Weekly*, 15 April 1893, USA

SETTING DATE: 1874

NOTABLE AS THE first case in which Sherlock Holmes was ever engaged and the one that persuaded him that he could forge a career in the art of detection. Holmes tells Watson of how he spent a month in Norfolk holidaying at the estate of the wealthy Trevor family. Victor Trevor was Holmes's only friend from the two years he spent at university. Trevor's father, a Justice of the Peace who had made his fortune from Australian gold, was amazed by Holmes's powers of deduction. Particularly shocking was Holmes's revelation that Trevor Snr had once been linked to someone with the initials J. A. (a deduction stemming from an old tattoo in the bend of his arm). Indeed, so shocked was Trevor that he promptly fainted.

Despite attempts to put the incident out of mind, Holmes felt the atmosphere was strained to such an extent that he decided to take his leave of the family. However, before he had had time to go, a visitor appeared at the house whose mere presence disturbed Trevor Snr. This stranger transpired to be a man named Hudson, who had been Trevor's shipmate three decades earlier. Trevor offered Hudson a position in the household and the name of Beddoes was mentioned between the two men. Within an hour, Trevor was discovered on a sofa comatose through alcohol. The following day Holmes returned to his digs in London to work on some chemistry experiments.

Seven weeks later a telegram arrived from Victor exhorting Holmes to return to Norfolk. Trevor Snr had suffered a stroke seemingly brought on by shock. Holmes learned that Hudson had been made gardener and then butler but showed no gratitude, cursing, drinking and taking advantage of his master until Victor turfed Hudson out one night. Trevor Snr attempted to persuade his son to apologise but when he wouldn't, Hudson left. Victor witnessed his father ravaged by a 'pitiable nervousness'. Just as he seemed to be improving slightly, a letter arrived that brought on the stroke. The contents of the letter seemed to be only harmless nonsense about the supply of game, orders for fly-paper and the 'preservation of your hen pheasant's life'.

Holmes employed his code-breaking skills to get to the bottom of the murky case, at the heart of which lay the *Gloria Scott*, a ship bound for Australia many years before. The reference in the story to a chaplain standing 'with a smoking pistol in his hand' is widely considered the origin of the phrase 'smoking gun' to mean incontrovertible evidence of wrong-doing.

OPPOSITE: The *Gloria Scott* was a bark, a type of ship traditionally distinguished by its three masts and the absence of a mizen top-sail.

THE ADVENTURE OF
THE MUSGRAVE RITUAL

FIRST PUBLISHED: The *Strand Magazine*, May 1893, UK; published in the US edition of the *Strand Magazine* one month after UK publication and in *Harper's Weekly*, 13 May 1893, USA

SETTING DATE: 1879

ANOTHER TALE IN which Holmes narrates events to Watson. The case begins with a visit to Holmes (then residing in Montague Street) by Reginald Musgrave, who had known the Detective during their college days. Two of Musgrave's staff (a maid, Rachel Howells, and the butler, Richard Brunton) have gone missing from his estate at Hurlstone. The disappearances occurred shortly after Musgrave had given Brunton his marching orders when he was caught prying into the family's secret papers in the early hours one night. Among these documents was the Musgrave Ritual, a riddle dating from the seventeenth century and including the question and answer: 'Whose was it?/His who is gone.'

It was this document that had the particular attention of Brunton. He begged Musgrave to give him a month's notice before he had to leave the house. An infuriated Musgrave granted him a week. It was a few days later that the butler went missing, his bed still made and his belongings untouched. Howells, his former sweetheart, flew into a hysterical fit when questioned and a servant was appointed to watch over her. However, Howells took her opportunity when the guard-servant fell asleep and beat a hasty exit through the window. Her footprints traced a path to the edge of an eight-foot-deep lake. A drag of the mere revealed no body but did yield an unpromising sack filled with a mass of twisted, rusting metal and a collection of dull-looking pebbles or coloured glass.

RITUALIA MUSGRAVIENSIA

Sir Arthur Conan Doyle

An endearing and unusual view of Holmes for a Latin translation of 'The Musgrave Ritual', published by The Battered Silicon Dispatch Box.

Holmes is quick to realise that the solution lies in the Ritual, which he considers far less trivial than Musgrave himself does. By untwisting its meaning, Holmes brings proceedings to a macabre conclusion.

The opening scenes in 221B are full of domestic detail, including Holmes's habit of keeping his tobacco in a Persian slipper, of pinning his unread post to the mantelpiece with a jack-knife, and of firing Boxer cartridges into the wall in the pattern of a 'patriotic V.R.'. Patience, thy name was Hudson!

THE ADVENTURE OF
THE REIGATE SQUIRES

FIRST PUBLISHED: The *Strand Magazine*, June 1893, UK; published in the US edition of the *Strand Magazine* one month after UK publication and in *Harper's Weekly*, 17 June 1893, USA

SETTING DATE: 1887

KNOWN IN THE USA as 'The Reigate Puzzle'. The story begins with Watson explaining how Holmes's health and spirit had almost been broken by two months of intensive investigation into 'the question of the Netherland-Sumatra Company and of the colossal schemes of Baron Maupertuis'. Watson brings him home from France and arranges for a restorative stay in Reigate, Surrey, at the estate of an old friend from the Afghan campaigns, one Colonel Hayter.

Alas, Watson's plans for a restful break are soon knocked off course when the Detective learns that the local area has recently witnessed a mysterious crime. A burglary at the Acton estate had seen the robbers escape with a motley collection of loot, including a book, candlesticks, a paperweight, a barometer and a ball of twine. Holmes's interest piqued, Hayter's butler then reports that a robbery at the local Cunningham estate has resulted in the murder of a coachman, William Kirwan. He was shot through the heart. The investigation is being led by Inspector Forrester and a key piece of evidence is uncovered, a torn note clutched in William's hand.

Forrester hopes to benefit from Holmes's expertise and the Detective indeed makes some startling observations about the note using his expert knowledge of graphology.

A long-running feud between the Actons and the Cunninghams provides another line of enquiry, and Holmes's interview with Cunningham and his son Alec – who claims to have witnessed a deadly arm-to-arm struggle between William and the burglar – is particularly instructive. In a bid to protect the integrity of a vital piece of evidence, Holmes employs his acting skills to fake a fit. He also conveys the appearance of a once great man whose faculties are failing. He will later utilise Watson's thespian abilities in pursuit of the miscreants. The Detective has to endure a bodily attack before the story is over but it is clear that the thrill of a case has reinvigorated Holmes better than any rest.

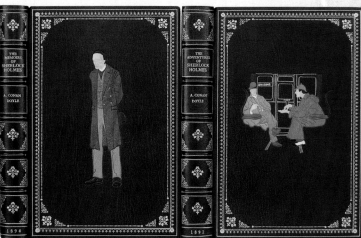

These 1890s editions of *The Adventures* and *The Memoirs* were rebound by the Chelsea Bindary for Peter Harrington Books, a rare books dealer in London.

THE ADVENTURE OF
THE CROOKED MAN

FIRST PUBLISHED: The *Strand Magazine*, July 1893, UK; published in the US edition of the *Strand Magazine*
one month after UK publication and in *Harper's Weekly*, 8 July 1893, USA

SETTING DATE: 1889

Darjeeling was an important British military station nestling among the Bengali hills and was a favourite summer destination because of its relatively cool climate.

HOLMES VISITS THE recently married Watson at his digs in Paddington and, as is his wont, persuades the Doctor to desert his wife to catch the tail-end of one of his investigations. One Colonel James Barclay of the 'Royal Mallows' (or 'Royal Munsters' in some versions), stationed at Aldershot, has been murdered. The finger of suspicion points at his wife, Nancy.

Holmes briefs Watson on the evidence as it stands, gleaned largely from a certain Major Murphy and from the Barclays' domestic staff (the household living in a villa off camp). Their marriage was regarded as strong among the other officers, although there was a suspicion that Barclay's feelings for his wife were stronger than hers for him. He was also prone to apparently unprovoked fits of depression.

The previous Monday, Nancy had attended a meeting of a charitable organisation to which she belonged, in the company of her next-door neighbour, Miss Morrison. The meeting lasted around forty minutes and she returned home presently, where she ordered some tea be brought to the morning room. Shortly afterwards, the coachman witnessed the Colonel join his wife, the last time he was seen alive.

When the maid arrived with tea, she discovered the room locked from the inside and heard an argument raging. Nancy repeated the phrase 'You coward!' and, mysteriously, used the name 'David'. The Colonel's words, in contrast, were indiscernible. The exchange ended with a cry from the Colonel, a loud crash and a piercing scream from Nancy. The coachman ran to the garden and gained access to the room via a French window. He discovered the mistress fainted and her husband killed, prostrate in a pool of his own blood. His face was contorted with fear and the apparent murder weapon, a club, was found nearby. None of the household recognised it as from the victim's own weapon collection. After the police and a doctor were called for, it was then discovered that there was no sign of the key for the door.

Holmes arrives on the scene the following morning. The missing key convinces him that a third party had been present. He uncovers some telling footprints, including those of no 'creature that we are familiar with'. Emphasising the precarious situation in which Nancy finds herself, Holmes persuades Miss Morrison to shed what light she can on events. Holmes quickly wraps things up, in the process learning of a dark episode in the aftermath of the Indian Mutiny.

The story is also notable for Holmes uttering the word 'Elementary!' (though decidedly not 'Elementary, my dear Watson!').

HOLMES AND ME 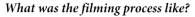 DOUGLAS WILMER

Douglas Wilmer became a well-known actor in film and on television in the 1950s. From 1964 to 1965 he played Holmes for the BBC opposite Nigel Stock as Watson. His performance remains much revered among Holmesian enthusiasts.

How did you come to play Holmes?

I got the role because I was a reasonably well-known TV actor – probably rather overexposed at the time. The cut of my countenance and the fairly incisive way I had meant I had played a lot of barristers and people like that. I wasn't exactly surprised to be asked to play Holmes and my face was apparently judged to be very like those of Sidney Paget's illustrations in the *Strand* magazines. Although on what they based that, I don't really know as he looks different in every single illustration and none of them comply with Conan Doyle's own descriptions.

I'd never played Holmes before but I had thought when I was reading the stories – which I did rather late in life during my first job as an actor – that I'd rather like to play him one day. As an actor, one always has to bring something of oneself to the role, in the way of one's personality or mannerisms. But I thought he was a perfectly believable character. A very real character. And of course when the stories were written people were convinced, or managed to convince themselves, that the character existed.

The story I liked best is not, generally speaking, one of the most popular ones I think. It's the story of Charles Augustus Milverton, the blackmailer. The whole thing was borrowed quite shamelessly by Doyle from his brother-in-law Hornung and has quite a strong element of Raffles about it. It seems to me to have a beginning, a middle and an end and to be well-shaped. It was certainly the one I enjoyed acting most.

Douglas Wilmer appeared as Sherlock Holmes in thirteen episodes of a BBC series. His performance has been praised for its exploration of Holmes's psychological depths.

What was the filming process like?

It was fraught with difficulty. The first episode was a pilot in a series called something like *Great Detectives*. It was done with a view to making a series out of them if they were any good. So the BBC hit on 'The Speckled Band' and asked me to play it. They decided it was good enough to sign up a series. Giles Cooper wrote that one and it was a very good one. We also had an absolutely marvellous director, Robin Midgely, who was never used again. We had six or seven directors and there was never any cohesion of purpose. One had to really drag the thing together to make it a cohesive whole with some consistency of style. With so many writers and directors it was doubly difficult.

There were a number of scriptwriters, ranging from the brilliant to absolutely deplorable. The first one, Giles Cooper, was of the first type but for that reason he was overworked and his work deteriorated slightly. In the end he went to pieces completely and produced a script for 'The Devil's Foot' which was meant to run to fifty minutes but had not much more than twenty minutes of playing time in it. One night he had a good dinner at the Garrick Club, took the train to Brighton, and when it had got up speed, jumped off. So that was the end of his scriptwriting. There were others who were not brilliant who should have jumped off trains before they wrote at all. I would be working on the script in conjunction with the stories and I noticed the most flagrant discrepancies. I did my best, though not always successfully, to remedy that. I was engaged in rewriting some of them until two o'clock in the morning. And then I had to learn the bloody stuff as well!

I used my previous experience of seeing other actors in the role to remedy certain things that had been left out or overlooked which I thought were important. One of these was the cocaine habit. It's OK now but then it was considered not quite on. I think that was rather a pity as it provided an interesting sidelight on the character.

People complained that I wasn't sympathetic but I didn't set out to be. I don't regard Holmes as a sympathetic character at all. It would have been hell to share rooms with him. I thought there was a tendency to play him like the captain of the cricket XI and I don't see him that way or as a Victorian paterfamilias. I see him as a much more complex character, with violent mood swings. I'm sure he was a manic-depressive. These were aspects I think were largely ignored and which I tried, as far as I was able in the limitations of the script, to bring out.

What about your Watson, Nigel Stock?
He was excellent and considerably better than Nigel Bruce, who was the *Buffoonus britannicus*. Stock was a real person. He did occasionally verge on the comic but I think it needed that to lift the character. But he never overstepped the mark. I thought he was an admirable Watson. He looked right. He sounded right. His personality was very right and I always consulted him on the scripts.

Are there any favourite Holmes portrayals that followed on from you?
I did think Bob Stephens was very good in *The Private Life of Sherlock Holmes*. It was a complete pastiche of course, but it was convincing. And I admired

Jeremy Brett very much in the beginning. I thought his performances were very promising and interesting. He certainly suggested that dark side. Whether he got it from me, I don't know. He came to dinner one night, twenty years before he played the character, and he was very complimentary and effusive about my performance. He said he admired it very much and, if he did as much as he said he did, I'm sure he incorporated a certain amount of it, even if only unconsciously. And he had very good Watsons. David Burke actually played the villain in the 'Beryl Coronet' we did.

In his later performances Brett was not a well man. He had all sorts of psychological difficulties. And his treatments aggravated each other which was very bad luck. To me, he began to suggest a sort of desperation where he was really beginning to overact. That was a pity. I thought he went way over the top. But at the beginning I thought he was wonderful.

An original artwork in the Park Plaza Sherlock Holmes Hotel on Baker Street, an enigmatic portrayal of a figure who might be Watson or even Moriarty. (Painting by Andrea Byrne)

HOLMES IN THE TOWN
AND IN THE COUNTRY

*'It is my belief, Watson, founded upon my experience, that the lowest
and vilest alleys in London do not present a more dreadful record of sin
than does the smiling and beautiful countryside.'*
'The Adventure of the Copper Beeches'

THERE IS A strange dichotomy at the very heart of Sherlock Holmes. Ask the man on the Clapham omnibus to describe the Great Detective, and he will probably paint a picture of a figure with a curved pipe, dressed in a cape and a deerstalker. Ask him where is Holmes's natural setting, and he'll almost certainly come up with the gas-lit streets of Victorian London (probably in the midst of a real pea-souper). A man of the city, decked out for a day in the country. But just whether Holmes is at heart a city gent or a country squire is not entirely clear.

Holmes counted among his ancestors a line of country squires and finished his life amid the rolling countryside of Sussex. But it was London that he made his home for the large part of his professional life. Most of the canonical comments upon London derived from Watson, who suggested an occasional weariness with the big city. However, like Holmes, there was no pressing reason for him to live there save for his own preference. In *A Study in Scarlet* Watson described naturally gravitating to London, as if he were somehow pulled in by forces independent of his own will. Even in those early days his attitude to the city was ambivalent. London was 'that great cesspool into which all the loungers and idlers of the Empire are irresistibly drained'. Whether he counted himself among these loungers and idlers is not clear though it seems likely that he spent his pre-Holmesian days whittling away his meagre army pension on carousing and gambling.

The town was certainly a place in which a man could lose himself (something Watson may have wanted to do in the weeks and months following his return from Afghanistan). Again in *A Study in Scarlet* he said that 'of all the mazes that ever were contrived, this city is the most confusing' and in 'The Red-Headed League' he spoke of 'an endless labyrinth of gas-lit streets'. *The Sign of Four*, meanwhile, saw him describe 'the great city' in rather menacing terms as he wrote of 'dense drizzly fog', the 'steamy, vaporous air' of the Strand and the 'murky, shifting radiance' that emanated from its shop windows. 'There was, to my mind,' he suggested, 'something eerie and ghostlike in the endless procession of faces.'

His description in 'The Man with the Twisted Lip' of the poor riverside neighbourhoods around London Bridge, replete with opium dens, again suggested a place of threat and foreboding. There was the 'murky river flowing sluggishly', the 'dull wilderness of bricks and mortar' and its 'vile' alleys. Holmes himself spoke of a trap-door at the back of one of the buildings 'which could tell some strange tales of what has passed through it upon the moonless nights'. Certainly the London of this period was not an easy place for a good many of its citizens. The county of London's population had grown from something like two million to four-and-a-half million over the course of the nineteenth century, and in the 1880s over a third of them were living in poverty. Charles Booth conducted a survey into *Life and Labour in London* between 1886 and 1902 and wrote that 'there are 10,000 people in the East End living in chronic want … Half the people in this area are on the margin of existence.' Yet were we to dwell only on Watson's words, we would be hard pressed to understand why anyone with the choice would have lived in the city. So what kept Holmes and Watson there?

Holmes's take on the city suggested that its endless fascinations made up for any shortcomings. Samuel Johnson famously observed that 'when a man is tired of London, he is tired of life', and that seems to have been a view in concordance with the Detective's own. In 'The Six Napoleons', Watson gave a sense of the huge variety of life on offer as he outlined a journey during which they 'passed through the fringe of fashionable London, hotel London, theatrical London, literary London, commercial London, and, finally, maritime London, till we came to a riverside city of a hundred thousand souls, where the tenement houses swelter and reek with the outcasts of Europe'. For a mind as busy as Holmes's there was much to keep it entertained.

In 'The Resident Patient' Watson explained that 'to my companion, neither the country nor the sea presented the slightest attraction to him. He loved to lie in the very centre of five millions of people, with his filaments stretching out and running through them.' It was this huge social complexity (and its associated potential for crime) that seems to have appealed to him most. 'To the scientific student of the higher criminal world, no capital in Europe offered the advantages which London then possessed,' he said in 'The Norwood Builder'. This statement contained considerable truth for London, with its rapidly expanding population, was most certainly a hotbed of wrong-doing. The *Eclectic Review*, published in 1854 (several years before Holmes was active as a detective), stated that: 'There is no longer any dispute that the aggregation of the population in large towns is accompanied by the development and rapid growth of certain forms of crime.' However, the idea that London's problems only got worse as the century progressed – an impression no doubt strengthened by the Holmes stories and the news-worthy Ripper murders – was a false one. The crime rate in fact reached its peak mid-century and fell away over its second half. Nonetheless, there was ample nefarious activity to occupy Holmes. Rarely did he speak so lyrically as when he addressed Watson in 'A Case of Identity': 'If we could fly out of that window hand in hand, hover over this great city … and peep in at the queer things which are going on … it would make all fiction with its conventionalities and foreseen conclusions most stale and unprofitable.'

But just as they viewed their cityscape from different angles, Watson and Holmes had significantly opposed takes on the countryside too. Watson, perhaps predictably, loved nothing more than a chance to escape the London greyness in exchange for some rural tranquillity. In 'The Solitary Cyclist' he wrote of how 'the heath-covered countryside, with the glowing clumps of flowering gorse, seemed all the more beautiful to eyes which were weary of the duns and drabs and slate grays of London'. It is easy to imagine the good doctor relishing a good long walk in the open air before dropping into an old country inn for a hearty meal and a glass of something red.

Holmes, though, saw the countryside in a somewhat more threatening light. His observations to Watson on their train journey to the Copper Beeches were most instructive. 'Think of the deeds of hellish cruelty, the hidden wickedness which may go on, year in, year out, in such places, and none the wiser,' he said. The wide open spaces with their capacity for isolation might appeal to a soul tired of the city but made Holmes think instead of 'the impunity with which crime may be committed there'. He even suggested, perhaps optimistically, that the swell of people in an urban conglomeration ensured a degree of self-regulation, arguing that 'the pressure of public opinion can do in the town what the law cannot accomplish'.

This sense of impending danger was, of course, not without attraction to a man who loved to solve crime. We can imagine that he rather enjoyed his lonesome stay upon the 'gloomy curve of the moor, broken by the jagged and sinister hills' in *The Hound*. Similarly in 'The Devil's Foot' Watson reported Holmes's fascination with the 'glamour and mystery of the place' which saw him spend long periods alone on the moors. And the countryside proved a most fruitful place for Holmes professionally, for a great many of his cases took him there and away from London.

However, it was London that most suited him. The vastness of the countryside (and the isolation that allowed for many of his toughest cases) was something that no individual could fully master. London, in contrast, was complex enough

to provide a challenge to his intellect but geographically compact enough to be subjected to his analytical processes. For instance, as Watson noted in 'The Empty House', 'Holmes's knowledge of the byways of London was extraordinary.' I have discussed elsewhere how Holmes's deductive techniques were most suited to spying the flaw in the expected order of things and then examining that flaw to solve his case. Inevitably, these defects would have been easier to spot in the condensed urban setting.

That Holmes retired to the countryside and indulged his passion for bee-keeping might suggest that, when all was said and done, his family's rural heritage won through. But in 'His Last Bow' he described his great work, a *Practical Handbook of Bee Culture*, as 'the fruit of pensive nights and laborious days when I watched the little working gangs as once I watched the criminal world of London'. Whatever the setting for his old age, his attentions were taken with the study of a social organisation akin to that of a great city. Finally, let us take Holmes's words in 'The Bruce-Partington Plans': 'The thief or the murderer could roam London on such a day as the tiger does the jungle, unseen until he pounces, and then evident only to his victim.' One can think of no other place the Great Detective would rather be.

THE ADVENTURE OF THE RESIDENT PATIENT

FIRST PUBLISHED: The *Strand Magazine*, August 1893, UK; published in the US edition of the *Strand Magazine* one month after UK publication and in *Harper's Weekly*, 12 August 1893, USA

SETTING DATE: 1887

IN MANY EDITIONS, the story starts with the Holmes 'mind-reading' scene from 'The Cardboard Box', added after Conan Doyle decided that the latter tale was too shocking to appear in collected editions.

The case is brought by Dr Percy Trevelyan, a gifted but unmonied practitioner. At least, that was the case until a figure called Blessington arrived on the scene and set Trevelyan up in practice on Brook Street. In return, he was to receive 75 per cent of the doctor's earnings and, himself in poor health, the benefit of an on-site physician.

The arrangement operated to both sides' satisfaction for several years until recently Trevelyan had noticed a change in Blessington. He became highly agitated after news of a West End burglary and was out of sorts for many days. As time went on he appeared to be returning to some semblance of normality. Then Trevelyan received a new patient, a Russian aristocrat suffering cataleptic fits. The nobleman arrived for his consultation with his son, who remained in the waiting room as Trevelyan made his examination. Blessington was out on his regular evening walk. Mid-examination, the nobleman went into a fit. Trevelyan went to find amyl nitrite to treat him but returned to discover both patient and son gone.

The two men returned the following evening, again when Blessington was out. The son claimed that on seeing his father walk from the consultation room the previous evening, he had assumed the appointment was at an end. It was only later that he realised something was amiss. Trevelyan conducted another examination and the Russians left. Blessington returned later and fell into a mad panic when he discovered footprints in his room. They could only have been those of the aristocrat's son, yet nothing seemed to have been taken or disturbed. It was at this stage that Holmes was called in.

Holmes, Watson and Trevelyan set out for Brook Street, where they are greeted by a fearful and armed Blessington. Eventually he calms enough to tell Holmes that he does not know who the Russians might be but suggests they are after the large sum of money he keeps in his room. Holmes believes Blessington is lying and refuses to proceed with the case. The next morning brings news that Blessington has been found hanged in his bedroom.

Inspector Lanner of the Yard assumes suicide but Holmes is convinced that this is not the case. With his knowledge of cigar butts and footprints and after some consultation of police records, Holmes has the conundrum licked.

OPPOSITE: A view of Brook Street, a well-to-do road leading off Grosvenor Square in Mayfair, in 1875. The street is home to the famous Claridge's Hotel.

THE ADVENTURE OF THE GREEK INTERPRETER

First Published: The *Strand Magazine*, September 1893, UK; published in the US edition of the *Strand Magazine* one month after UK publication and in *Harper's Weekly*, 16 September 1893, USA

Setting Date: 1888

A STORY MOST notable for the appearance of Mycroft Holmes, Sherlock's portly and intellectually brilliant brother. Holmes takes Watson to the Diogenes Club on Pall Mall in response to a summons from Mycroft. Also present is Mr Melas, a Greek interpreter and a neighbour of Mycroft. Melas narrates his strange story to the party.

The interpreter had received a call two evenings earlier from one Harold Latimer, who wished Melas to accompany him to a house in Kensington for some urgent translation work. Having been bustled into a waiting cab, Melas noticed that the windows were blanked out. Latimer then produced a bludgeon with the clear intention of intimidating his new acquaintance. He told Melas that he was not to know the location of their destination but that he would be rewarded for the inconvenience as long as he guaranteed his silence on the matter. Failure to stay quiet would have serious repercussions.

Their journey lasted over two hours and ended at a large, poorly lit property. Melas was led into a room occupied by a nervy, giggling figure (later revealed as Wilson Kemp). Another man was brought in, looking gaunt and ill-used but strong-spirited. This, it emerged, was Paul Kratides, a Greek. The kidnappers wanted Melas to act as intermediary in their attempts to make Kratides sign some documents.

Kratides was adamant he would not sign. He and Melas exchanged extra information during the course of their 'official' negotiations and it emerged that Kratides was from Athens, had been in London for three weeks and was being starved. However, a woman called Sophy appeared before the full story could come out. She was shocked to see Kratides, whom she called Paul, and the couple flew into an embrace before being separated.

Melas was ushered back into a cab, given five sovereigns and told to keep his counsel. He was then deposited far from home. The following day Melas shared his story with Mycroft and the police. An advertisement placed in the *Daily News* requesting information on Paul and Sophy receives a response from a Mr Davenport of the Myrtles, Beckenham. Holmes, Mycroft, Watson and Inspector Gregson go to interview Davenport but on the way discover that Melas has been taken off by a giggling man.

Holmes's party make their way to the Myrtles, which turns out to be the scene of Kratides's incarceration. Holmes notes ruefully that 'our birds are flown and the nest empty'. However, not before one last desperate act. The story's end is not among the canon's most satisfying, Watson himself noting that 'the explanation . . . is still involved in some mystery'.

THE ADVENTURE OF THE NAVAL TREATY

FIRST PUBLISHED: The *Strand Magazine*, October—November 1893, UK; published in the US edition of the *Strand Magazine* one month after UK publication and in *Harper's Weekly*, 14—21 October 1893, USA

SETTING DATE: 1889

THE LONGEST OF all the short stories in the canon. It also references 'The Second Stain', a story that would not be published for another eleven years.

The tale begins after Watson receives a letter from a school friend, Percy 'Tadpole' Phelps, who now works for the Foreign Office (the result of the nepotism of his uncle, Lord Holdhurst) and resides at Briarbrae in Woking. Two months previously, Percy was entrusted with copying a crucially important naval treaty, which has been stolen.

Percy had been working late at his office, copying the document, and was keen to catch up with Joseph, his brother-in-law-to-be, who was in town. Percy summoned the commissionaire (who sat guard at one of the two entrances to the office) to order coffee. It was the commissionaire's wife, however, who took the order. When the coffee had not arrived after a little while, Percy went to chase it up. He discovered the commissionaire asleep at his post and the kettle boiling beside him. At that moment the bell from Percy's office rang, sending the young civil servant into a spiral of panic. He rushed upstairs to find the treaty gone and no sign of the culprit.

Assuming the thief must have left via the unguarded side door, the commissionaire's wife became chief suspect after she was spotted leaving the building at the critical moment. The only other possible candidates seem to be the commissionaire and Charles Gorot, a seemingly unimpeachable colleague of Phelps. Initial police enquiries failed to implicate any of them. Percy returned to Woking, where he took to his sickbed with 'brain-fever' brought on by stress.

He has been nursed throughout by his fiancée, Annie Harrison. Percy has taken the room normally used by her brother, Joseph. It is Joseph who first greets Holmes and Watson at the house. An interview with Percy follows and Holmes picks up on several intriguing features of the case. Why on a wet night were there no footprints at the crime scene? What of the strange use of the bell-pull? And why has the treaty seemingly not made its way on to the international market? Its contents are soon to be announced, at which point its black-market value will plummet.

An interview with Lord Holdhurst convinces Holmes that no one could have overheard him and his nephew discussing the document. In the meantime, there has been an attempted break-in at Briarbrae, focused on Percy's room. Fortunately, Percy surprised the intruder at the window before he could get in. Holmes has formed his theory and sets up a night-time swoop on the culprit.

THE ADVENTURE OF
THE FINAL PROBLEM

FIRST PUBLISHED: The *Strand Magazine*, December 1893, UK; published in the US edition of the *Strand Magazine* one month after UK publication and in McClure's Magazine, December 1893, USA

SETTING DATE: 1891

THE STORY ORIGINALLY intended to be Holmes's last, great hurrah. It also marked the debut of Professor Moriarty, 'the Napoleon of crime'.

Holmes calls on Watson one evening, looking thinner than ever as he nervously secures the surgery against possible airgun attack. It seems that three attempts have already been made on his life that day alone. Responsibility lies with the gang led by Moriarty, a shadowy figure whose elimination, Holmes feels, would prove the pinnacle of his crime-fighting career.

Holmes narrates how he has been on the trail of the Professor and his forces for several months and has never been closer to delivering them all into the hands of justice. Yet he acknowledges Moriarty is blessed with an intellect that makes him the most formidable opponent of his life. The Professor, tired of Holmes's interference in his business, has already made a personal visit to warn Holmes of the dangers of continuing his pursuit.

Holmes asks Watson to accompany him to the Continent (no doubt testing the patience of Mrs Watson once again). He arranges for the two of them to meet covertly at Victoria station the next morning then leaves Watson via a back wall (to evade the attentions of Moriarty's men). So it is that the following day Watson finds himself in a first-class carriage, anxiously awaiting his friend's arrival. Holmes does him proud by donning one of his finest disguises.

Despite all his precautions, Holmes spots Moriarty on the platform as the train pulls away. He then reveals that 221B was set ablaze the previous night. The pair decide to change trains at Canterbury and then on to Newhaven in a bid to outfox the Professor. Once on the Continent news reaches them that most of the gang has been rounded up but not the ringleader. Watson, ever loyal, refuses the option to return home to safety.

After a joyous week wandering round the Rhône valley, the two men end up at Meiringen in Switzerland and decide to visit the nearby Reichenbach Falls. However, their journey is interrupted by a messenger requesting that Watson return to the hotel to attend to a sick English lady. Holmes is left to complete the expedition on his own and the tale ends with one of the greatest encounters in detective fiction.

OPPOSITE: Sidney Paget's dramatic portrayal of 'the end' of the world's greatest detective and his most formidable adversary as they tumble over the Reichenbach Falls.

THE LITERARY LINEAGE

'Your fatal habit of looking at everything from the point of view of a story
instead of as a scientific exercise has ruined what might have been an
instructive and even classical series of demonstrations.'
'The Adventure of the Abbey Grange'

SHERLOCK HOLMES IS without doubt the most famous creation in all of detective fiction, yet he was not the first of his type and, many would argue, did not emerge in a golden age for the genre. Few would have predicted what Holmes would become when he arrived, in *A Study in Scarlet* in 1887, to little fanfare and moderate sales. James Payn, editor of *Cornhill Magazine*, had condemned Conan Doyle's first offerings as nothing but 'shilling dreadfuls'.

Yet Holmes clung on, and with his introduction in the *Strand* became an overnight phenomenon. Before Holmes, detective fiction had a distinctly lowly reputation, being regarded as sensationalist and lowbrow. After him, it found a whole new respect, with skilled and imaginative writers eager to feed an unstintingly hungry mass market. A certain degree of snobbery may have lingered around the good old murder mystery but by the dawn of the twenty-first century high-quality detective fiction was at last recognised to be as legitimate and valuable as any other literary form. And with generally bigger sales to boot! So how did the Holmes stories, which even their creator considered catered for the less discerning reader, help transform the reputation of a whole genre?

In 1747 Voltaire's *Zadig* introduced a character with a proto-Holmesian style of logical deduction. However, Zadig's trick was to study natural occurrences to evolve theoretical narratives and his dealings were confined to philosophical, not criminal, detection. Until the nineteenth century there was little in the way of systematic policing and so, with no detective figures to provide inspiration, there was no such thing as detective fiction. Crime writing was confined to the gory and over-wrought narratives of the lives (and deaths) of real criminals. Such prose was epitomised by London's *Newgate Calendar*, a monthly account produced by the keeper of Newgate Prison. The *Calendar* would go on to inspire the Newgate novels of the 1820s–40s that retold the histories of selected malefactors of the previous century.

In 1794 William Goodwin published *Caleb Williams*, which does involve an individual uncovering the identity of a criminal. Yet it hardly qualifies as detective fiction, for the hero gets to the bottom of the mystery by the halfway point of the book, having reached his conclusions not through the consideration of a series of clues but by recognising his suspect's guilt-ridden emotional responses.

OPPOSITE: Conan Doyle writing at his desk while encamped at Bloemfontein in 1900, where he served as a surgeon in a field hospital during the Second Boer War.

The *Newgate Calendar* originally catalogued the monthly executions at Newgate Prison, pictured. It evolved into an often lurid record of the most infamous criminals of the age.

We must turn to Continental Europe to identify the first clear predecessor of Holmes, with the publication of the memoirs of Eugène François Vidocq in 1828 (a year before the establishment of the Metropolitan Police Force). Vidocq, a real person, was for the early part of his life a bad lot. Backed into a corner, he became a police informant and eventually an investigator, rising to become head of the national criminal investigations department. He also founded the world's first private detective agency. Not afraid of self-promotion and skilled at spinning a dramatic yarn, his memoirs verge distinctly into fiction. It has even been argued that he himself was the perpetrator of several crimes that he subsequently 'solved'. Yet he is a prototype for Holmes in several ways.

Vidocq was quick to recognise the importance of minutely studying the scene of crime and utilised several strands of forensics, including ballistics and plaster-casting footprints. He also kept highly detailed records of crimes (prefiguring Holmes's indexes) and liberally employed disguises. Here was a detective who set about solving crime by using his initiative, cunning and the most modern scientific methods available to accumulate data and sift through clues before bringing a wrong-doer to justice. Vidocq proved an inspiration for both Jean Valjean and Inspector Javert in Victor Hugo's *Les Misérables* and was a clear influence on two other giants of detective fiction: Edgar Allan Poe and Émile Gaboriau.

Poe created C. Auguste Dupin, a Parisian amateur detective and arguably the first 'great' fictional detective. Dupin appeared in three stories between 1841 and

1844: 'The Murders in the Rue Morgue', 'The Mystery of Marie Rogêt' and 'The Purloined Letter'. By logical reasoning and the consideration of apparently minor details, he reconstructed trains of events in order to solve the mystery. He was the archetypal thinking machine and considerably less rounded, and thus emotionally appealing, than Holmes would be.

Not only is Dupin's method echoed in Conan Doyle's tales, but the tone also. Consider the beginning of 'The Purloined Letter', related by Dupin's anonymous companion narrator:

> . . . I was enjoying the twofold luxury of meditation and a meerschaum, in company with my friend C. Auguste Dupin, in his little back library, or book-closet, au troisième, No. 33, Rue Dunôt, Faubourg St. Germain. For one hour at least we had maintained a profound silence; while each, to any casual observer, might have seemed intently and exclusively occupied with the curling eddies of smoke that oppressed the atmosphere of the chamber.

A change of name and geographical location and we could be forgiven for thinking that we are watching Holmes and Watson in 221B, awaiting a new case. Conan Doyle made no secret of his admiration, referring in his letters to 'those admirable stories of Monsieur Dupin' and describing Poe as 'the supreme original short story writer of all time'. Dupin is name-checked in rather tongue-in-cheek fashion in *A Study in Scarlet*. After Watson has told Holmes that he puts him in mind of Dupin, Holmes archly observes, 'Now, in my opinion, Dupin was a very inferior fellow.'

Continuing the tradition of French masterclasses in deductive reasoning, Alexandre Dumas's hero D'Artagnan showed his skills in *Le Vicomte de Bragelonne*, published between 1847 and 1850. Dispatched by the king to uncover the story behind a recent duel, D'Artagnan surveyed the scene of the confrontation and arrived at a complete narrative that Dupin himself might have envied. Then in 1866 Émile Gaboriau published *L'Affaire Lerouge*, which introduced Le Père Tabaret to the world. However, it was M. Lecoq, a disciple of Tabaret and the subject of a series of subsequent novels by Gaboriau, who won greater fame. Lecoq owes a great deal to Vidocq and was for several decades a superstar of the genre. Lecoq is no precursor of Holmes in terms of detective powers but he shared Holmes's disdain for the official police and was certainly influential on Conan Doyle in terms of structure. Indeed, Conan Doyle spoke of his admiration for 'a neat dovetailing of his plots'. *A Study in Scarlet* and *The Valley of Fear* in particular follow the Gaboriau template, with the detection work hap-

Edgar Allan Poe was a distinguished literary stylist and his creation, C. Auguste Dupin, is widely regarded as the first great fictional detective.

With *The Woman in White* in 1860 and *The Moonstone* in 1868, Wilkie Collins was instrumental in developing, respectively, the English mystery novel and the English detective novel.

pening in the first phase of the book, while the second half is taken up with the backstory that explains how the crime came to be committed. Holmes, though, would have turned his nose up at such a comparison for to him, 'Lecoq was a miserable bungler'.

The scene in Britain somewhat lagged behind. There was still a taste for the gruesome tales of wrong-doers, epitomised in the 1830s by the florid prose of Edward Bulwer-Lytton and Harrison Ainsworth. The influence of the cheap, lurid serialised fiction of the 'penny dreadfuls' was felt all the way through the century. Indeed, Henry Baskerville himself would later admit that 'I seem to have walked right into the thick of a dime novel.' However, the establishment of organised police forces and the formation of a specialist detective force in 1842 was followed by the emergence of numerous private detective agencies taking advantage of the relaxation in divorce legislation to pry into private lives. So British society gradually got used to the idea of the detective.

In 1849 a detective named Waters published the apparently true-life recollections of his professional life. In the 1850s newspapers benefited from tax breaks, leading to an explosion in the number of titles available and an upsurge in crime reporting. 1862 saw the appearance of Charles Felix's *The Notting Hill Mystery*, which may legitimately claim to be the first detective novel (of sorts) in English, with an insurance investigator hero looking into the mysterious death of a woman. This was followed six years later by Wilkie Collins's *The Moonstone*, featuring Cuff, a professional detective who nonetheless does not manage to solve the crime. The book is littered with possible suspects and clues to consider and firmly took the threat of crime away from the dirty back alleys of the 'penny dreadfuls' and inserted it ominously into the domestic setting. In many ways it laid out the rules of the game for years to come.

In the late 1870s Anne Catherine Green introduced her city detective, Ebeneezer Gryce, to the world. The first great female author of detective fiction, within fifty years the genre would be dominated by women. However, at this period, it was still resolutely a man's world. In 1886 a naturalised Australian, Fergus Hume, published *The Mystery of a Hansom Cab*, a page-turner centred on an assassination on the streets of Melbourne. Reputedly the best-selling crime novel of the Victorian age, Hume had rather hastily signed away his rights for just £50.

So the scene was set for the debut of Holmes the following year. Aside from Conan Doyle's ingenious plotting and his mastery of characterisation within the short story format, perhaps Holmes's lasting appeal rests with the fact that he is both a creation belonging to a distinct historical period and at the same time an enduring archetype.

Certainly, Holmes and Watson would struggle in the modern world. They operate most happily in the fairly rigid social structures that existed in the Victorian period and during the opening years of the twentieth century. Holmes is at his best when he identifies the glitch in the social structure, which leads the way to the evil-doer. A criminal act becomes an instance of social abnormality – spot the abnormality and the truth will follow. Necessarily, for the abnormality to emerge, everything else must fall under the definition of 'normal'. For Holmes to be at his most effective, men and women need to know their roles, upstairs and downstairs must retain a wary distance from each other, and England is a rock of civility while abroad is a place where they do things differently. To a Victorian audience, comprising a rapidly growing middle class, the stories offered the frisson of excitement associated with crime and then the reassuring spectacle of a man of reason restoring order. A perfect literary construction for that period and one that retains strong resonance today.

In creating Holmes, Conan Doyle was not making a huge literary leap forward in terms of style or structure. Rather it was a natural, if crucial, step in the evolution of crime fiction. First, it established crime fiction as a respectable and massively popular genre, transcending barriers of gender and class. Though Conan Doyle may have remained rather sniffy about crime fiction as opposed to the historical fiction he wanted to write, he made writing mysteries a more dignified enterprise. And by developing the Holmes–Watson partnership, he created a template still in use today. The pairing of the brilliant yet flawed detective with a humbler but dependable and sympathetic sidekick reappeared time and again throughout the twentieth century, from Christie's Poirot and Hastings to Colin Dexter's Morse and Lewis.

Inevitably, Conan Doyle's success inspired an immediate rush of literary rivals of varying quality. The likes of Jacques Futrelle's Professor Van Dusen, Hesketh Prichard's November Joe and Baroness Orczy's Old Man in the Corner all owed much to Holmes. Arguably the greatest of his near-contemporaries was G. K. Chesterton's Father Brown, a Catholic priest whose deductive skills appeared in several volumes of much admired tales. For some Father Brown represents the pinnacle of detective fiction, though other readers have found that his bouts of moral and metaphysical angst detract from the thrill of the chase. Holmes also inspired a number of anti-heroes almost as an antidote to the masterful detective. Most famous of all was A. J. Raffles, the Amateur Cracksman, the creation of Conan Doyle's brother-in-law, E. W. Hornung. Raffles is a gentleman thief, complete with a sidekick, Bunny, who had been Raffles's 'fag' at school and was something of a dumbed-down Watson. Conan Doyle was never a huge fan of Raffles, finding his championing of the amoral distasteful. In France, Maurice Leblanc created Arsène Lupin, a rather more Robin Hood-like figure, who stuck it to those who deserved it and famously outwitted a certain Herlock Sholmès.

For many critics, the Golden Age of detective fiction broadly covered the 1920s and 1930s, when Dorothy L. Sayers (creator of Lord Peter Wimsey), Margery Allingham (Albert Campion) and Ngaio Marsh (Roderick Alleyn) ruled the roost, along with the queen of them all, Agatha Christie. While it might be difficult to claim that the Holmes stories deal in gritty realism, they did at the very least give a nod to social reality. The Golden Agers by comparison created a cosy world of country house murders. The solution often seemed little more than an opportunity to give the detective an intellectual workout. There was a strong sense that in the absence of a just-slaughtered corpse, similar satisfaction might be derived from a quiet half-hour with the recently invented challenge of a crossword.

This is not necessarily a criticism of the Golden Agers. Writing with the horrors of the First World War a recent memory, it was not surprising that escapism was the order of the day and that the puzzle became everything. Yet to a modern reader, it seems to have been a wasted opportunity to further develop the combination of involving characters and cerebral games that Conan Doyle had done so much to advance. Nonetheless, Christie did give a nod to her predecessor, employing Hercule Poirot to make this rather arch observation in *The Clocks* (1963): 'It is the author, Sir Arthur Conan Doyle, that I salute. These tales of Sherlock Holmes are in reality far-fetched, full of fallacies and most artificially contrived. But the art of the writing – ah, that is entirely different. The pleasure of the language, the creation above all of that magnificent character, Dr Watson. Ah, that was indeed a triumph.'

The development of detective fiction in the United States took a very different course during the same period, with the emergence of 'hard-boiled' fiction by the likes of Raymond Chandler and Dashiell Hammett. Hammett, incidentally, had worked for the Pinkerton Detective Agency, which featured in two Holmes stories, *The Valley of Fear* and 'The Red Circle'. For the 'hard-boiled' writers there would be no polite middle-class murders, but instead a world of grit and ruthlessness. As Chandler put it, their detectives inhabited streets 'dark with something more than night'. Sam Spade and Philip Marlowe, the leading protagonists of Hammett and Chandler, at first glance seem to have little in common with Holmes. It is hard to imagine Holmes particularly enjoying their wise-cracking and world-weary company. But on closer inspection, we again see men who have trouble forming enduring relationships and who find their release in personal vices (principally alcohol). Unlike the Poirots and Marples of the world, their satisfaction comes not from solving riddles but from the pure thrill of running down their prey. As Chandler was to note: 'The perfect detective story cannot be written. The type of mind which can evolve the perfect problem is not the type of mind that can produce the artistic job of writing.' Conan Doyle, who rather sneered at the genre, might have agreed but few writers have come closer to achieving the feat than he did with Holmes.

An honourable mention should also be given to Nero Wolfe, a detective created by the American novelist Rex Stout and who featured in thirty-three novels and thirty-nine short stories from the 1930s to the 1970s. Wolfe, unlike most of his American contemporaries, had many obvious parallels with Holmes, being intellectually brilliant, rather eccentric and having his stories narrated by a staunch companion, Archie Goodwin. Indeed, several leading Holmes scholars have even tried to argue that Wolfe was the progeny of a union between Holmes and Irene Adler!

Curiously, if an opinion poll of the 1950s is to be believed, Holmes briefly lost his position not only as the most famous detective in the world but even as the most famous detective in Baker Street. His usurper was the now largely overlooked Sexton Blake. Appearing first in 1893, Blake's career encompassed novels, comic strips, radio, TV and film. In an 85-year career over 200 authors were responsible for 4,000 stories. Blake was a creation who moved with the times, evolving from a Holmes clone into a well-travelled man of action as the twentieth century progressed. However, the BBC series *The Radio Detectives* seemed to have the measure of Blake when they described him as 'the poor man's Sherlock Holmes'.

It is almost certainly true to say that Conan Doyle established (or at least cemented) so many of the core principles of detective fiction that no subsequent author can claim to be uninfluenced. The trend in the second half of the twentieth century was away from private detectives towards police procedurals (though often with a maverick hero kicking against the system). Nonetheless, the assimilation and evaluation of evidence perfected by Holmes is a tradition that has continued with all the greats, from Georges Simenon's pipe-smoking Maigret to P. D. James's Dalgliesh, Ruth Rendell's Wexford and Ian Rankin's Rebus. The latter operates in the tougher quarters of Edinburgh that has some parallels with the grim cityscape in which Holmes felt most at home (and that Watson so memorably called 'that great cesspool into which all the loungers and idlers of the Empire are irresistibly drained').

With sales in excess of four billion, Agatha Christie brought the detective novel to a massive new audience. In 1926 the mystery of her own brief disappearance captivated a nation.

In our era that prizes psychological insight in its literature, Holmes's troubled personality serves as a template for any number of his successors. Holmes was always more than just a reasoning machine and with his drug addictions, his inability to hold down relationships and his disregard for authority, he was a thoroughly modern creation. We see him echoed in the likes of Rebus, Morse (the real-ale-swigging, classical-music-loving eternal bachelor with a healthy disrespect for the senior ranks) and in Henning Mankel's Kurt Wallander (the heavy-drinking divorcee, with a track record of law-breaking and a tendency to insomnia).

Of course, many authors have overtly acknowledged their debt to Conan Doyle by kidnapping Holmes (and a host of other canonical figures) to use in their own books, with a few working remarkably well. Often the most successful have endeavoured to pick up on psychological aspects of the Detective and expand on these features in directions that Conan Doyle himself did not. Nor does a ripping good crime to solve go amiss. Though certainly not an exhaustive list, notable successes include Nicholas Meyer's *The Seven-Per-Cent Solution*, Laurie R. King's Mary Russell series that began with *The Beekeeper's Apprentice*, Michael Dibdin's *The Last Sherlock Holmes Story*, Michael Chabon's *The Final Solution*, Caleb Carr's *The Italian Detective* and Mitch Cullin's *A Slight Trick of the Mind*. Though absent in person, Holmes's presence further resonates through Alan Moore's flamboyant *The League of Extraordinary Gentlemen*. More recently, Anthony Horowitz has breathed new life into the Great Detective in novels endorsed by the Conan Doyle estate.

Colin Dexter's *Morse* novels reached a new level of popularity when they were dramatised for television, starring John Thaw as Morse and Kevin Whately as Lewis, Morse's Watson.

SHERLOCK HOLMES'S WRITINGS

~

Holmes wrote a great number of articles and monographs during his career. Below is a summary of some of his most significant work:

Practical Handbook of Bee Culture, With Some Observations Upon the Segregation of the Queen

'The Book of Life', a magazine article in which he explained his theories of deductive reasoning

'On the Surface Anatomy of the Human Ear' for the *Anthropological Journal*

'The Polyphonic Motets of Lassus'

'Upon Tattoo Marks'

'Upon the Dating of Documents by Handwriting Analysis'

'Upon the Distinction between the Ashes of Various Tobaccos'

'Upon the Influence of a Trade upon the Form of a Hand'

'Upon the Subject of Secret Writings'

'Upon the Tracing of Footsteps (with Some Remarks upon the Uses of Plaster as a Preserver of Impresses)'

Holmes also referred to several works that he had planned to write. These delights included 'The Chaldean Roots of the Cornish Language', 'The Use of Dogs in Detective Work', 'Malingering' and 'The Typewriter and its Relation to Crime'.

House, played by Hugh Laurie, has been a great success on television, the series making many knowing nods to its literary forefather.

Though not strictly a pastiche or parody, one of the finest novels of recent years to give a nod to Holmes was *The Curious Incident of the Dog in the Night-time*. Written by Mark Haddon (and taking its title from the famous line in 'Silver Blaze'), it is a beautifully written story about a Holmes-loving boy with behavioural problems (he is often seen as autistic though this is not explicitly stated in the book), who sets out to unravel a murder mystery.

Meanwhile, the hugely successful *House* TV series has been among the most obvious homages to Holmes in the 'noughties'. House – a 'misanthropic diagnostician' – is teamed with Dr James Wilson, their very names a nod to Conan Doyle. House, who solves mysteries that present themselves in his hospital, shuns close human contact, is addicted to Vicodin and is an expert in non-verbal diagnoses in the style of Joseph Bell. He even lives in an apartment numbered 221B. The setting may have changed and the dialogue may be snappier, but the key ingredients are still the same.

While it may well have galled Conan Doyle to think that Holmes would remain his best-known creation, he may have found some comfort knowing that his legacy endures and continues to inspire popular and well-respected work across media.

THE HOUND OF THE BASKERVILLES

FIRST PUBLISHED: The *Strand Magazine*, August 1901–April 1902, UK; The *Strand Magazine*, September 1901–May 1902, USA

SETTING DATE: 1889

SURELY THE MOST famous detective story of them all, and deservedly so. Written for an audience who at the time had an insatiable appetite for more tales of Holmes (who had recently been killed off at the Reichenbach Falls), this one has everything. Holmes's deductive powers are on top form and Watson is never more admirable as his lieutenant. The mystery itself is a particularly knotty one, with its suggestion of the supernatural, and of all the four novella-length stories, it is the plot of *The Hound* that feels least stretched.

An evocative depiction of the mysterious man on the tor, whose identity Watson eventually uncovered.

The story begins with Holmes teasing Watson into deducing the identity of a visitor who has mistakenly left his walking cane at 221B. Dr James Mortimer soon appears on the scene. A resident of Dartmoor in Devon, he comes bearing two distinct documents. The first dates from 1742 and recounts the legend of the Hound of the Baskervilles, a spectral beast who took the life of the evil Hugo Baskerville in 1648 and has plagued Hugo's descendants ever since. Holmes's initial boredom with such a fanciful story is pricked when he is given the second document, a recent newspaper report of the death of Charles Baskerville, whose body was found on an open piece of ground devoid of evidence of any other human presence. There were, however, the prints of a massive hound.

Charles's only known descendant, Sir Henry, is soon to arrive from his home in Canada to take over the family pile. Mortimer is beside himself with worry as to what to do. Almost immediately there is the mysterious theft of one of Sir Henry's boots from his hotel in London. It is agreed that Watson should accompany Baskerville and Mortimer to Devon while Holmes remains in London.

In Dartmoor we are introduced to a rich cast of characters. First, there are Mr and Mrs Barrymore, the faithful and long-serving servants of Sir Charles. Then there are the nature-loving neighbours, the Stapleton siblings (brother and sister). When Miss Stapleton mistakes Watson for Sir Henry she pleads with him to leave Dartmoor. And what of Frankland, who terrorises the locals with his love of serial litigation? Add into the mix the unworldly

howls sporadically heard across the moor and an escaped convict called Selden, and the encroaching sense of doom grows.

Much of the story is narrated via Watson's notes back to Holmes in London and through a series of diary entries. However, it is only when he manages to track down a strange lonesome figure spotted dwelling on the moor that the mystery begins to resolve itself.

ABOVE: The first edition of the defining Holmes story, *The Hound of the Baskervilles*, published by George Newnes Ltd in 1902.

LEFT: Paget's classic illustration of the hound meeting its gruesome end on Grimpen Mire at the hands of Holmes.

HOLMES AND ME ⬤ CALEB CARR

Caleb Carr is a writer and military historian. His novels include The Alienist *and* The Angel of Darkness, *both set in late-nineteenth-century New York and featuring the forensic psychologist Dr Laszlo Kreizler. His worldwide sales run into the millions. In 2005 he published* The Italian Secretary, *a Sherlock Holmes pastiche commissioned by the Conan Doyle estate.*

Caleb Carr, the much respected novelist and historian, was well aware of the peculiar challenges intrinsic in writing a Holmes pastiche.

How old were you when you first read the Holmes stories?

I was about eight years old. They were among the first serious things that I read. I grew up in a very crazy household and the stories' appeal was that process of using reason to deal with people and the extreme things they do. I had two brothers and we grew up among some fairly outlandish characters, the original members of the Beat Generation. Kerouac, Ginsberg and William Burroughs were all friends of my father and lived in our house when I was young. When you're six years old that's a very stressful environment. They really were quite out of hand. I was drawn to any fictional characters that imposed order on things, a sense of morality. Because all they did was constantly call everything into question.

What particular challenges did you face in writing a new Holmes story?

The big challenge was to make it faithful. When I was asked to do it they said I should try to be faithful but try to add something of my own. That threw me into a bit of a loop for a while. Because I wanted it to be as faithful as possible but I knew that they didn't just want a carbon copy.

I wasn't originally going to do anything connected to the supernatural, even though I've always been fascinated by that part of Conan Doyle's life. I understood why he got involved with Spiritualism and the fairy hoax. There was some kind of pathos in that story that I found very humanising. At times you could almost lose sight of him as a human because he was so larger than life and he lived by these principles that he exhorted other people to live by. When his son died in the war it was such a crushing thing for him and he got more heavily involved with that stuff, seeing mediums to try and talk to his son.

There are a lot of fans who really don't think Holmes should or would be involved in any supernatural stuff. They quote the line about 'no ghosts need apply' but on the other hand there are lots of stories where he concedes the possibility of other dimensions in life. And that conveniently gets forgotten. So that was another reason to bring in the supernatural element. But I knew that would be hard. It had to play a crucial role but not *the* crucial role. The story would have to work without it. And that was a difficult line to walk. That's where the ghost of David Riccio came from.

Holmes and Watson are often seen (and represented) as fairly one-dimensional characters. Did you feel you had to 'flesh them out' a lot?

I think that the nuance is there. I don't think Conan Doyle always brought it out himself but it's there to be tapped into. There's a great deal of psychological expansion you can do on these characters while remaining faithful to the original purpose. I think Nick Meyer's book [*The Seven-Per-Cent Solution*] proved that. But you should elaborate from a position of integrity. We've had so many weird stories around Sherlock Holmes just for the sake of screwing with it. To screw with an icon – that I can't stand.

Conan Doyle put a lot into them in the beginning and that's where the potential was. If you just read the later stories you get a very different idea. Those are kind of two-dimensional. But you need to read the whole lot to realise that in the beginning he created characters with enormous psychological and dramatic possibilities. He just got tired of them. And that's perfectly understandable.

I did feel the need to flesh out the relationship between Sherlock and Mycroft a little bit. And I think that over time people had forgotten that Watson was supposed to be an active, strong counterbalance to Holmes. Not just this Nigel Bruce buffoon. So I felt Watson had to have as big a role as possible.

You have been quoted as saying that Holmes's rationalism has a particular resonance in this era of fundamentalist religious politics. Could you expand on that a little?

Sometimes I wonder if I wasn't wishing that more than stating it. Certainly the years since the book was published haven't convinced me that we're moving towards rationalism any faster than we were then. If anything it's become apparent that we're going to have to suffer some catastrophe as a result of people reverting to the medieval ways of thinking religiously. I guess what I meant at the time was that you had all these popular culture things, like the TV show

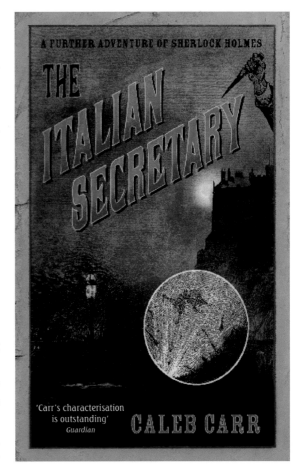

The cover of the British edition of *The Italian Secretary*.

CSI, about the scientific dissection of crime. Forensics has become the most pervasive thing in crime drama and fiction. There was a sense of people gravitating towards a reasonable explanation to all these outrageous, horrible things that were being done. At the time I really thought that might prove a more mitigating influence over the insanity that was driving the violence. I'm not so sure I now feel as hopeful as I did at that time. It's only been three or four years but the jury is out.

Ever since Conan Doyle wrote the stories and up until the last five or ten years, Holmes was the most recognised fictional character in the world. And now we have a new character: Harry Potter. That fact to me is enormously significant. There is a huge adult audience for Harry Potter. Everybody tries to lay it off on the kids but it's not just kids buying all those books. And that reflects a desire for a very simple-minded, facile, undisciplined magic. It's almost lazy. When you consider all the fiction that has been written and the stuff that knocked Holmes off his pedestal is Harry Potter . . . Objectively it seems absurd but when you look at the world right now it doesn't.

Did the Holmes stories inform your approach to your Dr Kreizler novels at all?

When I read Holmes the one thing that was missing for me was the psychological dimension. Holmes and Conan Doyle made a big thing about being able to solve a crime solely on physical evidence, without knowing anything about the people involved. What we know now is that there is a whole category of crimes – stranger-based crimes – that have no evidence trail. If you ignore motivation and profiling, they will remain unsolved for ever. It was true at that time too but Conan Doyle chose never to involve Holmes in or write about the Jack the Ripper crimes. I think he knew it was something he was profoundly uncomfortable with and he didn't want to get into it. The idea of the Alienist was really to create a character to solve all the cases Sherlock Holmes could not solve.

What for you is the essence of Holmes?

So many people say it's his rational side and the incredible brain. For me, it is his humanity. We don't know what the nature of the torment is but to me he is so clearly a tormented soul. I don't really need to know and I'm not dissatisfied that Conan Doyle never wrote what his personal secrets were. He didn't want to and that's fine. But it is important that he wrote him as a person who had that dimension. And it's what Watson recognises about him. Even though most of the time it's implicit, he realises this guy cannot really function in the world. He becomes his enabler for interacting with the world. To me, that's the essence of it. Even supposedly pure reason has its psychological causes and dimensions. That's what I really like about him.

THE ADVENTURE OF THE EMPTY HOUSE

FIRST PUBLISHED: The *Strand Magazine*, October 1903, UK; *Collier's*, 26 September 1903, USA

SETTING DATE: 1894

BACK BY POPULAR demand! Ten years after the events at Reichenbach Falls, Holmes reappears to fight his foes on the streets of London.

The tale begins with Watson narrating the tale of Ronald Adair, son of the Earl of Maynooth, who has been murdered in a hotel on Park Lane. This was a classic 'closed room' mystery, with the door locked from the inside and the only other entry/exit route a window twenty feet above a flower bed that showed no sign of human interference. The killing (with a bullet from a revolver) at first appeared motiveless – Adair seemed to have no enemies and his body was discovered surrounded by money so robbery was ruled out. However, it does emerge that he had run a rather successful gambling partnership with one Colonel Moran.

Watson has kept up his interest in the more out-of-the-way crimes since the loss of his great companion. So it is that he visits the crime scene, where he (literally) bumps into a decrepit old book collector. The bibliophile reappears a little later at Watson's digs and playfully reveals himself to be Holmes, apparently returned from the dead. Watson responds in a suitably stunned manner.

Holmes then fills Watson in on what really happened at the Reichenbach Falls and how he has spent the subsequent three years, when he went undercover to escape the attentions of Moriarty's henchmen. Returned to London, Holmes throws himself straight

Charing Cross Station, the great rail terminus a stone's throw away from Trafalgar Square, was the scene of an attack on Holmes.

back into the city's dark underworld. He takes Watson to the empty house of the title (with its prime view of 221B) and, with the assistance of a waxwork (courtesy of Monsieur Oscar Meunier of Grenoble) and the sterling efforts of Mrs Hudson, ensnares a mortal foe. At the same time, he gives Lestrade the opportunity to wrap up the Adair murder. For, as Holmes points out to the Inspector, 'three undetected murders in one year won't do'.

And so, much to Conan Doyle's disappointment, the Holmes carousel began to spin again. Though perhaps not among the finest tales in terms of mystery and detection, it reintroduces all the key characters on excellent form and is very satisfying for all that.

THE ADVENTURE OF
THE NORWOOD BUILDER

FIRST PUBLISHED: The *Strand Magazine*, November 1903, UK; *Collier's*, 31 October 1903, USA
SETTING DATE: 1894

HOLMES IS LAMENTING the absence of suitable criminal opponents in London when John Hector McFarlane, a young solicitor, bursts into 221B in the hope that the Detective might be able to save his reputation. What began the previous day with McFarlane receiving a visit from a builder, Jonas Oldacre, ended with him as prime suspect for Oldacre's murder.

Oldacre had requested that McFarlane should draw up his will, which to his astonishment made him the sole heir of a large estate. The job in hand required McFarlane to visit the builder's property in Norwood. Having stayed quite late studying legal

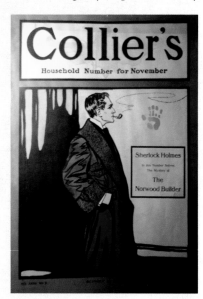

The American *Collier's Magazine* featured the illustrations of Frederic Dorr Steele, probably the most famous of all Holmes illustrators after Sidney Paget.

documents, McFarlane claimed he left the victim safe and well to retire to a nearby inn. Taking a train back to London the following morning, he read of the murder of Oldacre and that the police were on his trail.

The evidence against McFarlane does indeed seem compelling. His cane was discovered in Oldacre's room and a fire set in the grounds of the house still harboured the stench of burning flesh. Lestrade, as should be expected, is convinced of McFarlane's guilt and even Holmes is struggling to come up with an alternative solution.

However, when he learns that McFarlane's mother had once been Oldacre's fiancée before she broke off the engagement on account of his cruelty (in that instance to animals), Holmes suspects all is not as it seems. His analysis of Oldacre's roughly drafted will and the discovery that Oldacre had made a series of large payments to a certain Mr Cornelius only muddies the waters. Holmes suspects that the suspiciously acting housekeeper could hold the answers.

However, when traces of Oldacre's clothes are found in the remnants of the fire and a bloody fingerprint discovered in the hallway, the momentum seems to be back with Lestrade's theories. Nonetheless, the thumbprint proves to be this tale's 'dog that didn't bark' and sets Holmes on the right path. With Lestrade, Watson and three constables in attendance, Holmes prepares for an incendiary conclusion to the mystery.

THE ADVENTURE OF THE DANCING MEN

FIRST PUBLISHED: The *Strand Magazine*, December 1903, UK; *Collier's*, 5 December 1903, USA

SETTING DATE: 1898

THE STORY BEGINS with an archetypal scene at 221B, Holmes labouring over a particularly malodorous experiment before breaking hours of silence to astound Watson with a neat bit of deduction. Just how did Holmes know that at that very moment Watson was deciding not to invest in South African securities? The answer, of course, turns out to be elementary.

The mystery of the dancing men begins when Hilton Cubitt of Ridling Thorpe Manor in Norfolk posts a note asking for help in deciphering a strange code (consisting of little dancing men in various poses) that has thoroughly unsettled his previously idyllic marriage to Elsie.

Elsie was raised in America, and just before their wedding the previous year had made Cubitt promise never to ask her about her past. Assured that there was nothing of which she was personally ashamed, and that the problem lay rather with some 'very disagreeable associations', Cubitt did the decent thing and vowed silence on the subject.

All had been well until the arrival of a missive from the United States. This Elsie had burnt but then the strange code began to appear around the property, sometimes written on paper, other times graffitied on walls or doors. The effect on Elsie was dramatic and, though clearly frightened, she refused to share her fears with her husband.

Holmes asks Cubitt to send him all available instances of the code and employs his cryptographic skills. He soon realises the need for urgent action and so he and Watson head for Norfolk. Alas, they discover Inspector Martin already there, with Cubitt

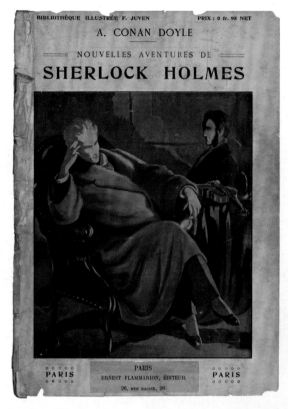

An edition of *The New Adventures of Sherlock Holmes*, illustrated by G. da Fonseca and published in Paris in 1909.

shot dead through the heart and Elsie suffering a grave bullet wound to the head. Martin believes Elsie killed her husband before attempting suicide.

As ever, Holmes is less easily convinced. A ballistic analysis and a disturbed flower bed suggest a third party was present. And what of the discarded pile of money at the crime scene? Using intelligence garnered from the coded messages, Holmes soon has the culprit in his sights.

THE ADVENTURE OF
THE SOLITARY CYCLIST

FIRST PUBLISHED: The *Strand Magazine*, January 1904, UK; *Collier's*, 26 December 1903, USA
SETTING DATE: 1895

THE ARRIVAL OF Miss Violet Smith is rather a nuisance to Holmes, whose attentions are taken up with the 'peculiar persecution' of John Vincent Harden, the well-known tobacco millionaire. Miss Smith lives with her mother, following the death of her father which has left them somewhat hard up.

When an advert appeared in a newspaper requesting information about the women's whereabouts, they responded and were met by Carruthers and Woodley, two fellows recently arrived from South Africa where they were cohorts of Violet's Uncle Ralph (of whom the women had heard nothing for a quarter of a century). Ralph had died in poverty shortly after hearing of his brother's death and had extracted a dying promise from these two gentlemen that they would make sure the Smith girls were looked after.

So it was that Carruthers employed Violet as his daughter's music teacher at an exceedingly generous £100 a year. Based at Chiltern Grange in Farnham in Surrey, she was allowed weekends off to return to her mother. All went well until Woodley – 'a dreadful person' – visited and aggressively pursued Violet, promising her a life of wealth if she would marry him. What her fiancé, Cyril Morton, would have thought is anyone's guess. After physically

assaulting Violet, Woodley received a hiding from Carruthers and hadn't been seen since.

To get to and from the railway station at weekends, Violet cycled, and she had recently noticed a mysterious figure with a black beard shadowing her about two hundred yards behind. Holmes sends Watson to scout out the situation and there he discovers that the bearded bike-rider emerges from and returns to Charlington Hall. Holmes, however, is less than impressed with Watson's efforts. They then receive a note from Violet that Carruthers has proposed but she has refused him.

Holmes takes matters into his own hands and heads for Surrey. On a mission for information at the local pub, Holmes shows a willingness to mix it with a ruffian who turns out to be Woodley. Returning to 221B a little battered but otherwise well, Holmes receives another note from Violet. Carruthers's proposal and the reappearance of Woodley have forced her to resign her post. Holmes whips Watson into action as he suspects the story may yet have a sting in the tail. When Violet goes for an earlier than expected train, it seems like Holmes's efforts may come to naught. But a dramatic finale in Farnham sees Holmes win out in the end.

ABOVE: Miss Violet Smith being pursued. J. K. Sterley unveiled his Rover in 1885, widely regarded as the first 'modern' bicycle.

OPPOSITE: A. Wessels Co. of New York published *The Return of Sherlock Holmes* in 1907 with illustrations by Charles Raymond Macauley.

HOLMES AND ME  DAVID BURKE

*David Burke is a well-known actor on stage and screen. His career on television
began in the early 1960s. From 1984 to 1985 he played Dr Watson opposite Jeremy
Brett in the celebrated Granada series.*

What factors informed your characterisation of Watson?

He seemed to me a very innocent man, really bordering on the naive. Nigel Bruce
had played the role mainly for comedy. I thought it was a very nice characterisation
but perhaps went a little too far towards the comic. But he and Rathbone made a
very good team. Then Nigel Stock had played the role for the BBC opposite Douglas
Wilmer. I was actually in one of those episodes – 'The Beryl Coronet'. Nigel Stock was
a very fine actor who I admired greatly.

So I was aware of who else had played Watson. I tried to bring a balance to it. To
be able to play the comic aspect of it, to accentuate the contrast between the rather
intolerant, driven Sherlock Holmes and the laid-back, gentle character of Watson.

How was the experience of making the series?

Working with Brett was a delight. He was a very nice man, a kind person. When
you're playing a sidekick in a television series, it is very easy for the actor in the
main role to use their position to give you an awkward time if they so choose. But
Jeremy was a real gentleman. He was slightly crazy in a nice way, which worked
well for his character.

I do think he is the best Sherlock Holmes we've ever had. And that's largely
because of his utter eccentricity. Although he was totally – well not totally but
largely – unlike Holmes, he very much understood that aspect of him. He made it
very viewable. I think television detectives need a degree of eccentricity about them if
they're to hold the interest of the audience. I think you find that in all the great ones.

Why did you leave the series when you did? Any regrets?

That's an interesting one. I spoke to Michael Cox in recent times and I said 'Do
you know why it was I left?' He said he knew one of the reasons was that my wife
had just had a baby and I really wasn't around very much. But the thing that really
clinched it happened a couple of months before we finished the first thirteen episodes. I was driving to Manchester with Jeremy and he said to me: 'You know,
if they offer us another series, we must on no account do it. It would be a great
career mistake.' I didn't actually ask him why it would be a big career mistake. I
just thought, 'He must know, he's more experienced than I am.'

Brett and Burke breathed
new life into the Conan Doyle
stories, starring together
in thirteen episodes of the
acclaimed Granada series.

When I got home I told my wife that I'd be home all the time when the eighteen months that I'd committed to were up because we wouldn't be doing any more. She was pleased, of course. And after I'd made that promise I couldn't go back on it. Lo and behold, about a month later Jeremy said, 'We're doing another series, you know.'

I said, 'But Jeremy, you told me you weren't doing any more.'

'Ah well, I don't know what I said, dear boy. But anyway, you will be on board won't you?'

So I told him that I'd promised my wife and couldn't go back on it. Jeremy was very disappointed, bordering on angry, that I wasn't going to do another series. That's why I left. It was really at his initiative, rather than my own. But there were no regrets. Because of my wife and having a young family, it was the right decision.

Also, I've always been a character actor at heart and I love the variety of moving from one part to another. When you get into a long-running series – and remember these ran for ten years – you can't do that. You're playing the same part, day in and day out. Dr Watson is a nice character but there's not an awful lot of scope in him. You find yourself endlessly saying, 'Oh good heavens, Holmes! How did you work that out?' And there are only so many ways you can do that before you start to get a little bored.

Many actors have felt burdened by their association with the Holmes stories. Was that the case for you?

I don't think I became identified with the role. I didn't do it for long enough for that to happen and he isn't as prominent a character anyway. But people certainly can get identified with a role and it can blight their careers. Personally, I think Jeremy stayed in it for far too long. I think it affected his health. It was an extremely strenuous job for him to do because every day he had a load of lines to remember. You couldn't really improvise them, it had to be precisely rendered and he wanted it to be so. The general public rarely thinks about actors learning their lines but it actually forms a large part of the job. And it doesn't get any easier as you get older.

By then Jeremy was having to get up at some ungodly hour in the morning because his car arrived at seven o'clock and he had to make sure he was ready for the day. At the end of the day he'd be dreadfully tired and I think he used to have a few glasses of champagne to drink himself to sleep. During the whole time he was doing Holmes, he was living in the Midlands Hotel. Now, a hotel existence is all right for at most a couple of months at a time but to do it year after year . . . it's no sort of life at all. There's no social life. Jeremy was a very gregarious, sociable sort of person and I think his social life almost ceased during those ten years. On the other hand, he was passionately interested in playing Holmes and I don't think he could bear the thought of somebody taking it over. So he stayed with it and paid the price.

THE ADVENTURE OF THE PRIORY SCHOOL

FIRST PUBLISHED: The *Strand Magazine*, February 1904, UK; *Collier's*, 30 January 1904, USA

SETTING DATE: 1901

THORNEYCROFT HUXTABLE, THE principal of the preparatory Priory School at Mackleton in the north of England, arrives at 221B and immediately collapses on the bearskin hearth rug. When he comes to he tells how one of his pupils, Lord Saltire – son of the Duke of Holdernesse – has been kidnapped. The Duke is offering a £5,000 reward for the boy's safe return and a bonus £1,000 for the identity of the kidnappers. The situation is further complicated by news that Heidegger, the German teacher, is also missing along with his bike.

Saltire had seemed happy enough in his two weeks at the school, despite whispers from James Wilder, the Duke's secretary, that his parents had separated, his mother now in the South of France, and that Saltire was closer to his mother than his father.

The evidence suggests Saltire must have departed at night via the ivy that grew by his window. He took with him a letter he had received from his father that day (contents unknown). The German master appears to have been in a rush for he left behind his shirt and socks. Holmes decides the case is serious enough to abandon his London work and accompany Huxtable back to the school.

Here Holmes interviews the Duke, who reveals that there has been no ransom demand and that he

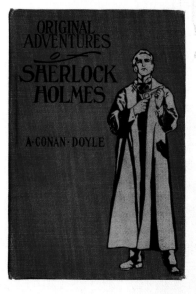

A limited edition of selected stories, published in New York by R. F. Fenno & Company around 1900.

is convinced that his wife has no part in the disappearance. He also rules out the possibility that the letter, which was posted by Wilder, has any relevance. An investigation of the grounds around the school leads Holmes to assume that the boy must have been taken cross-country. When his cap is found in the possession of some gypsies, the police round them up.

Holmes and Watson discover some tyre tracks and then the body of Heidegger, his head smashed in. Holmes is convinced the master had been pursuing the boy, not taking him. A lunch at the nearby Fighting Cock Inn focuses the Detective's thoughts, particularly in relation to the strange cow tracks he has seen on the moor despite the absence of any cows. A peek at the local smithy does not go down well with Hayes, the inn's landlord. Holmes has soon got to the bottom of things, with the Duke's colourful past at the centre of it all, and pockets £6,000 for his troubles.

This tale has received criticism from some readers because one of Holmes's key deductions (concerning the direction of cycle tracks) is considered to be without scientific basis.

THE ADVENTURE OF BLACK PETER

FIRST PUBLISHED: The *Strand Magazine*, March 1904, UK; *Collier's*, 27 February 1904, USA

SETTING DATE: 1895

WATSON RELATES HOW Holmes was really at the top of his form during 1895. The tale opens with Holmes returning to 221B from a butcher's, armed with a barbed-headed spear. He has convinced himself that even using his full strength, he cannot transfix a pig with a single blow. Good information to have.

His experiment is related to a case on which the estimable Inspector Stanley Hopkins has consulted him. At Forest Row in the Weald one Peter Carey, an old whaler and seal hunter and previously the master of the *Sea Unicorn* of Dundee, has been discovered murdered, skewered to a wall with a harpoon.

Carey seems to have been a man difficult to like. His wife and daughter are positively grateful for his demise. He was a drunkard with a propensity for violence (in one case beating up a vicar). He slept in an outhouse away from his family that he had designed to look like a ship's cabin and this was where he was killed. Slater, a local stonemason, revealed that he had spotted the figure of a man other than Carey in the cabin on the night of the murder. Carey's daughter had heard screaming at around two o'clock in the morning but had presumed her father was simply having another drunken episode.

When Carey was found the next day, he was dressed. The presence of two glasses and some rum suggested he had been expecting company. A sheathed knife and a notebook containing information about stocks (dated 1883 and initialled 'J. H. N.') were discovered in the

room. There is little other evidence to be had, save for a sealskin tobacco pouch with a 'P.C.' insignia. This despite the fact that Carey was not known as a smoker.

By the time Hopkins returns to the cabin with Holmes, there is evidence of a failed break-in. Convinced that the burglar will try again, they lie in wait. Sure enough, one John Hopley Neligan arrives, gains entry and examines a logbook. Neligan, however, pleads his innocence of the murder and Holmes suspects he is telling the truth. Holmes assumes the identity of one Captain Basil to place an advert for a harpooner. One of his three applicants is destined to hold the key to the case, a tale of greed and blackmail.

While whaling had been an important industry for British fleets during the eighteenth and early nineteenth century, it had gone into sharp decline during Queen Victoria's reign.

The RETURN of
SHERLOCK HOLMES
By A. CONAN DOYLE
Illustrated by Frederic Dorr Steele

THE ADVENTURE OF THE SIX NAPOLEONS

This is the eighth story of the new Sherlock Holmes series, which began in October. The preceding Adventures were those of The Empty House, The Norwood Builder, The Dancing Men, The Solitary Cyclist, The Priory School, Black Peter, and of Charles Augustus Milverton. During the summer months the publication of this series will be suspended, to be resumed in the autumn, the next story, "The Adventure of the Three Students," to appear in the Household Number for October, dated September 24. There will be twelve stories in the completed series

IT WAS no very unusual thing for Mr. Lestrade of Scotland Yard to look in upon us of an evening, and his visits were welcome to Sherlock Holmes, for they enabled him to keep in touch with all that was going on at the Police Headquarters. In return for the news which Lestrade would bring, Holmes was always ready to listen with attention to the details of any case upon which the detective was engaged, and was able occasionally, without any active interference, to give some hint or suggestion drawn from his own vast knowledge and experience. On this particular evening Lestrade had spoken of the weather and the newspapers. Then he had fallen silent, puffing thoughtfully at his cigar. Holmes looked keenly at him.

"Anything remarkable on hand?" he asked.

"Oh, no, Mr. Holmes, nothing very particular."

"Then tell me about it."

Lestrade laughed.

"Well, Mr. Holmes, there is no use denying that there *is* something on my mind. And yet it is such an absurd business that I hesitated to bother you about it. On the other hand, although it is trivial, it is undoubtedly queer, and I know that you have a taste for all that is out of the common. But in my taste for 'all that is out of the common.' But in my opinion it comes more in Dr. Watson's line than ours."

"Disease?" said I.

"Madness anyhow. And a queer madness, too! You wouldn't think there was any one living at this time of day who had such a hatred of Napoleon the First that he would break any image of him that he could see."

Holmes sank back in his chair.

"That's no business of mine," said he.

"Exactly. That's what I said. But then when the man commits burglary in order to break images which are not his own, that brings it away from the doctor and on to the policeman."

Holmes sat up again.

"Burglary! This is more interesting. Let me hear the details."

Lestrade took out his official notebook and refreshed his memory from its pages.

"The first case reported was four days ago," said he. "It was at the shop of Morse Hudson, who has a place for the sale of pictures and statues in the Kennington Road. The assistant had left the front shop for an instant when he heard a crash, and, hurrying in, he found a plaster bust of Napoleon, which stood with several other works of art upon the counter, lying shivered into fragments. He rushed out into the road; but, although several passers-by declared that they had noticed a man run out of the shop, he could neither see any one nor could he find any means of identifying the rascal. It seemed to be one of those senseless acts of Hooliganism which occur from time to time, and it was reported to the constable on the beat as such. The plaster cast was not worth more than a few shillings, and the whole affair appeared to be too childish for any particular investigation.

"The second case, however, was more serious and also more singular. It occurred only last night.

"In Kennington Road, and within a few hundred yards of Morse Hudson's shop, there lives a well-known medical practitioner, named Dr. Barnicot, who has one of the largest practices upon the south side of the Thames. His residence and principal consulting room is at Kennington Road, but he has a branch surgery and dispensary at Lower Brixton Road, two miles away. This Dr. Barnicot is an enthusiastic admirer of Napoleon, and his house is full of books, pictures, and relics of the French Emperor. Some little time ago he purchased from Morse Hudson two duplicate plaster casts of the famous head of Napoleon by the French sculptor, Devine. One of these he placed in his hall in the house at Kennington Road and the other on the mantel-piece of the surgery at Lower Brixton. Well, when Dr. Barnicot came down

this morning, he was astonished to find that his house had been burgled during the night, but that nothing had been taken save the plaster head from the hall. It had been carried out and had been dashed savagely against the garden wall, under which its splintered fragments were discovered."

Holmes rubbed his hands.

"This is certainly very novel," said he.

"I thought it would please you. But I have not got to the end yet. Dr. Barnicot was due at his surgery at twelve o'clock, and you can imagine his amazement when, on arriving there, he found that the window had been opened in the night and that the broken pieces of his second bust were strewn all over the room. It had been smashed to atoms where it stood. In neither case were there any signs which could give us a clew as to the criminal or lunatic who had done the mischief. Now, Mr. Holmes, you have got the facts."

"They are singular, not to say grotesque," said Holmes. "May I ask whether the two busts smashed in Dr. Barnicot's rooms were the exact duplicates of the one which was destroyed in Morse Hudson's shop?"

"They were taken from the same mold."

"Such a fact must tell against the theory that the man who breaks them is influenced by any general hatred of Napoleon. Considering how many hundreds of statues of the great Emperor must exist in London, it is too much to suppose such a coincidence as that a promiscuous iconoclast should chance to begin upon three specimens of the same bust."

"Well, I thought as you do," said Lestrade. "On the other hand, this Morse Hudson is the purveyor of busts in that part of London, and these three were the only ones which had been in his shop for years. So, although, as you say, there are many hundreds of statues in London, it is very probable that these three were the only ones in that district. Therefore a local fanatic would begin with them. What do you think, Dr. Watson?"

"There are no limits to the possibilities of mono-

Holmes had just completed his examination when the door opened

mania," I answered. "There is the condition which the modern French psychologists have called the 'idée fixe,' which may be trifling in character and accompanied by complete sanity in every other way. A man who had read deeply about Napoleon, or who had possibly received some hereditary family injury through the great war, might conceivably form such an 'idée fixe,' and under its influence be capable of any fantastic outrage."

"That won't do, my dear Watson," said Holmes, shaking his head, "for no amount of 'idée fixe' would enable your interesting monomaniac to find out where these busts were situated."

"Well, how do *you* explain it?"

"I don't attempt to do so. I would only observe that there is a certain method in the gentleman's eccentric proceedings. For example, in Dr. Barnicot's hall, where a sound might arouse the family the bust was taken outside before being broken, whereas in the surgery, where there was less danger of an alarm, it was smashed where it stood. The affair seems absurdly trifling, and yet I dare call nothing trivial when I reflect that some of my most classic cases have had the least promising commencement. You will remember, Watson, how the dreadful business of the Abernetty family was first brought to my notice by the depth which the parsley had sunk into the butter upon a hot day. I can't afford, therefore, to smile at your three broken busts, Lestrade, and I shall be very much obliged to you if you will let me hear of any fresh developments of so singular a chain of events."

The development for which my friend had asked came in a quicker and an infinitely more tragic form than he could have imagined. I was still dressing in my bedroom next morning when there was a tap at the door and Holmes entered, a telegram in his hand. He read it aloud:

"Come instantly 131, Pitt Street, Kensington, Lestrade."

"What is it, then?" I asked.

"Don't know—may be anything. But I suspect it is the sequel of the story of the statues. In that case our friend the image-breaker has begun operations in another quarter of London. There's coffee on the table, Watson, and I have a cab at the door."

In half an hour we had reached Pitt Street, a quick little backwater just beside one of the briskest currents of London life. No. 131 was one of a row, all flat-chested, respectable, and most unromantic dwellings. As we drove up we found the railings in front of the house lined by a curious crowd. Holmes whistled.

"By George! it's attempted murder at the least. Nothing less will hold the London message boy. There's a deed of violence indicated in that fellow's round shoulders and outstretched neck. What's this, Watson? The top steps swilled down and the other ones dry. Footsteps enough, anyhow! Well, well, there's Lestrade at the front window, and we shall soon know all about it."

The official received us with a very grave face, and showed us into a sitting-room where an exceedingly unkempt and agitated elderly man, clad in a flannel dressing-gown, was pacing up and down. He was introduced to us as the owner of the house, Mr. Horace Harker of the Central Press Syndicate.

"It's the Napoleon bust business again," said Lestrade. "You seemed interested last night, Mr. Holmes, so I thought perhaps you would be glad to be present, now that the affair has taken a very much graver turn."

"What has it turned to, then?"

"To murder. Mr. Harker, will you tell these gentlemen exactly what has occurred?"

The man in the dressing-gown turned upon us with a most melancholy face.

"It's an extraordinary thing," said he, "that all my life I have been collecting other people's news, and now that a real piece of news has come my own way I am so confused and bothered that I can't put two words together. If I had come in here as a journalist I should have interviewed myself and had two columns in every evening paper. As it is, I am giving away valuable copy by telling my story over and over to a string of different people, and I can make no use of it myself. However, I've heard your name, Mr. Sherlock Holmes, and if you'll only explain this queer business I shall be paid for my trouble in telling you the story."

Holmes sat down and listened.

"It all seems to centre round that bust of Napoleon which I bought for this very room about four months ago. I picked it up cheap from Harding Brothers, two doors from the High Street Station. A great deal of my journalistic work is done at night, and I often write until the early morning. So it was to-day. I was sitting in my den, which is at the back of the

10...

THE ADVENTURE OF THE SIX NAPOLEONS

FIRST PUBLISHED: The *Strand Magazine*, May 1904, UK; *Collier's*, 30 April 1904, USA

SETTING DATE: 1900

INSPECTOR LESTRADE CALLS at 221B to reluctantly seek assistance in solving what, on the face of it, seems to be a rather silly affair. An unidentified individual has taken to smashing identical busts of the Emperor Napoleon. The first victim of these strange attacks was Morse Hudson, who owns a shop that sold them. Next was a Dr Barnicot, who discovered that his two statues – and nothing else – had been taken and smashed in burglaries at both his home and his surgery.

Lestrade's first and predictably wayward instinct is that there is a crazed obsessive on the loose. However, things take a nasty turn when that night brings news of another smashed Napoleon and this time an accompanying corpse. Horace Harker, a journalist who owned the sculpture, had been disturbed by noises coming from the downstairs of his house. Going to investigate, he discovered an open window and the statue gone. When he opened his front door he found a dead man on his doorstep. The victim was around thirty, poorly dressed and sunburned. Beside him was a wood-handled clasp knife and in his pocket a photo of a 'simian' man.

Holmes realises that the perpetrator is in search of something specific but decides it would

LEFT: Napoleon at Wagram, depicting the famous battle of 1809, was painted by (or possibly after) Horace Vernet, Holmes's esteemed artist ancestor.

OPPOSITE: 'The Adventure of the Six Napoleons' appeared in *Collier's* on 30 April 1904. Frederic Dorr Steele used the actor William Gillette as the model for his Holmes.

be better if the culprit believes the police consider him to be a madman. He tells Lestrade to convey that opinion to Harker, which he knows will then find its way into the press. Holmes tracks down the shops that sold the busts and from them traces the manufacturer, Gelder & Co. All the broken busts came from the same batch of six. It emerges that the man in the photo is an Italian called Beppo who has recently been employed at the factory but was considered rather unsavoury. His cousin still works there.

That evening Lestrade reveals that the dead man is one Pietro Venucci, a member of the Mafia. The race is on to track down the remaining Napoleons and Holmes proves up to the job. It is ultimately a rare instance of Holmes and Lestrade working in unison. Harker, meanwhile, has managed to gather himself sufficiently to get his take on the story into print.

THE ADVENTURE OF CHARLES AUGUSTUS MILVERTON

FIRST PUBLISHED: The *Strand Magazine*, April 1904, UK; *Collier's*, 26 March 1904, USA
SETTING DATE: 1899

An unusual case in which there is no mystery as to who is the foe, only to how he might be stopped. Milverton – 'the worst man in London' – is, along with Moriarty and Grimesby Roylott, among the most fully realised of all Holmes's enemies.

Holmes has been approached by Lady Eva Blackwell, a stunning young débutante, whose marriage to the Earl of Dovercourt is two weeks away. However, the chances of the wedding taking place hang in the balance. Some rather indiscreet letters penned by Blackwell have fallen into the hands of Milverton, an unscrupulous professional blackmailer.

Holmes invites this dastardly fellow to 221B for talks. Milverton demands the huge sum of £7,000 and rejects out of hand a counter-offer of £2,000. Holmes is uncharacteristically riled by the interview, and with Watson in tow, the three men almost conclude with a scuffle before Milverton leaves to visit other 'clients'.

Holmes decides to take a different tack and pays a visit to Milverton's impressive pad on Hampstead Heath disguised as a plumber. Here he ingratiates himself with Agatha, the maid, even promising her marriage. A cruel game but one he feels necessary in these peculiar circumstances. With Agatha in his confidence, Holmes soon picks up intelligence on the workings of the household and the location of Milverton's papers.

Holmes then decides to take the law into his own hands and plans a night-time break-in. Watson, of course, will not let him face the danger alone. Yet the Detective has made a crucial miscalculation as to how deep a sleeper Milverton is. In an exciting climax, a further terrible crime is committed.

221B Baker Street, London, an interpretation of the Great Detective's lodgings by Texan artist Trish McCracken, was created after close study of the canon.

HOLMES AND THE CURIOUS AFFAIR OF THE MISSING WOMAN

'Woman's heart and mind are insoluble puzzles to the male.'
'The Adventure of the Illustrious Client'

INTELLIGENCE, WEALTH, A successful career, sporting ability and a prime London address. He was even quite a snappy dresser, deerstalker excepted. Yet rather than having to fight the ladies off, Holmes stands out as one of the most famous bachelors in literature. So what was he doing wrong? Or perhaps that is not the question at all. Maybe the single life was a very conscious choice or the result of a stunted emotional life. Others, inevitably, have wondered whether actually the Great Detective was not so much interested in women but would have sooner set up home with Watson given the chance.

This latter theory is one that has gained momentum in recent years, a natural and not illegitimate question about a man who spent his adult life avoiding

'You insult me, Mr. Holmes': The Detective was not one to spare a lady's feelings but the widely touted accusation that he was a misogynist is harsh.

emotional interaction with women in favour of an intense friendship with a man. In *Strangers: Homosexual Love in the Nineteenth Century* (Picador, 2003), Graham Robb makes the argument that 'everyone already knows, instinctively' that Holmes is gay. Robb convincingly builds a case that the stories do contain a distinct gay vocabulary. Mycroft's Diogenes Club is referred to as the 'queerest club in London' in the same year that references to 'snob queers' were made during Oscar Wilde's trial for sodomy. It is also interesting to note that in 'The Final Problem', Holmes was attacked in Vere Street, which in 1810 had been at the centre of a landmark episode in Britain's gay history. In that year a group of men were arrested on charges of homosexuality in a molly house on Vere Street, with eight eventually convicted, of whom two were hanged and six pilloried. Doyle, never a fool, would surely have been aware of such connotations. There are other textual references that hint at a physical intimacy between the Detective and the Doctor. At one point we see 'Holmes's hand steal into [Watson's]' and in a later story the two 'slept in a double-bedded room'. In 'The Dying Detective', Holmes prompted the Doctor into action with the extraordinary exhortation 'Quick, man, if you love me!'

What is beyond doubt is that, for all the occasional bickering and Holmes's sometimes distant manner, there is a highly tender relationship between the two men. It can be seen in casual domestic details, such as the fact that Holmes kept Watson's chequebook in his drawer and was guardian of its key. However, there are far more explicit examples, such as Holmes's assertion in *The Hound of the Baskervilles* that 'I shall be very glad to have you back safe and sound in Baker Street once more.' Holmes arguably was never more passionate than when he feared that Watson had been shot dead in 'The Three Garridebs', when assuring the assailant that 'If you had killed Watson, you would not have got out of this room alive.' This passion is characterised by a surly jealousy at the end of *The Sign of Four*, when Holmes responded to the news of Watson's engagement to Mary Morstan with the line 'I really cannot congratulate you.' Yet while there is plentiful evidence of great affection, emotional tenderness is not proof of sexual proclivity, and in truth there is precious little in Conan Doyle's words to suggest a *Brokeback Mountain*-style subtext.

For the vast majority of the canon, the relationship with Watson is devoid of any sexual tension and the two men seemed to have little to do with each other for weeks, months, even years at a time between cases. The domestic descriptions of the two going about their business in 221B Baker Street remind us more of Morecambe and Wise platonically sharing a flat (and indeed a bed) in one of their Christmas specials, or Ernie and Bert sparring with each other in *Sesame Street*. To Holmes, Watson is his steadfast and reliable companion, 'a trusty comrade'. 'I am lost without my Boswell,' he said in 'The Adventure of the Second Stain', putting

Holmes made an unlikely cover star for this 1951 edition of the male-interest magazine, *Men Only*.

Watson kindly but firmly in his place; a trusted witness to Holmes's brilliance, but not quite an equal.

Watson himself certainly has an eye for a pretty face, rarely missing the chance to celebrate the beauty or charm of at least one woman per story. As Holmes noted, 'Now, Watson, the fair sex is your department.' Watson never entirely lost faith in seeing Holmes settled down but when he occasionally sensed a glimmer of hope, as with Violet Hunter in 'The Copper Beeches', those hopes were soon dashed. As Watson regretfully noted in 'A Scandal in Bohemia', 'He never spoke of the softer passions, save with a jibe and sneer.'

It is not that Holmes never had sensitive feelings but they were rare and fleeting. In 'The Solitary Cyclist', he said of the appealing Miss Violet Smith that 'It is part of the settled order of Nature that such a girl should have followers.' He also clearly had a soft spot for Miss Maud Bellamy in 'The Lion's Mane'. Nor is Holmes repugnant to women. In 'Charles Augustus Milverton' he had no problems in turning on the charm to secure an engagement with Milverton's maid in double quick time. Though the attachment was only a tool for Holmes to solve his case, rather than an act rooted in love, it does not take away from the ease with which he successfully went about wooing.

Yet the only woman to gain anything like a kind of permanence in Holmes's life is dear Mrs Hudson, who was essentially an asexual surrogate mother figure. Though she may have occasionally tutted at 'the worst tenant in London', she saw to all Holmes's domestic needs despite his acerbic tongue, antisocial behaviour and parade of often dubious visitors. And that's to say nothing of the dangerous chemical experiments going on upstairs. The only other women who were broadly tolerated over a long period were Watson's wives (if we accept that there must have been two), probably because they didn't actively obstruct the adventures of our heroes. (That said, there is the sneaking suspicion that Watson would have regularly had to purchase the Victorian equivalent of petrol station flowers to make up for all those moonlit flits and extended stays away from home.) But for Holmes, an acceptable woman was one who didn't get in the way.

With nothing to suggest the contrary, the most reasonable conclusion is that Holmes was completely celibate, fearful that emotional attachment might reduce his powers. As Superman relied on kryptonite, Holmes's abilities relied on him keeping his distance from women, at least in his own mind. Thus he was highly guarded around them, variously noting that 'Women have seldom been an attraction to me, for my brain has always governed my heart,' and that 'I am not a whole-souled admirer of womankind.'

While it is unlikely that Holmes would have had much truck with self-help books, he was nonetheless an early advocate of the *Men Are from Mars, Women*

This poster for the Belgian release of Billy Wilder's *The Private Life of Sherlock Holmes* alludes to the film's distinctly more sexualised Sherlock.

United Artists
Entertainment from
Transamerica Corporation

het private leven van

UN FILM DE
BILLY WILDER
la vie privée
de SHERLOCK
HOLMES

"THE PRIVATE LIFE OF SHERLOCK HOLMES

AVEC
ROBERT STEPHENS · COLIN BLAKELY ·

PROD. & REGIE   SCENARIO
BILLY WILDER · BILLY WILDER AND **I.A.L.DIAMOND**

D'APRÈS   MUSIC
SIR ARTHUR CONAN DOYLE · MIKLOS ROZSA · PANAVISION · COLOR by DeLuxe

SHERLOCK HOLMES

IMPR. LICHTERT - Bruxelles 7

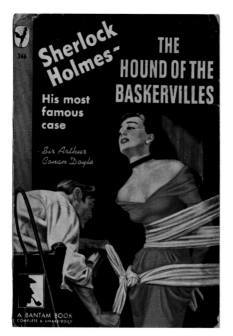

Holmes was given a Wild West makeover in this 1949 American edition published by Bantam Books, New York. The illustration was by Bill Shoyer.

Are from Venus theory of gender incompatibility. As a man who based his life on methodical, logical deduction, he was completely unable to get to grips with the unpredictability of a woman. If it is a woman's prerogative to change her mind, Holmes would have rather seen the prerogative banned. In exasperation he concludes that 'the motives of women are so inscrutable . . . How can you build on such a quick-sand?' On numerous occasions he presented femalekind as the antithesis of the reasoning male. 'The emotional qualities are antagonistic to clear reasoning,' he said in *The Sign of Four*, while in 'The Adventure of the Abbey Grange' he warned Watson that 'The lady's charming personality must not be permitted to warp our judgement.' Later in *The Sign of Four* he was more explicit still: 'I should never marry myself, lest I bias my judgement.'

Holmes in many ways represents the Victorian ideal of reason conquering dangerous emotion. Despite his independent spirit, he was a man of order. He was forever mulling over maps and indexes and almanacs. Everything was categorised and labelled and in its place and by knowing what's what he could eliminate doubt and uncertainty from the world. How often did he solve crimes by spotting the detail that is not quite just as it should be? Yet he seemed terrified that a beautiful face or a glimpse of ankle was going to throw him off his game.

In him we can see echoes of *Peter Pan*, *Swallows and Amazons* and even *Just William*, all creations which he pre-dates. He is the boy who never grows up, rushing around hither and thither, solving crime, righting wrongs and sticking one in the eye to all the usual institutions of authority. He doesn't need his life complicated with girls and all that stuff. He is a man operating in a man's world but part of his enduring attraction for us is the eternal child within him. There is certainly something of the playground in Holmes's retort to Watson's observation that a client, Mary Morstan, was very attractive: '"Is she?" he said languidly. "I did not observe."'

Yet while there is something indisputably childlike in Holmes, he was patently not an immature thinker. He had a considerable understanding of relationships and emotions, which he used in making his deductions about the motivations and actions that lay at the bottom of so many of his cases. When he played the cold fish, perhaps it is too simple to suggest that he was simply running away from emotions he did not comprehend.

It is hard to imagine Holmes as the sort of husband you would want for your sister, and equally difficult to believe that Holmes wouldn't have known that himself. What Mrs Holmes would have reacted kindly to his going missing for three

THE UNEXPLAINED CASES

~

In the canonical tales, there are over a hundred passing references to cases, many of which are presumably detailed in Dr Watson's dispatch box kept in the bank of Cox and Co. (Charing Cross). They leave us with a host of intriguing questions and have served as the basis for many pastiche works. Just what was that cormorant trained to do …?

* The Abernetty Family (and the depth to which the parsley had sunk into the butter)
* The Amateur Mendicant Society
* Bert Stevens, the Mild-Mannered Murderer
* The Bogus Laundry Affair
* The Camberwell Poisoning Case
* Colonel Warburton's Madness
* The Colossal Schemes of Baron Maupertuis (Netherland-Sumatra Company)
* The Darlington Substitution Scandal
* The Disappearance of Mr. James Phillimore
* The Dundas Separation Case (in which a husband 'had drifted into the habit of winding up every meal by taking out his false teeth and hurling them at his wife')
* The Giant Rat of Sumatra (featuring Matilda Briggs)
* The Little Problem of the Grosvenor Square Furniture Van
* The Madness of Isadora Persano (with a remarkable worm unknown to science)
* Merridew of Abominable Memory
* The Most Winning Woman (who poisoned three little children)
* The Nonpareil Club Card Scandal
* The Peculiar Persecution of John Vincent Harden
* The Politician, the Lighthouse and the Trained Cormorant
* The Repulsive Story of the Red Leech and the Terrible Death of Crosby the Banker
* Ricoletti of the Club Foot and his Abominable Wife
* The Singular Affair of the Aluminum Crutch
* The Two Coptic Patriarchs
* The Woman at Margate with no Powder on her Nose
* Wilson, the Notorious Canary-Trainer

years after supposedly falling to his death over the Reichenbach Falls? Particularly if she were to find out he had been careering round Nepal disguised as a Norwegian explorer in the meantime. In turn, Holmes seemed distinctly underwhelmed by the attractions of marriage as an institution. Take 'The Adventure of the Retired Colourman', when he said of one of the protagonists: 'A competence, a wife, leisure – it seemed a straight road which lay before him.' Apart from charging this vision of domestic bliss with a distinct sense of anticlimax, he went on to say: 'But is not all life pathetic and futile? . . . We reach. We grasp. And what is left in our hands at the end? A shadow. Or worse than a shadow – misery.' A career as a marriage guidance counsellor was unlikely.

Did that sharp mind of his also conclude that were he to allow his judgement to be 'warped' by attraction, he would be drawn to the 'wrong' type of woman? Take these couple of off-the-cuff observations from *The Sign of Four*. 'Women are never to be entirely trusted – not the best of them,' he said and then, intriguingly, 'I assure you that the most winning woman I ever knew was hanged for poisoning three little children for their insurance money.' We can be confident that Watson would always end up with someone decent and upstanding but can we be so sure that Holmes wouldn't end up with a bad 'un?

One woman, Irene Adler in 'A Scandal in Bohemia', stood apart for her ability to get under Holmes's skin. 'The daintiest thing under a bonnet on the planet', she was a feisty American opera singer who was the lover of the King of Bohemia. When he announced he was to marry another woman, considering Adler 'not on my level', he feared she would reveal their affair. It was the king who employed Holmes to recover a tell-tale photo from her but it was Adler to whom Holmes warmed. And it was she who ultimately outwitted the Great Detective. She was beautiful, cunning, independent, dangerous when scorned, threatening the future of one of Europe's great houses. When Holmes talked elsewhere of having been 'beaten four times – three times by men, and once by a woman', we must assume that Adler was this woman. She is just the sort of character of whom we might expect Holmes to have been most wary. But while Watson decided Holmes felt no 'emotion akin to love for Irene Adler', she was to Holmes 'always the woman . . . [who] eclipses and predominates the whole of her sex'. Holmes retained her photo at the end of the story. For a man so averse to sentimentality it was a grand gesture indeed. And so we are left to wonder whether he avoided relationships because he had deduced that the women most likely to attract him were also the ones most able to destroy him.

Finally there remains the possibility that Conan Doyle had in mind a sting in the tail for his hero. In *The Hound of the Baskervilles*, Watson notes that 'Evil indeed is the man who has not one woman to mourn him.' Surely Holmes, the man who 'never loved', would be left to wonder who would be there to weep for him?

Irene Adler, the woman who could justly claim to have the measure of Holmes, as featured in Alexander Boguslavsky's series of Conan Doyle cigarette cards in 1923.

PROFESSOR MORIARTY

PERHAPS THE FIRST great fictional master criminal, Moriarty gives an insight into how Holmes himself might have been had he turned to the bad. He appeared in only two stories, 'The Final Problem' and *The Valley of Fear*, and was mentioned in just five others. Yet the genius of this creation is that he exerts a constant ominous presence. Just as Holmes became almost obsessed in his pursuit of this 'Napoleon of crime', so it is that Moriarty infiltrates the reader's consciousness so completely that the possibility of his shadow hangs over virtually every story. He is like a spirit, flashing in and out of the reader's peripheral imagination.

Holmes considered Moriarty to be 'the organizer of half that is evil and of nearly all that is undetected in this great city'. Aside from Moriarty's malevolence, what made him such a delicious challenge to Holmes was his huge mental capacity. Holmes gave him the greatest of all compliments when he called him his 'intellectual equal'. Physically, Moriarty cut rather an eerie figure. He is described as tall and thin, with a pale, domed forehead, sunken grey eyes and a 'face [that] protrudes forward and is forever slowly oscillating from side to side in a curiously reptilian fashion'.

Moriarty's great skill was to evade for so long all suspicion of his criminal influence despite being 'the organizer of every deviltry, the controlling brain of the underworld'. As Holmes noted: 'The man pervades London, and no one has heard of him. That's what puts him on a pinnacle in the records of crime.' To the world at large he was simply 'ex-Professor Moriarty, of mathematical celebrity'. (It is worth noting that Conan Doyle loathed mathematics while a schoolboy so it was perhaps inevitable that his most devilish creation should have come from a mathematics background.) Holmes, however, eventually grasped the reach of this 'genius . . . philosopher . . . abstract thinker'. He traced the threads of countless crimes back to Moriarty, 'the poisonous, motionless creature' lurking at the centre of the web.

Like any great general, Moriarty surrounded himself with capable lieutenants. They ranged from the relatively lowly, like Parker in 'The Empty Room' ('a garroter by trade, and a remarkable performer upon the jew's-harp'), to 'his chief of staff' Colonel Sebastian Moran, a former army man and 'the best heavy-game shot that our Eastern Empire has ever produced'.

Moriarty, a resolutely single man, came from a privileged background and gained recognition throughout Europe when only twenty-one for his 'treatise upon the binomial theorem'. This led to him being appointed to the mathematics chair at one of England's smaller universities. He also authored a much respected work entitled

The Dynamics of an Asteroid. With the world seemingly at his feet, he became the subject of unspecified 'dark rumours' that precipitated his resignation from the teaching post and saw him move to London. It was at that juncture that he devoted himself to a life of criminal enterprise.

For Holmes, bringing down Moriarty's empire was his crowning achievement. Watson related in 'The Final Problem' that 'if [Holmes] could be assured that society was freed from Professor Moriarty he would cheerfully bring his own career to a conclusion'. While Holmes maintained a healthy disrespect for Moriarty (for instance, studiedly addressing him as 'Mr Moriarty' rather than 'Professor Moriarty'), he did acknowledge that he presented the single greatest challenge to his detecting abilities. For a while it seemed as if they were so perfectly matched that they had cancelled each other out in the most final way possible at the Reichenbach Falls. Fortunately, the Great Detective came off rather better than first believed. Yet still Moriarty found his way into Holmes's consciousness: 'I am not a fanciful person,' said Holmes, 'but I give you my word that I seemed to hear Moriarty's voice screaming at me out of the abyss.' Perhaps it was only to be expected that 'the greatest schemer of all time' would leave his nemesis one final, enduring memory to haunt his nightmares.

Holmesians have long enjoyed proposing possible real-life models for Moriarty. In *The Valley of Fear* Holmes likened him to Jonathan Wild. Wild operated in the London of the early eighteenth century, running a gang of apparent 'thief-takers' who, in lieu of an organised police force, brought to justice many criminals. For this work Wild was something of a popular hero but the twist was that the thief-takers were themselves criminals. One of Wild's ruses involved his men stealing property then claiming they had recovered it (and apprehended the miscreants). Wild was then richly rewarded for returning the stolen property to its rightful owners. It was alleged that virtually every thief in London was under his control. Should a man outlive his usefulness, Wild thought nothing of turning him over to the hangman (receiving yet another financial reward for his civic work). However, the truth eventually caught up with him and he was hanged in 1725, his name to become synonymous with corruption and hypocrisy.

Another possible template for Moriarty was Adam Worth, who was dubbed 'the Napoleon of the criminal world' by Scotland Yard before Holmes ever used the phrase. Worth was born in Germany in 1844 but his family moved to the USA while he was still a child. There he progressed from petty theft to more serious robberies until he fled to Europe to avoid the grip of the American justice system. He lived in France and England, where he robbed, defrauded and ran illegal gambling establishments. Over time he built up a complex web of underworld contacts whom he used for countless robberies and house breaks

OPPOSITE: An unsettling advertising poster for *Moriarty* (also known as *Sherlock Holmes* outside of the UK), a 1922 release with John Barrymore as Holmes.

ENGLAND, 1922

WILL DYSON

Gainsborough's portrait of the Duchess of Devonshire was audaciously stolen from a gallery in Bond Street by Adam Worth in 1876.

(under the proviso that violence should not be employed). In 1876 he famously stole Thomas Gainsborough's portrait of the Duchess of Devonshire from the gallery of Agnew & Sons in London. Conan Doyle has Moriarty owning a picture by Greuze entitled *La Jeune Fille à l'Agneau*, which many critics have read as an oblique reference to Worth's exploit. After outwitting the police forces of two continents for so long, things began to unravel for Worth in 1891 when a bungled robbery in Brussels saw him arrested. Still the police were unable to prove the extent of his criminal activities but he nonetheless received a seven-year sentence for the Belgian fiasco. He was released early for good behaviour and in 1901 reunited Agnew & Sons with their Gainsborough in return for a hefty $25,000. This master gentleman criminal, who outwitted the forces of law and order so efficiently, died early the next year a free man.

Among the host of other contenders for Moriarty's inspiration, a particularly strong case has been made for Roland de Villiers. De Villiers was the alias of George Ferdinand Springmuhl von Weissenfeld, who was born into a wealthy German background. For a large part of Victoria's reign he lived in London fraudulently amassing huge sums while remaining quite out of reach of the law. He was finally arrested after a dogged pursuit by one Chief Inspector Sweeney of Scotland Yard, who recalled the events in his memoirs of 1904.

A SELECTION OF NOTABLE NEMESES

THOSE WITH EVEN the most passing acquaintanceship with Holmes probably know the name of Professor Moriarty but there are plenty of other memorable villains to conjure with. It is by no means the case that all those guilty of wrong-doing are considered monsters by the Great Detective. Some actually command a degree of sympathy from both him and the reader. But others are almost completely devoid of virtue and serve as powerful ciphers for the latent fears in Holmes's society and our modern world too.

Of course, no list of Holmes's greatest adversaries would be complete without a mention of the magnificent Irene Adler. However, it is fair to say that she ranks more as a grand opponent than a malicious foe. So for more information on Miss Adler, see the chapter 'Holmes and the Curious Affair of the Missing Woman'. Let's start here, though, with a man who is a member of that small band of canonical baddies who dared attempt a premeditated attack on Holmes's life: Sebastian Moran (introduced to us in 'The Adventure of the Empty House'). Indeed, he had the impudence to try to kill him twice.

Sidney Paget's famous depiction of Holmes's great nemesis, Moriarty, suggestive of the crime lord's 'strangely reptilian' demeanour.

Moran was the right-hand man of Professor Moriarty and was thus considered by Holmes as 'the second most dangerous man in London'. The son of Sir Augustus Moran, a former British minister to Persia, Sebastian came from a background of privilege and promise. Educated at Eton and Oxford, he served with distinction in the army, being mentioned in dispatches for his role in the 1879 Battle of Charasiab in the Second Anglo-Afghan War.

He was in particular known for his remarkable attributes as a marksman and for apparently pursuing a man-eating tiger down a drain in India. But then something went wrong and he was forced out of the army, returning to London and joining forces with Moriarty. To the outside world, he continued to appear a man of decorum, inhabiting smart London neighbourhoods and enjoying membership of exclusive clubs. But this was a mirage, blurring a life of serious criminality. It is this that makes him such a memorable antagonist. Here was a man who apparently represented the familiar social order but who

Barry Moser's depiction of Dr Grimesby Roylott, one of the fiercest and most devilish opponents that Holmes ever encountered.

was in fact intent on undermining it. In Holmes's world, that is the most dangerous sort of malefactor. Dare it be said, just as Moriarty may represent 'Holmes-gone-criminal', Moran can be viewed as the man Watson might have become if Stamford had introduced him to Moriarty and not Holmes.

Such a threat to the social structure is similarly represented by Baron Adelburt Gruner, whose crimes were detailed in 'The Adventure of the Illustrious Client'. The Austrian aristocrat coupled his sociopathic tendencies with good looks and an 'air of romance and mystery' that allowed him to reel in women who then faced grim fates. He was 'a purring cat who thinks he sees prospective mice'. Holmes found him 'an excellent antagonist' and admired the artistry of his crimes but detested the threat he posed to the natural order, a threat only accentuated by a 'swarthy' foreign exoticism.

Holmes's distrust of foreign 'otherness' was also apparent in 'The Adventure of the Speckled Band', where we see Dr Grimesby Roylott, the last remnant of one of England's oldest families, turned into a monster after a prolonged period living in India. However, it seems unlikely that his horrific temper could really be blamed on his many years in 'the tropics'. We can all get overheated and tetchy but Roylott's ruthless cruelty is perhaps unrivalled anywhere else in the canon. The victims of his crimes were members of his own family, those who had been entrusted into his care. If Holmes (and by extension, Conan Doyle) sought to protect the broad social order (even when they were critical of aspects of it), this attack on the family – its fundamental unit – was by far the most dire. All the more so given that the principal victims were charming and defenceless young females who appealed to the Great Detective's sense of gallantry.

If Roylott was irredeemably horrible, Jephro Rucastle in 'The Adventure of the Copper Beeches' was not far behind him, despite a first impression that was a little more charming. In common with the dismal doctor, he executed a plan of cold ruthlessness against a member of his own family for personal gain. Indeed, so difficult is it to see good in him that when Rucastle is left an invalid as a result of his own nefarious doings, his fate as a 'broken man' prompts no sympathy from either reader or narrator.

But perhaps the most pernicious exponent of social undermining comes in the form of Charles Augustus Milverton, a blackmailer so unpleasant that he gets a story named after him (a rare honour indeed). 'I've had to do with fifty murderers in my career,' Holmes notes, 'but the worst of them never gave me the repulsion which I have for this fellow.' Milverton, plump and described as having 'something of Mr. Pickwick's benevolence in his appearance', had spent years buying up incriminating personal letters in order to 'compromise people of wealth and position'. He then demanded vast sums, often from young ladies who had done nothing worse than been a little too forthcoming with their feelings. Not only was Milverton a torturer of souls, but he gnawed away at the social fabric, launching assaults on privacy and mining expressions of (usually female) sexuality for his own advantage. In an age where, it is said, a finely turned piano leg might cause polite company to flush, no wonder Holmes regarded Milverton as such an abomination.

The stories are littered with an army of colourful villains but those detailed here are, along with Moriarty, some of the most base and unscrupulous. None of them are Jack the Ripperesque demons driven by unfathomable forces. Instead, they are each cool and calculating, carrying out despicable acts for their own benefit. As such, they represent serious threats to the normal social order – that order which Holmes devoted his entire life and energies to keeping in delicate balance.

THE ADVENTURE OF THE THREE STUDENTS

FIRST PUBLISHED: The *Strand Magazine*, June 1904, UK; *Collier's*, 24 September 1904, USA

SETTING DATE: 1895

STAYING IN AN unspecified university town (presumably either Oxford or Cambridge), Holmes is rather put out when his studies into early English charters are interrupted. He is approached by Hilton Soames, a lecturer at St Luke's College, to help with a little local trouble. Soames had been preparing a Greek paper to be used in an exam the following day for the valuable Fortescue Scholarship. At 4.30 he had gone to meet a friend for tea, leaving a draft of the exam (a text of Thucydides) on his desk in a locked office.

However, when he returned an hour or so later, he discovered a key in the door and realised that somebody had tampered with his papers. They had been in a single neat pile but there were now pages in three different places around the room. Astonishingly, Holmes is able to tell Soames exactly what these three locations were. Some mischief is afoot and the good name of the university is at stake.

The key in the door belongs to Bannister, a trusted servant. He has professed no involvement in the skulduggery but tells of how he had entered the office to ask whether he should make tea. When he found the room unoccupied he retreated but must have left the key in the door. On hearing that the papers had been interfered with, Bannister had come over faint and collapsed into a chair. Soames has made some useful observations including the presence of a broken pencil lead, some pencil shavings, a three-inch score mark on his desk and a saw-

A view of Tom Quad at Christ Church College, Oxford, the largest college quad in the city.

dust-speckled blob of black dough or clay.

Holmes's investigation of the crime scene leads him to conclude that whoever the cheater was had hidden in Soames's bedroom. Suspicion falls on the three students who live in the building. One of them, Daulat Ras, had visited Soames earlier but the tutor is sure the papers were safely out of sight. Das is, however, to be seen nervously pacing his room. The other students are the athletic and financially impoverished Gilchrist on the lower floor and the brilliant but disagreeable Miles McLaren on the top floor.

Holmes arises at six a.m. on the day of the exam to do some last-minute cramming before revealing just who is responsible for the dastardly crime.

THE ADVENTURE OF
THE GOLDEN PINCE-NEZ

FIRST PUBLISHED: The *Strand Magazine*, July 1904, UK; *Collier's*, 29 October 1904, USA

SETTING DATE: 1894

AN ATMOSPHERICALLY STORMY night is interrupted by the appearance of Stanley Hopkins from the Yard. He is seeking Holmes's help in solving a mystifying murder that occurred at Yoxley Old Place near Chatham in Kent.

The property belongs to the elderly and infirm Professor Coram. Coram's young secretary, Willoughby Smith, has been stabbed with a sealing-wax knife. Yet all investigations suggest that Smith had no enemies. The only real clue lies with his dying words spoken to the maid, Susan Tarlton, who found him in the study. 'The Professor – it was she,' he had told her.

Interviewed by Hopkins, the maid furnished further details about the circumstances of that day. With the Professor in bed, she was hanging curtains when she recognised the foot tread of Smith going into the study. A moment later came an unearthly scream. Gathering her composure, she rushed to the study and there found Smith, his carotid artery cut. The pair of golden pince-nez were clutched in his hand.

In a not entirely satisfactory survey of the crime scene, Hopkins discovered footprints

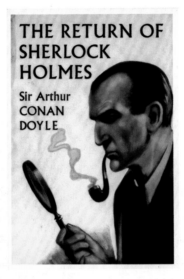

The distinctive dust jacket for John Murray's edition of *The Return of Sherlock Holmes*.

running beside the garden path but, because of adverse weather conditions and the culprit's attempt to disguise their tracks, he could not tell in which direction they were going or what size they were. When Holmes and Watson arrive, Holmes sees rather more detail at the scene. He particularly notes a corridor lined with coconut matting and realises that although the Professor's study appears undisturbed, burglary was the motive. But most useful of all are the pince-nez. From this single clue Holmes constructs a complete description of the person he believes is responsible for the murder.

The Detective then engages in a marathon of Egyptian cigarette smoking during an interview with Coram. Coram claims to have no idea as to the circumstances of the murder, suggesting his secretary may have committed suicide. When the housekeeper tells Holmes that Coram's appetite has been particularly voracious since the killing, Holmes decides on a reinterview and the culprit is soon uncovered.

THE ADVENTURE OF
THE MISSING THREE-QUARTER

FIRST PUBLISHED: The *Strand Magazine*, August 1904, UK; *Collier's*, November 1904, USA
SETTING DATE: 1896

AT THE START of this story Holmes is once again at a low ebb. Watson is concerned that in the absence of professional challenges, his friend will fall back into the drug mania from which he has been slowly weaned. Rescue comes in the form of Cyril Overton, captain of the Cambridge University rugger team (Overton is distinctly from the school of rugger rather than rugby), who has been directed towards Holmes by Scotland Yard. The team's star winger, Godfrey Staunton, has most uncharacteristically disappeared off the face of the earth the day before the varsity match against Oxford. Without him Cambridge is destined to lose.

Though by his own admission lacking any real knowledge concerning the oval ball game, Holmes takes on the case. Staunton, who had seemed out of sorts the previous night, was last seen leaving Bentley's Private Hotel in London in the company of a rough-looking bearded fellow. In his hotel room Holmes finds an intriguing portion of a telegram sent by the missing man, with the words '. . . Stand by us for God's sake'.

Staunton's uncle, the rich but miserly Lord Mount-James, appears on the scene. He claims to know nothing of his nephew's whereabouts and is less than keen to have to fork out any money on an investigation. That is until Holmes speculates that Staunton may have been kidnapped to get to his uncle. An alternative theory concerns a varsity match gambling scam. Can Staunton's friend, one Dr Armstrong, shed any light? It is left to a lop-eared beagle/foxhound cross called Pompey to bring the case to a close.

The first varsity match between Oxford and Cambridge took place in 1872. For the record, Oxford won in 1896, the year of this story.

THE ADVENTURE OF THE ABBEY GRANGE

FIRST PUBLISHED: The *Strand Magazine*, September 1904, UK; *Collier's*, 31 December 1904, USA

SETTING DATE: 1897

A NOTHER BROODING NIGHT on Baker Street. Watson is awoken by Holmes, who utters the immortal phrase 'The game is afoot!' Inspector Stanley Hopkins has once again sought the assistance of the Detective, this time in relation to the murder of Sir Eustace Brackenstall at his home, the Abbey Grange, located at Marsham in Kent. It seems he has been killed during a particularly brutal robbery by the notorious Randall gang.

On arrival Holmes interviews Lady Brackenstall, Sir Eustace's wife, about the previous night's proceedings. She begins by relating how she left her native Australia a year and a half earlier and got married about six months later. The union, though, had not been happy as Sir Eustace was a drunkard prone to violence (even setting fire to his wife's dog).

Just before eleven o'clock the previous night she had been doing her rounds of the home before going to bed. However, she interrupted a break-in in the dining room by a gang of three men (one older than the other two) and was knocked unconscious, tied in a chair with a bell-rope and gagged. Sir Eustace then appeared on the scene armed with a blackthorn cudgel but in the ensuing scuffle he

Sir Eustace Brackenstall lying dead on the floor of the dining room at Abbey Grange.

was cut down by a poker blow. Lady Brackenstall was lapsing in and out of consciousness but remembers seeing the intruders supping wine before loading up with silver.

Further evidence is provided by Brackenstall's maid and companion, Theresa Wright. She claims to have spotted the gang earlier in the evening without realising their intentions. Holmes's investigation of the crime scene presents several questions. Why use the bell-rope when pulling it down might have alerted the servants? Why did the thieves not steal more? And what of the beeswing in one of the wineglasses?

Holmes returns to London in the expectation that Hopkins will soon have wrapped things up. However, he is troubled by the tale of the Randall gang and mid-journey decides to return to the Grange. Another study of the crime scene yields more evidence and Holmes is soon on the track of a new suspect with links to Lady Brackenstall's past. Bypassing the niceties of the law, Holmes decides to impose his own form of justice.

THE ADVENTURE OF
THE SECOND STAIN

FIRST PUBLISHED: The *Strand Magazine*, December 1904, UK; *Collier's*, 28 January 1905, USA
SETTING DATE: 1894

ORIGINALLY ADVERTISED AS the 'Last Sherlock Holmes Story Ever to be Written'. Something that had been heard before . . .

Watson describes this as 'the most important international case' of Holmes's career. So it was that 221B played host to the Prime Minister, Lord Bellinger, and the Secretary of State for European Affairs, Trelawney Hope. A document has been stolen from Hope's locked dispatch box in his bedroom at Whitehall Terrace. Reluctant to give too much detail, they eventually tell Holmes that it was received from a foreign leader six days previously and that its contents, if revealed, could lead to a devastating war. The letter was stolen while Hope was out of the house for a few hours yet no one, not even his wife, knew of its existence.

Holmes quickly comes up with a list of the most likely suspects from London's espionage community. However, Watson reports that one of the leading contenders, Eduardo Lucas, was murdered the previous evening at his home near Whitehall. Holmes is then surprised to receive a visit from Hope's beautiful but frightened wife. She has come without her husband's knowledge and is desperate to know the contents of the missing envelope (information Holmes does not furnish).

Several frustrating days ensue, with Holmes convinced that the solution to the puzzle lies with Lucas's murder. Then a breakthrough occurs. It is reported in the press that one Mme Fournaye has been picked up by the Parisian police in connection with the death. Lucas, it seems, also went by the name of Henri Fournaye.

Holmes is convinced that were the letter loose, there would have already been repercussions. He is sure it remains hidden somewhere. Holmes and Watson are summoned by Lestrade to the scene of Lucas's dispatch. A strange discovery has been made:

the location of a bloodstain on the carpet does not match the corresponding stain on the wood floor. Holmes instructs Lestrade to interrogate the guarding officer, who admits he had earlier let an individual into the house. Holmes knows just who the visitor was.

Culprit and motive are soon within his grasp and with a dramatic flourish he reunites the letter with its rightful owner. Discretion has been maintained and war averted.

Holmes and Watson looking particularly debonnair as they stride purposefully down the street.

HOLMES AND ME 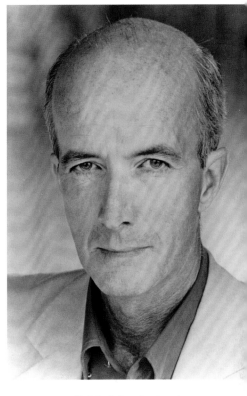 BERT COULES

Bert Coules is a prolific writer for radio. In a long association with the BBC he has worked on productions as diverse as The Thirty-Nine Steps, Mutiny on the Bounty, Rebus *and* Brother Cadfael. *Between 1989 and 1998 he was head writer on the BBC project to dramatise for the first time the entire canon of Doyle's novels and stories. The canonical stories saw Clive Merrison in the role of Holmes and Michael Williams as Watson. Andrew Sachs took over as Watson in two spin-off series.*

What drew you to the Holmes stories in the first place?

I can't recall now if it was the books that came first or the BBC's famous radio versions of the late fifties and early sixties – which starred Carleton Hobbs and Norman Shelley – that first captured my imagination. Both remain clear and vivid memories from the time I was ten years old or so. I think what I loved more than anything, at an age when I was deeply into Batman and Superman and the like, was that Holmes was like a superhero whose main power was that he was *clever*. That appealed very much to the awkward, over-weight, bad-at-games kid that I was: I couldn't be muscle-bound, I couldn't be faster than a speeding bullet, I couldn't have all those cool gadgets and live in a cave, but just possibly I could learn to use my brain . . .

Bert Coules's series starred Clive Merrison, the only actor to have played the Great Detective in adaptations of every single canonical story.

What challenges did you face in transferring the stories from page to airwaves?

How long have you got? But, in brief, the same challenges as in writing any radio drama – to be entertaining, to be gripping, to make the stories and the characters come alive in sound only. To make clear what was happening without bashing the listener over the head with obvious on-the-nose spelling-it-out writing. To use the unique properties of radio, its intimacy, its capacity to employ atmosphere with the most minimal means. Plus, in this case, to be true to the well-loved originals while at the same time presenting them in a fresh light for a contemporary audience.

The same principles applied for the non-canonical stories, really, with the added desire to explore areas which Doyle either wouldn't or couldn't, for whatever reason. I wrote an episode centred on Spiritualism, for example, which was a subject that Doyle held far too important to trifle with.

I'm proud of the fact that people have enjoyed the non-canonical stories and compared them favourably to the way I presented the Doyles. With the *Further Adventures*, as with the canonical stories, there are elements which I think work OK, and some which I think are less successful.

What is it that makes Holmes still popular for a modern audience?

It's not Holmes, it's Holmes and Watson. It's their relationship which is at the heart of the stories' continued popularity. It's one of the great literary friendships and beautifully drawn by Doyle for all his casual inconsistencies and hasty writing and protestations that he was just turning out ephemeral light fiction. And stories about good people doing their best to overcome evil are always relevant, aren't they? Every age needs its heroes.

The late Victorian period in which the earlier stories are set (and where most people, I think, believe that *all* the stories are set) exerts a very powerful pull: all that gaslight and fog and cosy open fires and hansom cabs clopping down Baker Street, and social certainty, where everyone not only knew their place but was happy to inhabit it. In reality, of course, it was a harsh, horrible time for the vast majority of people. And while the stories don't attempt to hide this, for some reason the social realism of Doyle's writing has never been prominent in his readers' minds in the same way that Dickens', for example, has in his.

Historically, Holmes and (especially) Watson have often been presented as rather one-dimensional characters in productions for radio, theatre and screen. In your plays, they are fully formed. Looking at the original stories, did you find them as such or did you have to 'join up the dots'?

The characters have depth in the original tales, but they're like a painting that's accumulated layer on layer of grime and dirt and varnish over the years. More people know Holmes and Watson from films, plays, TV, radio and even advertising than from reading Doyle. One of the aims of the BBC project was to wash away the grime and present what Doyle created.

Having said that, Watson in particular did seem to call for a bit of extra emphasising. In the texts (or most of them), he's ever-present simply by virtue of being the storyteller who presents the action to the reader. We tend to see most of what happens through his eyes and his interpretation. Since we wanted to break away from the rather old-fashioned style of radio drama which uses lots of direct narration, our Watson was in danger of slipping more into the sidelines than we wanted, and we worked hard to prevent that happening.

There's also a tendency, I think, with any pop-icon figure not to think of them as 'real' but simply as a collection of idiosyncrasies. We worked hard to present Holmes as more than just The Great Detective.

What do you make of Holmes's relationship with Watson?

It's tempting but simplistic to say that the two men together form a functioning human being: Watson is the heart and Holmes is the head. It's more inter-dependent than that.

Watson is in many ways the exact opposite of Holmes. Watson is the ultimate Victorian everyday respectable gentleman. But one of the main things that brings them together and keeps them together is that to a certain extent Watson would love to be Holmes, and Holmes needs to be Watson. Without Watson, Holmes would probably kill himself, deliberately or otherwise. And without Holmes, Watson would probably die of boredom.

Holmes knows, I think, that Watson is as essential a part of the partnership as he is. There are many of the stories in which Watson brings a level of knowledge and intelligence that Holmes is not capable of bringing. Watson is the public face. Watson is the one who interacts with the clients far more than Holmes does. And although he doesn't have the same sort of intelligence and insight as Holmes, he is a perfectly intelligent, insightful man in his own right. Holmes, for all his sarcasm and even occasional sneering, knows this perfectly well, and does acknowledge it from time to time.

One of the great things which ties the two men together is Watson's writing – which in itself is an aspect of his character that's often overlooked or ignored. Holmes's criticism of Watson's romantic treatment of what he sees as his exer-cises in science and logic is a thread that runs right through the canon, sometimes to comic effect and sometimes very much the opposite. It's a clever strand, since within the central fiction of the canon, without Watson's writing we wouldn't have the stories at all, and so wouldn't know about Holmes's objections to them. Doyle the postmodernist!

Holmes is in it for the intellectual pursuits, Watson is in it as much for the human side of what Holmes does. Holmes can look at a weeping woman client sitting in the corner of the sitting room, telling her case, and analyse her in entirely abstract terms. Watson looks at her and sees a woman in distress, who needs to be helped. The woman needs them both, and so did Doyle, and so, to be poetic about it, do we.

Finally, what for you is the essence of Holmes?

Holmes is dysfunctional, brilliant, tortured, heroic and frightening. And lonely.

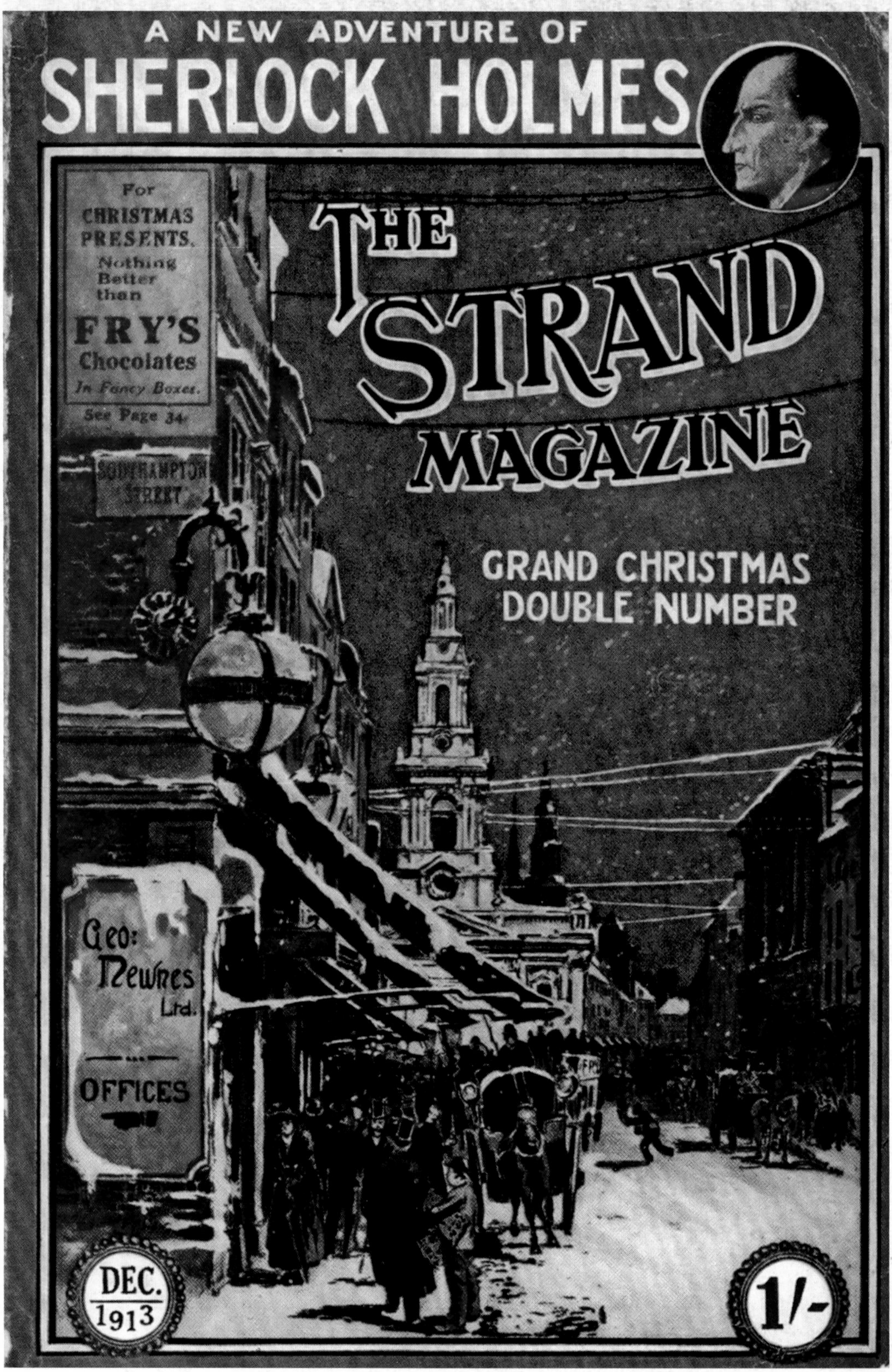

A NEW ADVENTURE OF

SHERLOCK HOLMES

SOUTHAMPTON
STREET

THE
STRAND
MAGAZINE

GRAND CHRISTMAS
DOUBLE NUMBER

Geo:
Newnes
Ltd.

OFFICES

DEC.
1913

1/-

THE *STRAND MAGAZINE*

SHERLOCK HOLMES MADE his first appearance in *A Study in Scarlet*, which was published in *Beeton's Christmas Annual* in 1887. Three years later the second Holmes story, *The Sign of Four*, appeared in *Lippincott's Monthly Magazine*. But the *Strand Magazine* was to prove the spiritual home for Conan Doyle's creation, an ideal setting for the short stories that established the reputation of the Great Detective.

The *Strand Magazine* was founded in 1890 by George Newnes and its first edition, dated January 1891, was edited by Herbert Greenhough Smith. Under Greenhough Smith's astute guidance for nearly 40 years, the magazine focused on factual articles, short stories and serials by an enviable roster of writers. The impressive roll call included G. K. Chesterton, Agatha Christie, Winston Churchill, Graham Greene, Rudyard Kipling, W. Somerset Maugham, E. Nesbit, A. J. Raffles, Dorothy L. Sayers, Georges Simenon, Leo Tolstoy, H. G. Wells and P. G. Wodehouse. The editor even secured a royal seal of approval when he received permission from Queen Victoria to reproduce an illustration she had made of one of her children.

ABOVE: 12 Burleigh Street, off the Strand and near Covent Garden, was the original home of the *Strand Magazine*.

Targeted at a mass market readership and hoping to attract every member of the family, the *Strand* aimed to have a picture on every page. Its initial price was a very reasonable sixpence – about half the going rate for comparable titles of the time. First month sales were around the 300,000 mark but it was not long before circulation rose to half a million.

Conan Doyle was quick to see how he and the magazine might be good for each other. His agent, A. P. Watt, had already sent Greenhough Smith a Conan Doyle short story – 'The Voice of Science', a gentle parody of intellectual life in the provinces – which was published in March 1891. But the aspiring author now recognised the potentially huge market for a series of self-contained stories that were unified around a recurring character. He had already had moderate success with Holmes in longer form stories and he was sure his detective would be well suited to the demands of the short story. 'A Scandal in Bohemia' appeared in the *Strand* in July 1891 and was an instant hit. So began a relationship that endured until the last story, 'Shoscombe Old Place', came out in April 1927.

Accompanied by the classic Sidney Paget illustrations, the public hunger for the adventures of Holmes and Watson seemed insatiable. By the time *The Hound of*

OPPOSITE: The December 1913 edition of the *Strand*, which contained 'The Adventure of the Dying Detective'. By this stage, Conan Doyle was no longer writing series but producing 'occasional scattered' stories.

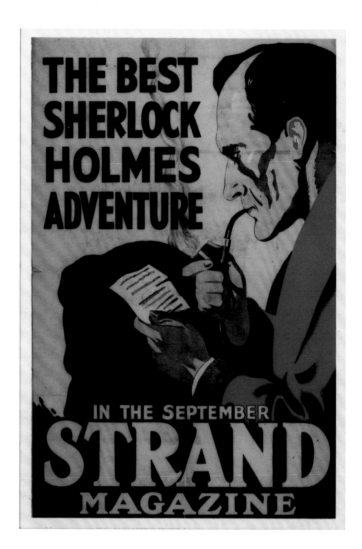

THE BEST
SHERLOCK
HOLMES
ADVENTURE

IN THE SEPTEMBER
STRAND
MAGAZINE

A promotional poster
for the venerable old magazine.

the Baskervilles appeared in serial form between 1901 and 1902, Conan Doyle was receiving the extraordinary sum of over £600 per episode. Greenhough Smith also gave his star author an outlet for his historical fiction, which Conan Doyle valued far higher than his detective fiction. The *Strand* published tales such as 'Rodney Stone' and 'The Adventures of the Brigadier General'.

Greenhough Smith eventually surrendered his editorship in 1930. Alas, the Second World War took a heavy toll on the magazine and it struggled to contend with high production costs and a dwindling readership. It was closed in 1950, with Macdonald Hastings serving as its last editor.

A new version of the magazine appeared in 1998, published from Michigan in the USA. Describing itself as 'The Magazine for Mystery & Short Story Lovers', it continues to print a strong mix of established and emerging crime and mystery writers.

SIDNEY PAGET

THOUGH ONLY ONE of many illustrators to turn his hand to depicting Holmes and Watson, it is Sidney Paget who most influenced the public perception of the Detective. As is now oft told, it was not Conan Doyle who made mention of Holmes careering round in a deerstalker and Inverness cape. Instead it is an image that flowed from Paget's pen (initially to accompany 'The Boscombe Valley Mystery') and entered the consciousness of the wider public. Today it is perhaps the defining image of Holmes for much of the world.

Sidney Edward Paget was born on 4 October 1860. His mother, Martha, was a talented musician while his father, Robert, worked as a vestry clerk of St James and St John, Clerkenwell, in London. Sidney was the fifth child of nine.

Sidney Paget was responsible for bringing Holmes and the deerstalker together. This illustration accompanied 'Silver Blaze' but the deerstalker first appeared alongside 'The Boscombe Valley Mystery'.

He studied at the Heatherley School of Fine Art, before joining the Royal Academy Schools in 1881. Two of his brothers, Henry and Walter, also studied there. It was one of Sidney's colleagues at the School, an architecture student called Alfred Morris Butler, who is often cited as the inspiration for his illustrations of Watson. Over his lifetime, Sidney had eighteen pictures exhibited by the Academy, of which half were portraits.

Much of his early career, though, was taken up by illustrating war subjects, particularly in Egypt and Sudan. He gradually made a name for himself providing illustrations for a host of magazines on both sides of the Atlantic. As well as the *Strand*, his drawings appeared in *Illustrated London News*, *Pall Mall Magazine*, the *Graphic*, *Pictorial World* and the *Sphere*. As well as Holmes, Sidney was also the chief illustrator of another literary detective, Arthur Morrison's Martin Hewitt.

The story goes that Sidney's elder brother Walter (the most famous of the brothers at this stage for illustrating, among other titles, *Robinson Crusoe*) was the *Strand*'s choice to illustrate Conan Doyle's stories but that the paperwork was sent to Sidney in error. Conan Doyle himself apparently felt Paget's pictures made Holmes more appealing than he had intended. However, it would seem that he was won over in time because he specifically asked for Paget to illustrate *The Hound of the Baskervilles* in 1902. As for Walter, it has long been held that he provided the inspiration for Sidney's drawings of Holmes – a story confirmed by Paget's daughter, Winifred, despite an explicit rejection of the tale in Sidney's entry in the *Oxford Dictionary of National Biography*.

In 1893, shortly after taking up his employ with the *Strand*, Sidney married Edith Hounsfield and the couple would have six children: two sons, Leslie and John, and four daughters, Winifred, Edith, Evelyn and Beryl. The family lived in Hertfordshire and Paget kept a studio in Kensington. Years later Winifred affectionately recalled the late nights he spent working to meet magazine deadlines and of how he would sometimes appear from nowhere, turning cartwheels on the lawn to entertain the kids before returning to his labours.

Sidney ultimately produced 356 drawings to accompany 38 Holmes stories. He was afflicted with a long-term chest problem that claimed his life on 28 January 1908. He is buried in St Marylebone Cemetery in East Finchley, North London.

Perhaps the only other Holmes illustrator who comes close to rivalling Paget is Frederic Dorr Steele, an American who first drew the detective in 1903 for *Collier's Weekly* and who spent the next several decades drawing him for a variety of publishers. As his model for Holmes he used the actor William Gillette, who had gained huge fame for his stage portrayal of the Great Detective.

Yet Paget is the artist whose influence was greatest for the most number of people. As the *Strand Magazine* so elegantly put it, 'his delineations of the famous "Sherlock Holmes" stories had their share in the popularity of that wonderful detective'.

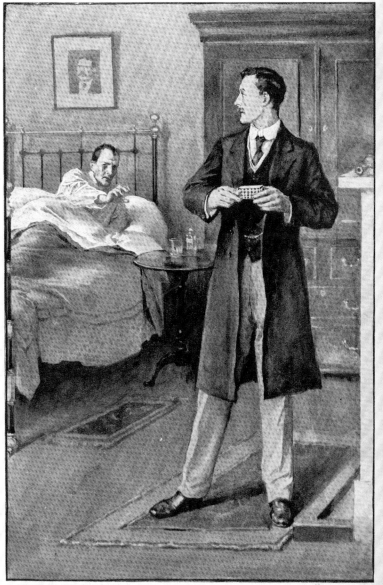

"PUT IT DOWN! DOWN, THIS INSTANT, WATSON—THIS INSTANT, I SAY!"

(See page 608.)

In 1913 Sidney Paget's brother, Walter, illustrated 'The Dying Detective' for the *Strand*, twenty-two years after George Newnes had first thought of him.

THE VALLEY OF FEAR

FIRST PUBLISHED: The *Strand Magazine*, September 1914—May 1915, UK; in book form by the George H. Doran Company, 1915, USA

SETTING DATE: 1888

HOLMES RECEIVES A heavily encoded note from Porlock, an informant within the organisation of Professor Moriarty. The story's early exchanges include a detailed analysis of the Professor's prominent role in the criminal underworld. Using a copy of *Whitaker's Almanac*, Holmes unpicks the letter's code, an exhortation to go to Birlstone in Sussex for the protection of an imperilled individual called Douglas. Alas, Inspector MacDonald of the Yard turns up with the news that Douglas has been gruesomely murdered that very morning.

It emerges that the amiable John Douglas was an American married to an English woman. It was Cecil James Barker, a visiting friend, who discovered the corpse. Douglas had been killed by shotgun wounds to the head. His wedding ring had been removed and nearby lay a note inscribed 'V.V. 341'. Holmes also logs that neither Barker nor Mrs Douglas reacts to the death in the expected way.

There are a series of other clues for the Detective to investigate. What of the curious symbol – branded, not tattooed – halfway up the dead man's arm? And how can the mystery of the missing dumbbell be explained? Watson's trusty umbrella has a major role to play in solving the case.

Although largely forgotten, Frank Wiles produced some iconic illustrations for the later stories in the *Strand*, including this one for *The Valley of Fear*.

Allan Pinkerton established his detective agency in 1850 and gained international fame for his role in derailing an assassination plot against Abraham Lincoln in 1861.

As with *A Study in Scarlet* and *The Sign of Four*, we must leave Britain's shores and cross the Atlantic to discover the background to the crime. The key lies in the coalfields of Pennsylvania and the activities of the Molly Maguires (members of a secret society of Irish origin) and the famous Pinkerton Detective Agency. With the crime unravelled by Holmes at the halfway point of the book, the second half of the story is spent narrating its American genesis.

HOLMES AND HIS POLITICS

*. . . the news of a revolution, of a possible war, and of an impending change
of government . . . did not come within the horizon of my companion.*
'The Adventure of the Bruce-Partington Plans'

CONAN DOYLE WAS a man of causes. Once a prospective MP, he used his social
standing to campaign on everything from divorce reform to miscarriages
of justice to a defence of Britain's action in the Boer War. Occasionally he used
the Holmes stories as a platform to highlight a cause of the moment. This is
perhaps most noticeable in 'His Last Bow', an overt anti-German propaganda
piece written a year before the end of the First World War. 'The Bruce-Partington
Plans' (1912) was an earlier attempt to raise awareness of the dangers of a fast
militarising German state and even 'The Naval Treaty', as far back as 1893, had
a subtext concerning the increasingly precarious political relationships between
the major European nations. Elsewhere, 'The Noble Bachelor' saw Holmes rather
uncharacteristically long for 'a world-wide country under a flag which shall be a
quartering of the Union Jack with the Stars and Stripes', a rather clumsy voicing of
the author's passion for all things American.

For the most part, though, Holmes was not an overtly political animal. That
said, he was a man of firm principles and strong beliefs that informed his day-
to-day dealings. For instance, he was most decidedly no respecter of class.
Take the moment in 'A Scandal in Bohemia' when he put the King of Bohemia
firmly in his place when discussing Irene Adler, the king's former lover. Watson

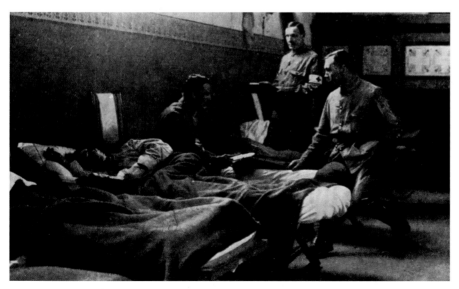

Conan Doyle at Bloemfontein
in 1900, attending Canadian
troops wounded during the
Boer War.

reported: '"From what I have seen of the lady she seems indeed to be on a very different level to your Majesty," said Holmes coldly.' Holmes's scepticism about the inherent virtue of the upper class was further revealed when he said 'There are certain crimes which the law cannot touch, and which therefore, to some extent, justify private revenge.' In 'The Speckled Band' he overlooked his own part in a death, rationalising that 'In this way I am no doubt indirectly responsible for Dr. Grimesby Roylott's death, and I cannot say that it is likely to weigh very heavily upon my conscience.'

In 'The Abbey Grange', Holmes mimicked the British courtroom to set free a man he believed acted with good will. With Watson as jury – 'I never met a man who was more eminently fitted to represent one' – the defendant was found not guilty and Holmes sent him on his way, claiming '*Vox populi, vox Dei.*' This Holmesian justice system made room for the repentant wrong-doer too so that a figure like Shinwell Johnson might leave behind his life as a 'dangerous villain' to become a trusted ally of the Detective in 'The Illustrious Client'.

It is thus possible to argue that Holmes was socially liberal for his age. He may have harboured a host of prejudices against individuals but by and large they were not rooted in the circumstance of their birth – young or old, rich or poor, male or female, anyone might find themselves an object of his respect or, alternatively, at the end of a tongue-lashing. However, Holmes's attitude to nationality and race was more ambiguous and must be viewed within the context of his own time. While quite able to see the faults of his own society (unsurprisingly for one immersed in its criminal underside), he was nonetheless a proud Englishman, sure in his heart that the English really were the best. As he said in 'His Last Bow': 'After all, you have done your best for your country, and I have done my best for mine, and what could be more natural?'

Allied to this patriotism was a definite feeling that 'Abroad' was a place where they did things differently and, on the whole, rather less well. *A Study in Scarlet* gives a good sense of the xenophobic backdrop against which Holmes worked. In it Watson quoted the *Daily Telegraph*'s view that the government should keep 'a closer watch over foreigners in England'. For many in Britain, foreign shores were places to go to earn a fortune before returning home. In numerous stories we see characters recently returned from fruitful lives in North America, Australia, South Africa and India. A great many of the crimes that Holmes solved had their roots in these distant and apparently lawless lands and the canon offers several uncomfortable racial stereotypes. Dr Grimesby Roylott in 'The Speckled Band' had his violent temper in part put down to 'his long residence in the tropics', while in 'The Twisted Lip' we are presented with the sinister figure of the Lascar. Daulat Ras in 'The Three Students' was 'a quiet, inscrutable fellow; as most of those Indians

OPPOSITE: Holmes giving instructions to Cartwright, a young lad of humble origins 'who showed some ability' and was employed by the Detective in *The Hound of the Baskervilles.*

THE
HOLMES/WATSON
FIREARM COLLECTION

Holmes' Webley Model 1880 single shot pistol he used for indoor target practice.

Eley's No. 2

"An Eley's No. 2 is an excellent argument, Watson."

Watson's old service revolver– Adam's Model 1872 Mark III.

Webley Police Model

"My old favorite" –Holmes

Webley Mark III .38 revolver– Police and Military

LEFT: Queen Victoria ruled from 1837 to 1901. While her reign is synonymous with a national golden age, her subjects were increasingly fearful of crime despite the streets becoming statistically safer.

are' and the Brazilian wife in 'Thor Bridge' was 'tropical by birth and tropical by nature . . . a child of the sun and of passion'. Elsewhere the indebted Sir Robert of 'Shoscombe Old Place' is described as in 'the hands of the Jews'.

Holmes himself was responsible for few of these appraisals but the regularity with which they appear is jolting for the modern reader. Most of all it serves to illustrate the ingrained thinking that passed with barely any comment a hundred and more years ago but which is rather more shocking today. That is not to justify the sentiments expressed but to give Holmes some sort of historical context.

OPPOSITE: An assortment of arms used by Holmes and Watson in the canon, illustrated by Larry Gosser. Holmes was willing to meet force with force when required.

CONAN DOYLE CHARACTERS

TONGA

This image of Tonga, the Andaman Islander from *The Sign of Four*, points to a kind of racial stereotyping still much in evidence in the early twentieth century.

Some critics have argued convincingly that Holmes is no racist. Most often quoted is 'The Yellow Face', in which Holmes showed compassion and respect for a white woman and her child born to an African-American. He certainly avoided any judgemental outbursts and the story finishes on a note of racial harmony. Yet even if we overlook the racial stereotyping that might be expected of the age ('a little coal-black negress, with all her white teeth flashing in amusement'), there is a sense that the ethnicity of the child and her father is a curse to be overcome. Even the mother is left to rue 'our misfortune that our only child took after his people rather than mine'.

Elsewhere, Holmes displayed considerably less sympathy for those of other races. Tonga, the character from the Andaman Islands in *The Sign of Four*, came from a race described in Holmes's 'authoritative' gazetteer as 'savage' and 'naturally hideous, having large, misshapen heads, small fierce eyes, and distorted features'. When Tonga was shot and killed, the death passed with barely any note. Perhaps even more suspect was the treatment meted out in 'The Three Gables' to Steve Dixie, a 'big nigger' who 'would have been a comic figure if he had not been terrific, for he was dressed in a very loud gray check suit with a flowing salmon-coloured tie'. Holmes played on his opponent's relatively limited intellectual faculties and seemed to take sport in outwitting him. Maybe this was fair practice if Dixie is considered as just another criminal in Holmes's sights but the focus on Dixie's race (in part down to Watson's narrative slanting) is deeply uncomfortable.

THE ADVENTURE OF WISTERIA LODGE

FIRST PUBLISHED: The *Strand Magazine*, September–October 1908, UK; *Collier's*, 15 August 1908, USA

SETTING DATE: 1895

A STORY PUBLISHED in the *Strand* in two parts: 'The Singular Experience of Mr. John Scott Eccles' and 'The Tiger of San Pedro'. John Scott Eccles, a bachelor of some social status, calls on Holmes and Watson about an 'incredible and grotesque' matter. Just as he is to embark on his narrative, Gregson of the Yard and Inspector Baynes of the Surrey Constabulary appear. They have been tracking Eccles in relation to the violent death of Aloysius Garcia of Wisteria Lodge near Esher.

Eccles and Garcia had become friends after meeting through an acquaintance called Melville. Garcia invited Eccles to come to Wisteria Lodge for a few days but the latter soon became aware of an odd tension after his arrival. Garcia had been distracted and when his servant handed him a note at dinner, his mood only blackened.

Eccles retired to his room around eleven o'clock. Garcia later appeared to ask him if he had rung for assistance but Eccles had not. The time, according to Garcia, was then around one o'clock. Eccles slept the night through and awoke to find his host and the household staff gone. Suspecting some kind of trick to avoid paying rent, Eccles enquired at the local estate agent's but discovered that the property was fully paid up. He then went to the Spanish embassy but Garcia was unknown there.

Baynes (to whom Holmes is uncharacteristically complimentary) has recovered the note to Garcia. Signed in a female hand from 'D', it makes puzzling references to 'our own colours, green and white'. Robbery is ruled out as a motive, so was a jealous lover responsible? And what of the theory that Garcia had made his one o'clock call on Eccles to establish an alibi?

Holmes, Watson and Baynes set out for the Lodge, where a constable reports having seen a devilish-looking man peering in at the window. Inside the house is a collection of odd artefacts including a mummified creature, a savaged bird, a pail of blood and some burnt bones.

Suspecting that the entire household is implicated in some ill-doing, Baynes arrests Garcia's cook (the figure seen by the constable) a few days later. Holmes is sure the answer lies elsewhere. He falls upon a local house belonging to the Hendersons, whose staff includes an English governess, a dark-skinned cook and a disgruntled gardener. Holmes soon has things figured out and the crime's origins are exotic indeed.

Holmes made some studies of voodooism at the Reading Room of the British Museum, just round the corner from his old digs in Montague Street.

THE ADVENTURE OF THE BRUCE-PARTINGTON PLANS

FIRST PUBLISHED: The *Strand Magazine*, December 1908, UK; *Collier's*, 18 December 1908, USA

SETTING DATE: 1895

IT IS A Thursday and there is a thick fog outside. Holmes attempts to keep his mind occupied by cross-indexing his book of references and studying medieval music. His brother Mycroft arrives to break the monotony. Mycroft, we learn, plays a pivotal role in the nation's affairs.

He wants Holmes's help in recovering three missing pages from the secret Bruce-Partington submarine plans, unaccounted for since Monday. The remaining pages were found on the body of Arthur Cadogan West, a youthful government clerk at the Royal Arsenal in Woolwich. His corpse was discovered on the tracks near Aldgate Underground station. Suggestively, no rail ticket was found with him. The last anyone had seen of Cadogan West was when his fiancée, a Miss Westbury, saw him run into the fog without explanation. They were due to have gone to the theatre.

The dead man inevitably fell under suspicion of stealing the papers for the purpose of selling them on. Yet there are many puzzling features to the mystery. If he was planning such an audacious crime, why had he arranged a rendezvous with his fiancée? And how had he died? What of the absence of bloodstains to correspond with his injuries?

Holmes learns that a passenger reported hearing a thud when travelling into Aldgate station and makes a study of the scene, including the points. An ingenious leap of imagination sees him conclude that the murder was committed elsewhere. A proposed interview with Sir James Walter, who was responsible for the safe keeping of the plans, is aborted when Colonel Walter, his brother, reveals that Sir James has died, apparently out of shame at events. A meeting with Miss Westbury is more useful. She tells of how her young man had been worried for some while in relation to his work.

Holmes then visits the office from which the papers were stolen and interviews the senior clerk, Sidney Johnson. He testifies that he locked the papers away on the Monday night and was last to leave the premises. A thief would have needed a set of three keys to get at the plans. Only Sir James had such a set. Holmes also notices something interesting about the window shutters. Then news comes through that one Hugo Oberstein has fled the country. A search of his house offers up much useful information and Holmes soon has a traitor and a murderer in his grasp.

'The Bruce-Partington Plans' was written at a time of intense rivalry between the British navy and the fast-growing German fleet.

THE ADVENTURE OF THE DEVIL'S FOOT

FIRST PUBLISHED: The *Strand Magazine*, December 1910, UK; The *Strand Magazine*, January–February 1911, USA

SETTING DATE: 1897

WATSON RELATES THIS case at the behest of the usually publicity-shy Holmes. It begins when Watson takes an exhausted Holmes for a recuperative holiday in Cornwall.

Inevitably, hopes of a quiet convalescence are soon wrecked when the local vicar, Roundhay, and his lodger, Mortimer Tregennis, arrive at our heroes' cottage. Mortimer had spent the previous evening playing cards at the house of his brothers (George and Owen) and sister (Brenda) in the village of Tredannick Wollas. He left them around ten o'clock but the next morning encountered a doctor on his way to an emergency call there. The housekeeper, Mrs Porter, had found the siblings still seated around the table where Mortimer had left them. Brenda was dead and the brothers were dementedly laughing, shouting and singing. All wore expressions of horror. Even the doctor had come over faint at the scene, as had Mrs Porter. There was no sign of a robbery or disturbance.

Mortimer reveals that an old family feud had long since blown over and remembers nothing odd from the previous night, save the suspicion of some unidentified movement in the garden. Holmes visits the house and makes an examination of the scene. Mrs Porter claims to have heard nothing untoward during the night. Holmes enquires why a fire was lit on a spring evening and Tregennis explains that it had been cold and damp.

Holmes is perplexed. What had terrified the family so? There are no footprints in the flower bed by the window to suggest that the source of their fright had been in the garden. Nor will Holmes

Holmes and Watson stayed in a cottage overlooking Mounts Bay, which is dominated by the imposing St Michael's Mount.

countenance the idea of a 'diabolical intrusion'. News arrives that a cousin of the family, a famed explorer and lion hunter called Leon Sterndale, has missed his passage to Africa to return to the village on hearing of the deaths.

Sterndale is keen to hear Holmes's theories on the incident. When Holmes, as was his wont, refuses to elaborate on his thoughts, Sterndale leaves in something of a huff. Holmes quietly follows him. The next morning Roundhay arrives to inform the Detective that Mortimer has been found dead in his room in the same manner as Brenda. They set out for Mortimer's lodgings, which is notably stuffy despite a window being open. A lamp burns on the table, from which Holmes takes some ash samples.

Holmes has formed his conclusions and sets out to validate them, at considerable risk to Watson and himself. Soon enough, a sad story of family politics is unravelled.

THE LEGACY OF THE GREAT DETECTIVE

Holmes and Watson have earned their title to be
'emancipated from the bonds of fact'.

S. C. Roberts

Holmes has become one of the world's most enduring 'brands'. Pictured here are (clockwise starting far left) adverts for Postum cereal, Booth's Gin and Schlitz Beer, alongside a Butler's rubber Holmes duck and a mug featuring a classic Penguin book cover.

Sherlock Holmes is among those rare figures who are instantly recognisable in virtually every corner of the world. Along with Mickey Mouse, Ronald McDonald, Harry Potter and a handful of others, the image of Holmes has largely transcended borders, age and gender. Put anyone (indeed anything) in a deerstalker, pop a curved pipe in the mouth and a magnifying glass in the hand, and most of the world will be able to pick up the reference.

It is then somewhat ironic that so much of the cultural shorthand for the Great Detective has grown and been mythologised from sources other than Conan Doyle's own stories. Neither the deerstalker nor the curved pipe were there in the canon, nor Holmes's most famous (non)utterance: 'Elementary, my dear Watson.' Perhaps that is all part and parcel of being a truly universal cultural icon; you become a possession of the world at large and no longer belong to a single author.

With such a profile, it is inevitable that Holmes's image has been used to sell everything from the predictable (pipes and tobacco) to the utterly random (motor oil), and pretty much everything in between. There have been adverts for gin and whisky, typewriters, crisps, cars, industrial machinery, wrinkle-free underwear, life insurance and carpet cleaner, to give the tiniest taste of a near-endless list. And that is to say nothing of those items created as souvenirs for the fans, which might be anything from pens to chocolates, neckties to clocks, Toby jugs to rubber ducks. For some, collecting Holmes paraphernalia is a very serious business indeed. In June 2007 a rare copy of the 1887 *Beeton's Christmas Annual* (in which Holmes made his debut) was auctioned for $156,000, while three years earlier Sidney Paget's famous illustration of the clash at the Reichenbach Falls sold for over $200,000 in New York.

THE VITRUVIAN SHERLOCK HOLMES (WITH PIPE)

Larry Gosser's Vitruvian Holmes, echoing the famous Vitruvian Man pen-and-ink drawing created by Leonardo da Vinci in 1487.

Holmes's durability and timelessness have proved irresistible to many other authors who have attempted to create their own take on the myth. There have been well over 400 full-length pastiches and parodies (and many more short stories), with the number forever growing. These have seen Holmes placed in disparate locations and historical periods, and ranging in age from boy to old man. Other authors have chosen to change the focus, with Watson, Mycroft, the Irregulars, Moriarty and even Mrs Hudson all being given the opportunity to take centre stage. Some do it wonderfully while a great many others would have been better served by never having tried at all. It was a trend that started remarkably early after the publication of *A Study in Scarlet* in 1887. Certainly by 1892, R. C. Lehmann (using the pseudonym Cunnin Toil) had written a series for *Punch* called 'The Adventures of Picklock Holes'. Other early parodies included Sheerluck Jones and Chubblock Holmes. Conan Doyle's son Adrian is another who attempted to write new Holmes tales, often in conjunction with John Dickson Carr. Below is a short list of some of the most famous writers who have 'had a go' at the Great Detective:

Isaac Asimov (who edited the anthology *Sherlock Holmes Through Time and Space*)

J. M. Barrie ('The Adventure of the Two Collaborators'; a story written by Conan Doyle's old friend and much enjoyed by him)

Anthony Burgess ('Murder to Music')

Agatha Christie (in 'The Case of the Missing Lady', her heroes Tommy and Tuppence try to pass themselves off as Holmes and Watson)

Stephen Fry ('The Adventure of the Laughing Jarvey')

Neil Gaiman ('A Study in Emerald')

Stephen King ('The Doctor's Case')

A. A. Milne ('The Rape of the Sherlock')

Mark Twain ('A Double-Barrelled Detective Story')

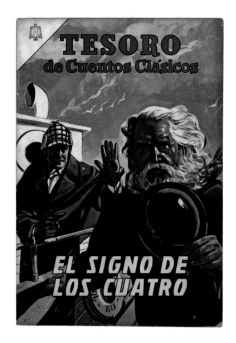

A comic book version of *The Sign of Four* published in Mexico by Editorial Novaro in 1965.

It was perhaps inevitable that Holmes would transfer from the prose story to the comic book, although the relationship between the Detective and the comic book artist has not always been an easy one. He did figure in a long-running syndicated newspaper strip (drawn by Mike Sekowsky and Frank Giacoia), but aside from this struggled to impose himself in the face of the superpowers possessed by his rivals. He had relatively short careers among the medium's heavyweights like DC Comics and Marvel, although he had slightly longer stints with the presses of Dell, Charleston and Classics Illustrated. Part of the problem was that Holmes's image was already so well established in the illustrations of Paget et al., and by the numerous film depictions, that comic artists could do little to make him new that wasn't somehow jolting. Nonetheless, he has managed an enduring comic book career that has seen him sent back to prehistoric times, propelled into the future and pitted against all manner of enemies, from the human to the supernatural to the alien. He was also the subject of many spoofs, a short roll-call of tribute acts including Gurlock Holmes, Hemlock Shomes, Herlock Sholmes, Padlock Bones, Padlock Homes, Sherlock Guck, Sherlock Hemlock and, indeed, Sherlock Lopez. Publishers continue to mine the character for inspiration, with Holmes still making guest appearances in other characters' stories and in his own graphic novels throughout the world.

Holmes has managed to attract an array of famous political fans (and critics) over the years. For instance, F. D. Roosevelt, the great American president, was responsible for *A Baker Street Folio: 5 Letters about Sherlock Holmes*. Rather more darkly, Hitler reportedly kept a German film adaptation of *The Hound of the Baskervilles* in his bunker. In 1973 Yugoslavia's President Tito said of Holmes: 'I think that such books can develop children's imagination and sense of justice.'

Less of an enthusiast was Stalin, whose 'stubborn refusal . . . to read any of the Sherlock Holmes adventures' was reported in the *Sunday Times* in 1950. Nor, it would seem, was he overly popular with Mao Zedong, given the *New York Times* headline of July 1958: 'CHINESE ASSAIL SHERLOCK HOLMES AS BOURGEOIS BRITISH WATCHDOG'. Holmes's political life in his homeland has been somewhat more understated, though he has on occasion found his way into parliamentary debate. Rab Butler, Chancellor of the Exchequer from 1951 to 1955, quoted 'Silver Blaze' to attack the opposition over omissions from their pre-election manifesto. 'It is rather like Sherlock Holmes and Dr Watson,' he said. 'What was significant about the action of the dog? The dog did not bark.'

A Soviet era cover for *A Study in Scarlet*. Holmes was a popular read, despite scepticism from the likes of Stalin.

For the most devoted Holmesians (or Sherlockians, if preferred), there are Sherlock Holmes societies operating around the world. At the last count there were over 400, with some having active memberships in the thousands. Holmes has inevitably infiltrated the internet, with a search on the networking site Facebook yielding over 500 results in 2008. However, until 1934 Holmes fanatics mostly found themselves pursuing their passion alone. It was in that year that two of the most famous societies of them all were founded. First were the Baker Street Irregulars, founded by the literary editor Christopher Morley in New York. Then in London the Sherlock Holmes Society came into being. It was to lapse during the Second World War, when its activities might have seemed rather frivolous, but had new life breathed into it with the Festival of Britain in 1951.

The Borough of St Marylebone thought long and hard about its contribution to the Festival. There was the possibility at one stage that it might theme its exhibition around slum clearance but the rather more attractive idea of Holmes won through (after much heated debate in the letters page of *The Times*, including missives from Dr Watson and Mrs Hudson themselves!). The exhibition was built around a collection of memorabilia at St Marylebone Public Library (now the basis of the Sherlock Holmes Collection), and what was meant to have been a

RIGHT: A postcard showing the remarkable 'reconstruction' of 221B Baker Street that became one of the most popular attractions of the 1951 Festival of Britain.

Holmes has a cultural resonance that transcends international barriers.
BELOW: An edition of *The Hound of the Baskervilles* in a Kiswahili translation by Hassan Ali, published by the Battered Silicon Dispatch Box.

BOTTOM: In 1996 the Japanese publisher Kodansha released this edition of *Holmes: The Great Detective*, translated by Holmes aficionado Masamichi Higurashi.

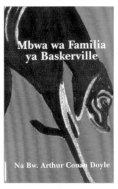

temporary reproduction of Holmes's living room has become a permanent fixture at the Sherlock Holmes Pub on London's Northumberland Street. The exhibition welcomed over 54,000 visitors and was reputedly the only part of the Festival that made its money back. Buoyed by this success, the Sherlock Holmes Society of London was reconstituted bigger and stronger than ever.

Most Holmes societies have regular meetings, talks and screenings, as well as visits to places of Holmesian interest. A great many also publish well-produced and much respected journals filled with news, reviews and articles of scholarship. The USA is home to by far the largest number of societies but the UK, Japan, Canada, Australia, Russia, India and Germany all have significant numbers. They are often imaginatively named after references within the canon. So it is that you can be a member of:

The Amateur Mendicant Society of Detroit
The Baritsu Chapter of the Baker Street Irregulars
The Bootmakers of Toronto
The Canadian Baskervilles
The Dancing Men of Providence
The Illustrious Clients of Indianapolis
L'Hotel de Dulong of Lyon
The Men with the Twisted Konjo of Tokyo

The Norah Creina Castaways of Lisbon

The Priory Scholars of Leicester

The Scandalous Bohemians of Akron

The Seventeen Steps of Los Angeles

The Speckled Band of Boston

The Sydney Passengers

Key to understanding how these societies work is the idea of 'playing the game'. Playing the game essentially involves suspending all disbelief in favour of taking Holmes to have been a real person and the canon our single source of biographical information about him. In this way Watson is treated as the true author of the tales and Conan Doyle simply Watson's literary agent. 'The game' has its roots in an influential address given by Ronald Knox to the Gryphon Club at Trinity College, Oxford in 1911. There he summed up the beauty of the game: 'we single out as essential what the author regarded as incidental'.

The idea of Holmes as a real person was one that caught on almost as soon as the first short stories were published. It is documented that when the tale of his demise at the Reichenbach Falls was published in the *Strand*, distraught readers wandered round London wearing black armbands. There were even reports of near-riots outside the *Strand* offices. An article in the *St James's Budget*, a London paper, dated 5 January 1894 must be among the first to report on the Detective as an actual person. Its sensational content concerned rumours that Watson had been arrested on suspicion of involvement in Holmes's demise. Whole lifetimes can be spent analysing the canon in often vain attempts to prove unprovable hypotheses. What happened to Holmes's parents? Where did he attend university? What *really* happened during the hiatus? How many wives did Watson have? Where exactly was 221B located on Baker Street? A great many scholars have dedicated themselves to this somewhat strange pursuit, among them such luminaries as D. Martin Dakin, William S. Baring-Gould, David Stuart Davies, Owen Dudley Edwards, Richard Lancelyn Green, Christopher Morley, Vincent Starret and Jack Tracy. To the outsider, playing the game can seem an exclusive and eccentric pastime, but for those prepared to throw themselves into it there is a lifetime's joy to be had. However, there are others who find the whole enterprise futile and believe that the

This advert for a party game made by Parker Brothers and based on the Great Detective appeared in *Harper's Magazine* in 1904.

greatest fun comes from taking the stories at simple face value. These are known as Fundamentalists.

A further indication of Holmes's status as a cultural phenomenon is the number of museums, statues and monuments dedicated to him. In this measurement he surely outstrips any other fictional creation. In London there is a museum on Baker Street and a statue just outside its Underground station, as well as the Sherlock Holmes Hotel further down the street. In addition, there is a plaque in the Criterion Bar on Piccadilly Circus (where Watson bumped into Stamford) and another at St Bart's Hospital commemorating the first legendary meeting between Holmes and Watson. The Swiss town of Meiringen is another important centre of pilgrimage, being the nearest town to the Reichenbach Falls, and pays homage to the Detective with its own museum and a statue outside its English Church. At the Falls themselves, on the very ledge from which Holmes and Moriarty supposedly fell, is another plaque with the following inscription: 'At this fearful place, Sherlock Holmes vanquished Professor Moriarty, on 4 May 1891.' Other memorials may be found in locations as disparate as Edinburgh, Moscow and Karuizawa in Japan.

That Holmes continues to be so widely referenced in literature, film, TV and even fashion and music (as evidenced by Lionrock's *An Instinct for Detection*) is remarkable. No mean achievement for an aloof detective whose spiritual home lay in the grimy gaslit streets of late Victorian London.

DEAR MR HOLMES…

There is perhaps no clearer evidence of the remarkable way that Holmes blurred the boundary between fact and fiction than the myriad letters sent to him over the years. Beginning while the stories were still debuting in the *Strand* and continuing to the present day, correspondence has emanated from an astonishing array of social groups – children, avid fans, police and lawyers requesting professional assistance, academics, members of the aristocracy … the list goes on.

In the early days, most of the post for Holmes found its way to Conan Doyle or else to Scotland Yard (where it was presumably set aside for the attention of Inspector Lestrade). However, some items were passed on to Dr Joseph Bell and even to the actor, William Gillette. Among the first notes was one sent in 1890 by a Philadelphian tobacconist requesting a copy of Holmes's monograph on identifying different types of ash.

While letters addressed to 221B Baker Street initially did not have a corresponding physical location at which they could be deposited, that changed in the 1930s when the Abbey National Building Society moved into new

A nine-foot-high, bronze statue of Sherlock Holmes, sculpted by John Doubleday, was unveiled outside Baker Street Underground Station in 1999.

headquarters. The Abbey Building covered a site given the postal designation 215–229 Baker Street. The post room was quickly deluged with letters for Holmes which were dutifully passed on to the Conan Doyle family or to the Holmes Collection located at nearby Marylebone Library. But from the late 1940s the building society employed a secretary specifically to deal with the Detective's post. Each missive subsequently received a reply on specially printed stationery.

In 1990 the Sherlock Holmes Museum set up shop just down the road, at 237–241 Baker Street. However, it made a formal application to use the famous 221B address and argued that it was the natural home for Holmes's mail. For the next decade, bank and museum feuded over ownership of the post until 2002, when the Abbey National moved its headquarters. The Abbey Building ceased operating as a commercial building in 2005 and since then the Royal Mail has delivered anything addressed to 221B to the museum.

Historically, the USA and Japan were the leading countries of origin for this correspondence. Attempting to work out which writers were merely 'playing the game' and which believed they were truly communicating with their hero is no easy task. Many of the letters are rather banal, simply seeking autographs or making general enquiries about Holmes's working methods or personal circumstances. Others are more intriguing though. What happened to my missing friend? Would Mr Holmes be interested to share my knowledge of bee-keeping techniques? Would he appreciate help in finding him a housekeeper for his country cottage over the festive season?

Then there are the requests for assistance in investigating real-life events, from common frauds and grisly murders to great affairs of state, including Watergate and the assassination of the Swedish Prime Minister, Olaf Palme. In 1913 one Felix de Halpert wrote to Conan Doyle via 221B asking him to look into the murder of a Polish nobleman, Prince Lubecki. He hoped Conan Doyle might help to clear the Lithuanian Baron, Jan de Bisping, accused of shooting Lubecki dead. In the event, Conan Doyle turned down the request – perhaps a wise move as it seems possible that Russian agents were behind the crime, believing the Prince to have been in possession of dangerous secrets. The case, nonetheless, remains officially unsolved.

THE ADVENTURE OF THE RED CIRCLE

FIRST PUBLISHED: The *Strand Magazine*, March–April 1911, UK; The *Strand Magazine*, April–May 1911, USA
SETTING DATE: 1902

A LANDLADY, MRS Warren, arrives at 221B in search of some information about a rather odd lodger who remains constantly out of sight. Why is he hiding away? The good lady and her husband are both uneasy with this strange situation.

She describes how a youngish, smartly dressed and bearded man who spoke good English (though with a foreign accent) had approached her about a room ten days previously. He paid an inflated £5 a week rent on condition that he have the room on his own terms – a key of his own and complete privacy.

He went out the first night and did not return until after midnight. Neither the Warrens nor their servant girl have seen him since, though they hear their lodger pacing the room.

Meals are delivered to a chair outside the door and all communication is via pencilled notes. Requests have included the *Daily Gazette*, matches (or at least a match) and soap. The lodger has received no visitors or correspondence. Holmes deduces from a cigarette butt brought by the landlady that this strange character even smokes in an unexpected fashion.

When Mrs Warren has gone, Holmes reveals that he believes the man who rented the room and the person now occupying it are different. He further suspects that the *Daily Gazette*'s agony column will prove crucial reading. The case is given a new sense of urgency when Mr Warren is kidnapped, bundled into a cab and deposited upon Hampstead Heath (ruffled but unharmed) an hour later. Holmes suspects a case of mistaken identity and heads for the Warren house. There he and Watson take up residence in a box room, armed with a mirror to catch sight of the lodger. The lodger's identity comes as something of a surprise. Their apparent horror at being spied on suggests a high-stakes game is in progress.

In an evening denouement Holmes cracks a code, bumps into Gregson of the Yard and an American Pinkerton agent, and bursts in on a gruesome scene.

The bustling streets of New York's Brooklyn borough held the secrets to unlock the Red Circle mystery.

THE DISAPPEARANCE OF LADY FRANCES CARFAX

FIRST PUBLISHED: The *Strand Magazine*, December 1911, UK; *The American Magazine*, December 1911, USA
SETTING DATE: 1901

WATSON HAS BEEN feeling a little old and rheumatic and has indulged in some sessions at the Turkish baths. Holmes has no time for such distractions though. So busy is he in London that he sends Watson to the Continent (first-class) to investigate the strange disappearance of the eponymous Lady. It is her former governess and enduring correspondent, Miss Dobney, who has consulted the Detective.

Lady Frances cuts a rather tragic figure. She is the sole survivor of the direct line of the Earl of Rufton but has been denied his riches because of her sex. She does, however, have a notable collection of jewellery. A 'drifting and friendless woman', she was last heard from five weeks ago at the Hôtel National in Lausanne, Switzerland. She cashed a large cheque there and another was cashed two weeks or so later in Montpellier, made out for £50 to her maid Marie Devine.

Watson learns at the Hôtel National that Lady Frances had hurriedly left after several weeks' residence, possibly related to her hounding by a tall, dark, bearded man. Devine had also resigned her position for reasons unknown. The track then leads Watson to Baden in Germany, where Lady Frances had resided for two weeks. There she befriended the Shlessingers, a missionary couple from South America. Lady Frances helped the wife nurse her invalid husband and had set off with them for London three weeks earlier. The strange bearded fellow had arrived on her trail only a week before Watson's arrival.

Watson's pursuit began in Lausanne, which remained a popular destination on the European 'Grand Tour' undertaken by wealthy travellers.

Watson then sets out for Montpellier, casually ignoring Holmes's strange request for a description of Dr Shlessinger's left ear. In France, Watson tracks down Devine, who reveals she left her post because she is about to be married and the £50 was a wedding gift. Mid-interview she espies the bearded man in the street. Watson gives chase but comes off worse in a scuffle and has to be rescued by a strangely familiar French labourer.

With the assistance of Holmes, the bearded gent is identified as one Philip Green, who harboured hopes of marrying Lady Frances. The action returns to London. Holmes receives news of the missionary's ear and puts in place a plan. However, does an imminent funeral mean Holmes is too late?

THE ADVENTURE OF THE DYING DETECTIVE

First Published: The *Strand Magazine*, December 1913, UK; *Collier's*, 22 November 1913, USA

Setting Date: 1889

Mrs Hudson has called on Dr Watson in his marital home with grave news. Holmes has been working on a case among the backstreets of Rotherhithe and has contracted a rare disease. For three days he has eaten and drunk nothing. He refuses medical help and she believes he is at death's door.

Watson rushes to 221B but receives a frosty reception from a near-demented Holmes. He threatens to dismiss him from the property if he tries to approach, saying that his disease originates from Sumatra and is both deadly and highly contagious. He even casts doubt on Watson's abilities as a doctor. Holmes summons the energy to lock Watson in the room, forbidding him to seek help elsewhere. The Detective tells him that at six o'clock he will be allowed to go and bring back a practitioner of Holmes's choice.

With two hours to kill, Watson absent-mindedly plays with a black and white ivory box on the mantelpiece before Holmes uncharacteristically orders him to leave his possessions alone. At six o'clock Watson is allowed to turn the gaslight up halfway and is given the address of a Culverton Smith, a recognised expert in the Detective's disease. Watson is to persuade him that

Holmes was a regular patron of Simpsons-in-the-Strand, as were the likes of Charles Dickens and the British Prime Ministers Benjamin Disraeli and William Gladstone.

Holmes is delirious (he is indeed rambling about oysters) and dying. Watson should then precede Smith back to 221B. The issue is further complicated by the revelation that Smith is not a fan of Holmes for he had previously implicated Smith in the death of his nephew.

Smith gives Watson his second cold reception of the day but his attitude thaws somewhat when he hears that Holmes is close to the end. He agrees to visit the Detective and so Watson makes his excuses and leaves so that he might arrive back first at 221B. Once there, Watson is commanded to hide behind the bedhead as Holmes reasons that Smith's opinion will be franker if he believes they are alone. The scene is set for a grim diagnosis and some spectacular revelations.

HIS LAST BOW

First Published: The *Strand Magazine*, September 1917, UK; *Collier's*, 22 September 1917, USA

Setting Date: 1914

WRITTEN IN THE third person, this story brings Holmes out of his Sussex retirement (where he has been working on his *Practical Handbook of Bee Culture*) on the eve of the First World War. Von Bork is a German agent, operating at the centre of a Moriartyesque web of intrigue. He has operated in England for four years unhindered, accumulating a vast wealth of intelligence while assuming the guise of a decent sportsman and thoroughly good chap.

At his home in Harwich on the East Anglian coast, he is denigrating the English character with his companion, Baron von Herling. His work is nearly done, save for one last meeting with Altamont, an Irish-American agent who hates the English. He is set to deliver Britain's naval signals into the hands of Germany.

With Von Herling departed and the housekeeper, Martha, retired for the night, Altamont appears in his chauffeur-driven car. Altamont proves a spiky customer, questioning the German's security arrangements and his country's track record for disposing of agents once they have outlived their usefulness. A stand-off ensues as Altamont wants his money before handing over his package, while Von Bork wants to examine the contents first.

Von Bork is right to be mistrustful for the intelligence is not that which he expected. In a grandstand finish, Holmes and Watson are united for a last hurrah. Martha too gets a pat on the back. Could this, by any chance, be Mrs Hudson by another name (as mischievously proposed by the Holmesian scholar Vincent Starrett)?

Written after three years of war with no end in sight, this story is underscored by Conan Doyle's desire to 'keep up the British end'. There is no great feat of deduction to amaze the reader and it has been widely criticised as a spy story (where it would have made more sense to keep Von Bork in the dark and continue supplying him with misinformation). To this extent it is quite unlike any other story in the canon and we should perhaps be grateful that there was another collection of stories round the corner with which to give the Great Detective a better send-off.

In this story Holmes had his one and only documented journey in a motor car, being chauffeured in a Ford of the type pictured here.

HOLMES AND ME 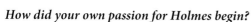 CATHERINE COOKE

Catherine Cooke curates the Sherlock Holmes Collection at Marylebone Library in London. She is a much respected Holmes scholar and a prominent member of several societies including the Sherlock Holmes Society of London and the US-based Baker Street Irregulars.

Could you tell me a little about the Collection?

In 1951 the government put on the Festival of Britain. After some wrangling, it was decided that Marylebone would put on an exhibition of Holmes. It was originally going to be books, journals, magazines, library-type material. Then it was decided to do a reproduction of Holmes's sitting room too. When the exhibition finished, we kept what books we'd got and they remained a small collection until the mid-1970s. At that time our librarian, Ken Harrison, thought it would be a good idea to do something with them. He found a member of staff with an interest in Holmes called Heather Owen. She ran it from the 1970s until 1982, at which point I got my claws into it and I've hung on ever since. We aren't just a Holmes collection but cover Conan Doyle's writings as a whole. They are a good mirror of late Victorian/Edwardian society.

How did your own passion for Holmes begin?

It was Douglas Wilmer. 1965. 'The Devil's Foot'. I had an older brother who wanted to watch it and I got hooked. I was very young at the time, I hasten to add! I'd quote my favourite stories as 'The Solitary Cyclist', 'The Devil's Foot' and, of course, *The Hound of the Baskervilles*. I've also come to understand *The Valley of Fear* a lot more since a trip to the Pennsylvania coalfields. My particular interest now tends to be more about the background, the origins of the stories; the inspiration if you want to put it like that.

I think Holmes has endured for a number of reasons. There is pure humour and entertainment in the stories. They were designed for short bursts of reading, for commuters on the train. Those were the days when commuting was taking off. And they have always been nostalgic. The first story was 1887 and they went through to the 1920s but there was only ever one motor car mentioned. Holmes hardly ever uses the telephone. The underground railway only appears once. It's always steam trains, hansom cabs, telegrams. It's really the world of the 1880s. By the time the stories became really popular in the 1890s, they were already nostalgic.

Catherine Cooke in costume during a Sherlock Holmes Society of London trip to Switzerland in 2005.

Conan Doyle had a rather dismissive attitude to Holmes and Watson. What is your take on them?

I think the characters are fairly well formed over the period, although I'd never try to compare them with a serious novelist writing serious work. The Sherlock Holmes stories – especially the later ones – were potboilers to keep the money rolling in. They are not well rounded in that sense. But I think there's a lot of humour in the relationship between Holmes and Watson.

Conan Doyle thought it was the historical novels that were really important. He also wrote four or five Professor Challenger novels, which implies he thought they were a fairly serious proposition. In the introduction to *The Lost World* he said his wish was to 'give one hour of joy to the boy who's half a man, or the man who's half a boy' but he couldn't see that about Sherlock Holmes, even though that's exactly what the Holmes stories do.

You're strongly involved in the Sherlock Holmes Society of London. How did it come about and what does it do?

There was a society in the early '30s that lasted for a couple of years. Its members included Dorothy L. Sayers. That really faded due to internal problems. Then the war killed it stone dead – people had better things to do. It was revived in 1951 by people who helped put on the exhibition. Membership got a big boost in the early 1980s with Brett's series and, though it's dropped off a bit, there are now about 1,000 to 1,200 members. I wouldn't like to say there's an 'average' member. They tend to be childless, although we do have members with children who sometimes come to the meetings too now they've grown up a bit. Other members include people who've done the children bit and we also have students. We had a very active bunch from Oxford University for a while, until they went off and got proper jobs, families, commitments and those sorts of things.

'Playing the game' is a key part of the Society. In the early '80s when we started regular trips, our first one was to Portsmouth where Conan Doyle began writing the stories. But Conan Doyle was not often mentioned in those days. We do admit these days that he wrote the stories. Sometimes! That said, there is usually a member of the Conan Doyle family around the Society, even if not directly involved. Dame Jean Conan Doyle was very supportive and Charles Foley, his great-nephew, comes to the annual dinner.

It hasn't always been the case though. Adrian and Denis, Jean's brothers, weren't hugely supportive. They both died before my time. But people who knew them have said Adrian especially was apt to slap a lawsuit on people. He was very protective of copyright. To sum up the attitude towards him, the Baker Street Irregulars used to drink an annual toast to the snake that once bit Adrian in Crowborough!

THE ADVENTURE OF THE MAZARIN STONE

FIRST PUBLISHED: The *Strand Magazine*, October 1921, UK; *Hearst's International*, November 1921, USA

SETTING DATE: 1903

ONE OF THOSE stories narrated not by Watson but by an unidentified third person. Watson has come to visit Holmes in Baker Street after an evidently fairly long time away. He is greeted by Billy, the decent young pageboy who fills a little of the lonely void in Holmes's life. Despite Watson calling at 7.30 in the evening, he finds Holmes asleep. He has evidently been going through a period of great activity, using all his powers of disguise to appear variously as a workman and an old woman.

It emerges that he has had meetings with both the Prime Minister and the Home Secretary relating to the burglary of a hugely valuable crown diamond, the Mazarin Stone. He has also had dealings with one Lord Cantlemere, whose scepticism as to Holmes's abilities of detection makes him look rather foolish.

By the window in 221B there is a facsimile of Holmes, posed in a dressing gown as if reading. It is to serve as a decoy to someone who Holmes suspects intends to make an attempt on his life. Holmes is initially unsure about the whereabouts of the jewel but has a clear idea of the culprit. He unexpectedly finds his chief suspect and would-be assassin at his door. Sending Watson off to get help from Scotland Yard, Holmes engineers a scene in which he manages to glean the location of the Mazarin Stone while avoiding attack from either his nemesis or his henchman. The tale finishes with an elaborate, and hard-to-swallow, practical joke with which Holmes is almost too pleased.

'The Mazarin Stone' recalls 'The Empty House' with the appearance of an effigy of the Detective. The story is actually a reworking of *The Crown Diamond*, a 1921 stage play by Doyle. Technology also has a role to play as Holmes makes cunning use of a gramophone. For many fans, 'The Mazarin Stone' is far from a classic and feels rather too much like an over-elaborate set piece.

The covers of Penguin's 2008 'Red Classic' editions of the complete canon play on the gothic horror of many of the stories, as well as echoing the Rathbone film posters of the 1930s and '40s.

THE PROBLEM OF THOR BRIDGE

FIRST PUBLISHED: The *Strand Magazine*, February–March 1922, UK; *Hearst's International*, February–March 1922, USA
SETTING DATE: 1901

WATSON TELLS OF how the papers relating to this story have long dwelt in his now legendary tin dispatch box held by the bank Cox and Co. of Charing Cross. The case is brought to Holmes – who had hitherto endured several months of unsatisfying casework – by one Neil Gibson, a millionaire known as 'the Gold King'

and a one-time American senator. His wife, Maria – a fiery Brazilian – has been found shot through the head on Thor Bridge, in the grounds of Thor Place in Hampshire. Gibson's appearance at 221B is preceded by that of his estate manager, one Marlow Bates, who suggests that Gibson is an 'infernal villain' whose wife was his 'chief victim'.

Everything, however, points to the guilt of the Gibson children's governess, Grace Dunbar. Not only was a note from her agreeing to meet Maria on the bridge found with the body, but a recently fired pistol has been discovered in her wardrobe. Gibson wants Holmes to prove her innocence. The Detective immediately surmises that Gibson harbours a romantic desire for Dunbar but nonetheless agrees to take on the case.

Where others see a mountain of incontrovertible evidence, Holmes is suspicious of such an excess. Would Dunbar really be so foolish as to hide the murder weapon in her wardrobe? Why would Maria have needed to take the note arranging the meeting on the bridge with her? Holmes makes a thorough investigation of the crime scene and, crucially, proves his mettle as a ballistics expert. Watson is on hand to offer up his revolver to prove Holmes's brilliantly deduced hypothesis correct.

"Suddenly Holmes sprang from his chair. 'Come, Watson, come!' he said. 'With the help of the God of justice I will give you a case which will make England ring.'"

A. Gilbert illustrated 'The Problem of Thor Bridge' for its appearance in the *Strand*. Gilbert also contributed drawings for 'His Last Bow' and 'The Mazarin Stone'.

THE ADVENTURE OF
THE CREEPING MAN

FIRST PUBLISHED: The *Strand Magazine*, March 1923, UK; *Hearst's International*, March 1923, USA
SETTING DATE: 1903

A contemporary view of Hradčany Castle, overlooking the Bohemian city of Prague where Presbury went missing for two weeks.

ONE OF HOLMES'S last cases before retiring, it is also one of the bizarrest and ultimately rather silly. 221B is visited by Trevor Bennett, the secretary and prospective son-in-law of the respected Professor Presbury of Camford. Presbury, in his early sixties, is engaged to one Alice Morphy, the young daughter of a colleague, and it is noted that his behaviour has become somewhat erratic since their betrothal. Presbury had gone missing for a fortnight, which he spent (Bennett learned from a friend's letter) in Prague. On his return, Presbury forbade Bennett to open certain correspondence that would be arriving for him. He also jealously guarded a wooden box he had brought back from his travels. While still quite in control of his mental faculties, Presbury had become increasingly secretive and prone to mood swings.

Then one night Bennett discovered the Professor crawling on hands and knees along a passageway. When Bennett addressed him, the Professor responded angrily and stalked off. In the midst of Presbury's narrative, his fiancée Edith arrives and tells of seeing her father peering in at her bedroom window in the middle of the night, despite her window being on the second floor and the absence of a suitable ladder. The clearly out-of-sorts professor has furthermore been subject to a series of attacks by his normally faithful wolfhound. Not for the first time, Holmes finds the behaviour of a dog particularly suggestive.

Holmes and Watson visit Presbury, claiming to have an appointment and calculating that since he is clearly living in some 'strange dream', he will go with it. However, the Professor is convinced that no such appointment ever existed and flies into a fury, leaving Holmes and Watson fearful of attack. Holmes nonetheless derives useful insights into Presbury's mental state from the incident.

Further observations about the creeping ivy leading to Edith's window, the Professor's 'thick and horny' knuckles and the identity of his strange correspondent provide Holmes with all the information he needs.

The influence of Robert Louis Stevenson's *Dr Jekyll and Mr Hyde* is clear and there is perhaps also a hint of the subconscious fear inherent in a post-Darwin society that man and beast are not so far apart.

THE ADVENTURE OF THE SUSSEX VAMPIRE

FIRST PUBLISHED: The *Strand Magazine*, January 1924, UK; *Hearst's International*, January 1924, USA

SETTING DATE: 1896

HOLMES RECEIVES A letter from a solicitors' firm, Morrison, Morrison, and Dodd, explaining that they have directed their client Robert Ferguson to him regarding an enquiry Ferguson has concerning vampires. A second note comes from Ferguson announcing, untruthfully, that he is acting for a friend and explaining that he is acquainted with Watson from their rugby-playing days.

Ferguson arrives the following day to explain his horrifying suspicions that his wife, another of Conan Doyle's fiery South Americans (this time from Peru), has been caught on numerous occasions by the nurse, Mrs Mason, sucking the blood of their baby son. She is Ferguson's second wife, his first marriage having produced a son, Jack, fifteen, who was crippled as a child. Despite his affectionate nature, Jack has been subject to beatings from his stepmother.

For a while Mrs Mason found that receipt of the odd sly backhander could appease her concern but eventually she became so worried that she told Ferguson of what she had witnessed. Ferguson, naturally, could not countenance such a notion until he saw for himself the baby's neck bleeding and his wife's mouth red with blood. Unable to explain herself, Mrs Ferguson took to her room, permitting contact only with her long-standing Peruvian maid, Dolores.

Holmes is sceptical that vampirism is at play, commenting that 'No ghosts need apply.' Indeed, he unravels this particular mystery before even setting out to Ferguson's Sussex estate, Cheeseman's. There Dolores explains that her mistress is in desperate need of a doctor. Watson obliges and finds Mrs Ferguson highly distressed, ranting about the presence of a fiend and all being destroyed.

Meanwhile, Holmes is introduced to the baby, to Jack and to Carlo, a sickly spaniel. He also makes a study of a collection of arms brought to England by Mrs Ferguson. His suspicions are all confirmed and he provides Ferguson with an explanation of events that breaks his heart in a most unexpected way.

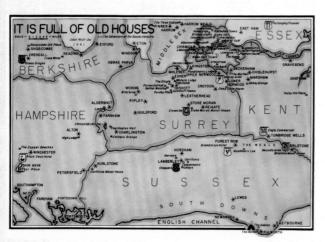

This map showing Holmes's activities in the southern counties was one of a series created by Julian Wolff, who headed the Baker Street Irregulars for 26 years.

HOLMES AND ME ⬤ EDWARD HARDWICKE

Edward Hardwicke was a much-loved stage and screen actor. When only ten years old he starred opposite Spencer Tracy in A Guy Named Joe. *In 1986 he succeeded David Burke in the role of Dr Watson for Granada and formed a celebrated partnership with Jeremy Brett over eight years and twenty-eight productions. This interview was conducted in 2008. He died in 2011.*

How did you come to get the role of Dr Watson?

I was working with Anna Calder-Marshall, who is married to David Burke, and I knew David anyway. He had been given the chance to go to Stratford and do a season at the Royal Shakespeare Company. At the same time, he had been offered another series of Sherlock Holmes. As I happened to be working with Anna, he said 'Look, get your agent to ring up about it.' That's how it happened.

As a youngster, my father was in Hollywood and I'd met his great friend Nigel Bruce, so I had a connection with Watson from way back then. I had read the stories like most people do but it never occurred to me that I might find myself doing them. But I was a fan. They are terrific and at the centre of it is that relationship, which is what I think makes them attractive to people. I think most good crime fiction has something similar to that. Watson is a kind of sounding board for Holmes.

Other than Burke's, did you look to any other actors' performances?

It was never a particular obsession with me. I read the stories and when they were at the cinema or shown on television, I would watch them. But never with any thought of doing them or having any connection with them at all.

I think the image that most people had, certainly to that point, was of the old Rathbone–Nigel Bruce films. I think they tend to forget that they were made in the period around and during the Second World War and they were made for an American market and so you have razor-sharp Basil Rathbone and then the rather gentle, bumbling Watson. There was a certain deliberate attempt to do that in those days but by the time we came to film we were in a different era. That is a wonderful thing about those characters – in a sense, they are like Hamlet. Every generation creates its own identity for them.

What influence did Jeremy Brett have on the productions?

I was very much the junior member because they had already made thirteen films when I joined. Jeremy had already put his stamp very strongly on the series. I think

Edward Hardwicke took on the role of Watson in 1986, going on to make twenty-eight appearances as the good doctor.

in reality it was very largely because the American audience liked him that we got another series, or indeed another three series, out of Granada.

Jeremy carried a well-thumbed copy of the collected stories on set. Quite rightly, when there was any dialogue actually in the stories, it had to be accurately put into the scripts. It was not left to the adaptor or writer to write his own dialogue. Jeremy was very anxious that we be as accurate and true to Conan Doyle as we possibly could. That's what he chased after all the time.

There was a wonderful team of people working on the films. They did extraordinary research, down to every pen and pencil that was used being accurate and of the period. It was a joy. The support you received as an actor was enormous. And you had great confidence that the fact you had been asked to do it meant you had something that they thought was correct for the character. It's wonderful for an actor to have that sort of back-up.

Had circumstances been different, would you have liked to have been able to film the whole canon?

I think it's questionable but we could have done more than we did. And I'm including David's thirteen films, which were the earliest and probably pick of the stories. Initially they didn't see the series going beyond thirteen episodes, so they chose the best ones. I think that completing the canon was something Jeremy was very keen to do but, bless his heart, his ill health affected that. I think there are certain stories that don't lend themselves to being adapted to film too. Watson is very often writing down the stories and that makes some of them difficult as you often have to represent him in a way different to the original story.

What do you think is the reason for the enduring popularity of Holmes and Watson?

That's an extremely difficult one. I do still get the odd letter about the series from all over the world. Granada hit a bit of a bull's-eye with it. It's still one of the biggest sellers they've ever had.

As for the enduring elements of those stories . . . Friendship is certainly one of the elements. They are two very different people with a friendship at the centre. Watson is a doctor and in a sense doctors and detectives have quite a lot in common. They look at various clues. I can see why Watson as a character would be fascinated by Holmes.

In another sense, they are in a way two aspects of one person. And they also represent a particular moment in our history. That Victorian/Edwardian moment which is very much part of the myth about the English.

Have you felt your association with such a famous character to be a burden in any way?

Not at all. Watson was a good friend to Holmes and he's been a very good friend to me. I have had a wonderful fifty years as an actor and Watson was the icing on the cake.

HOLMES ON STAGE, SCREEN AND RADIO

*The stage lost a fine actor, even as science lost an acute reasoner,
when he became a specialist in crime.*
'A Scandal in Bohemia'

Sherlock Holmes is the most filmed fictional character in history, with several hundred television and film productions to his name. Such a fact would surely have caused some amazement to Conan Doyle, who in the early 1890s had told a journalist: 'I am well convinced that Holmes is not fitted for dramatic representation. His reasons and deductions (which are the whole point of the character) would become an intolerable bore upon the stage.'

Charles Brookfield gave Holmes his first credited stage appearance in a short 1893 piece called *Under the Clock* at the Royal Court Theatre. That was followed by a Charles Roger production, *Sherlock Holmes*, which ran in Glasgow in May of 1894 with John Webb starring.

By autumn of 1897 Conan Doyle himself, never one to overlook a commercial opportunity, was seriously considering producing a play, which he had no doubt would be 'a lucrative if a humble piece of work'. Having laboured over a five-act structure, he struggled to find a suitable partner in the project, with the work rejected by both Sir Henry Irving and Sir Herbert Beerbohm Tree. The piece eventually found its way into the hands of an up-and-coming Broadway

A depiction of William Gillette playing Holmes in his smash-hit stage play. This picture accompanied a review in *The Illustrated London News* in 1901.

producer, Charles Frohman, who suggested it might be suitable for adaptation by William Gillette, a respected American actor-producer-playwright. Sherlock Holmes would turn him into an international star.

Gillette was not afraid to take Conan Doyle's script and mould it into his own. He famously wrote to Conan Doyle to ask permission to have Holmes fall in love with a woman, and received the response: 'You may marry or murder him or do what you like with him.' The show, now a four-act play incorporating strands from several of the published stories, had its official opening night on 6 November 1899 at the Garrick Theatre in New

TERRY'S THEATRE.

Sole Proprietor ... ... Mr. EDWARD TERRY.

Under the Management of Mr. YORKE STEPHENS.

Every Evening at 9
THE NEW CLOWN,

An Original Farce in Three Acts.

By H. M. PAULL.

Lord Cyril Garston	Mr. JAMES WELCH
Capt. The Hon. Jack Trent ...	Mr. CLARENCE BLAKISTON
Thomas Baker	Mr. GEORGE SHELTON
Mr. Dixon (Proprietor of Dixon's Royal Circus)	Mr. EDWARD SASS
Mr. Pennyquick	Mr. T. WIGNEY PERCYVAL
Billy (a Strong Man)... ...	Mr. RUSSELL NORRIE
Mr. Lamb (Landlord of the Riverside Inn)	Mr. JOHN WILLES
Figgis (a Clerk)	Mr. GUNNIS DAVIS
Boy	Master LEONARD PARKER
Policeman	Mr. W. BUSHELL
Maude Chesterton	Miss JANET ALEXANDER
Winnie Chesterton	Miss BEATRICE IRWIN
Rose Platt (Mr. Dixon's Niece) AND	Miss NINA BOUCICAULT

ACT 1. ... ... The Riverside Inn, near Bray
ACT 2. ... ... The Ring of Dixon's Circus
ACT 3. ... ... The Green Room of Dixon's Circus

Dresses by Mesdames. NOROC et Cie, 16A, Old Cavendish Street, W. ; Riding Habits and Circus Dresses by Messrs. JNO SIMMONS & SONS, 35, Haymarket ; Millinery by MAISON DE CRAM, 41, Chester Square, Belgravia.

The Band, under the direction of Mr. BRIGATA BUCALOSSI, will play during the evening the following selection of Music—

Selection	"The Toreador" ...	*Ivan Caryll and Lional Monckton*
Descriptive Piece ...	"A Hunting Scene" ...	... *Bucalossi*
	Early Morning The Meet The Chase A Joyous Return	
March... ...	"King's Own" ...	*B. Bucalossi*
Song	"The Honeysuckle and the Bee"	*Wm. H. Penn*
	(Published by Francis Day & Hunter)	
La Serenata ...	"Legende Valaque" ...	*Braga*
Serenata ...	"I Student" ...	*Ernest Bucalossi*
American Sketch ...	"Down South" ...	*W. H. Middleton*
Marsch	"Sternenbanner" ...	*C. M. Zehrer*
March	"The Union Jack" ...	*Percy J. Best*
Stage Manager ...	... ...	Mr. R. E. WARTON
Musical Director ...	... ...	Mr. BRIGATA BUCALOSSI

Box Office (Mr. A. HOLLINGSHEAD) open 10 to 10.   *Telephone 2702 Gerrard.*

Preceded every evening at 8.15 by
A Dramatic Criticism in Four Paragraphs and as many headlines by MALCOLM WATSON and EDWARD LA SERRE, entitled

"Sheerluck Jones,"

Or, WHY D'GILLETTE HIM OFF?

Being a hitherto unpublished commentary on the story of the famous detective and his connection with
" *The Strange Case of Miss Alice Baulkner.*"

Sheerluck Jones	Mr. CLARENCE BLAKISTON
Dr. Rotson	Mr. CARTER PICKFORD
John Toanfroman ...	Mr. J. EGERTON HUBBARD
Sir Edward Sleighton ...	Professor MacGILLICUDDY
Baron Pumpernickel ...	Mr. SIDNEY PINCH
Prof. MacGillicuddy (pronounced Machlicuddy)	Mr. J. WILLES
James Scarabee	Mr. RUSSELL NORRIE
Sidney Pinch	Mr. F. CREMLIN
Thomas Bleary	Mr. VICTOR BRIDGES
Braigin	Mr. A. JAMES
The Gas Collector ...	Mr. MARTIN HARPER
Carsons	Mr. LLOYD EARLE
Little Billee	Mr. GUNNIS DAVIS
Madge Scarabee ...	Miss BERRY DAYNE
Alice Baulkner	Miss GORDON LEE

Produced under the direction of Mr. JAMES WELCH.

The Place is the Strand.   The Time ― Any Time.

First Par.—A Musical Evening at the Scarabees.
Second Par.—Sheerluck finds his Match & Lights a Pipe with it.
Third Par.—The Trail of the Cigar.
Fourth Par.—The Pleasures of Home.

The Piano supplied by the PIANOTIST Co., 56, Regent Street, W.

N.B.—No one arriving after 8.15, and very few seated before that hour, can possibly understand the plot of the piece.

The Management desires to call the special attention of the audience to the novel light effects. For permission to reproduce these in the family circle by the method of rapidly opening and closing the eyes application to be made to the Acting Manager.

The light motives in the orchestra provided by Mr. Brigata Bucalossi.

Properties by their respective owners.

The costumes more by accident than design.

As the orchestra is only able to play one tune in the dark the indulgence of the public is requested should any similarity be detected in the musical finales to the various paragraphs.

Matinee—both Pieces—every Wednesday and Saturday at 2.30.

Sheerluck Jones was an early Holmes parody of 1901. It played at Terry's Theatre, established in 1887 by the actor-impresario Terry Edward O'Connor on the site of an old music hall.

York. It was an immediate success, with audiences if not with the critics, and ran for a further 235 performances before Gillette brought it to London's Lyceum Theatre in 1901 for a run of 216 shows. Such a hit was it that almost immediately a rival show, *Sheerluck Jones (or Why D'Gillette Him Off?)*, opened at Terry's Theatre off the Strand.

Gillette had a profound influence on the public perception of the Detective. Frederic Dorr Steele would look to Gillette as the model for his illustrations of the Holmes stories in *Collier's Weekly* in the coming years. The actor also scripted the line 'Oh, this is elementary, my dear fellow,' a short hop from the 'Elementary, my dear Watson' that would later be used on screen by Clive Brook. And it was Gillette who first had Holmes smoking a curved calabash pipe, apparently because he could not get his lines out while sucking on any of the models of pipe actually described in Conan Doyle's stories.

Aubrey Vincent, writing in the *Spectator*, recalled seeing Gillette, who 'spoke in an eerie, sinister drawl, rather high-pitched, and, with his head thrown back and eyes half closed, gave the impression that he was thinking of anything but the problem on hand'. Conan Doyle, I am sure uninfluenced by any royalty cheques, said of Gillette's adaptation, 'I must say I think he was very successful' and complimented his performance as touched by 'the genius of a great sympathetic artist'. Gillette would play the role a total of 1,300 times, finally hanging up his pipe and deerstalker in 1932. The play toured extensively throughout the English-speaking world, making a particular star of H. A. Saintsbury in Britain, as well as giving a break to a young Charlie Chaplin, who appeared as Billy the Page Boy. Gillette put the production on film in 1916 but sadly no copies remain.

Subsequently, Holmes has had a long and varied career on stage. Conan Doyle had another stab at dramatising his hero when he wrote *The Speckled Band* in 1910, which ran successfully with Saintsbury in the lead role and despite some trouble with poorly trained thespian snakes. Conan Doyle's next go, *The Crown Diamond: An Evening with Sherlock Holmes*, appeared for a short

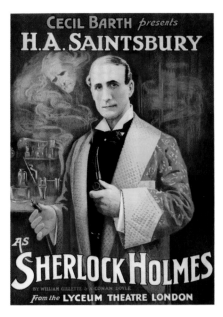

H. A. Saintsbury, born in London in 1869, played Holmes over 1,400 times. Charlie Chaplin expressed his gratitude for the support Saintsbury showed him as a young actor.

While William Gillette was the great star of the day, it was Charles Chaplin, far down the bill in this stage production, who would go on to become one of the most famous performers of the twentieth century.

run in 1921 at London's Coliseum. Despite its failings as a play, he was able to rework it into the short story 'The Adventure of the Mazarin Stone'.

It is a rare time indeed when there is not some version of Holmes being played on the stage somewhere, whether it be a straight play, a tongue-in-cheek parody or even a ballet. *The Great Detective* was a reasonably well-received show at the Sadler's Wells Ballet in 1953, while the musical *Baker Street* was a Broadway success in the 1960s. Another song-and-dance version, *Sherlock Holmes: The Musical*, opened in 1988 and has undergone several revivals. Meanwhile, Roger Llewellyn has honed his beautifully observed performance as Holmes (and assorted other canonical figures) in his one-man shows. He is fast approaching 500 performances around the world and shows no sign of letting up.

Holmes made the leap to film in 1900 with *Sherlock Holmes Baffled*, a curiosity running at less than a minute. Rather than a celebration of the Great Detective, it was a showcase for the wondrous potential of moving pictures. Five years later, Maurice Costello had the honour of being the first actor to be credited as playing Holmes on screen, in an eight-minute film called *Held for Ransom*.

Britain was curiously unwilling to take on the challenges of filming Conan Doyle's creation, so most of the early versions emanated from America, Italy and, most famously, Denmark. Between 1908 and 1910 Denmark's Nordisk Film Company produced thirteen films of variable quality. One, *Sherlock Holmes in the Great Murder Mystery*, involved Holmes going into a trance and identifying the criminal as an escaped gorilla. Viggo Larsen was the driving force behind this series, variously taking on the duties of writer, director and star. He then moved to the German Vitascope studio, where he worked on another Holmes series. Alwin Neuss and Georges Treville gave other notable performances as Holmes in Continental productions of the period.

It was not until 1914 that the first British film emerged, a version of *A Study in Scarlet*. Produced by the Samuelson Film Company, it starred James Bragington as Holmes. Bragington was a Samuelson employee cast on the basis of his physical similarity to the character rather than any notable performing skills. In 1916 the same company cast Saintsbury in *The Valley of Fear*, his one appearance on film to go with the thousand or so he made on stage. Universal had made their own version of *A Study in Scarlet* in 1914, starring Francis Ford, the brother of the renowned film-maker, John. The world's first black Sherlock Holmes, played by Sam Robinson, appeared in Ebony Film Corporation's *A Black Sherlock Holmes* in 1918.

Eille Norwood, a Yorkshireman born Anthony Brett, was the first man to become a bona fide film star playing the Great Detective. The first of two notable Bretts to play Holmes, he was almost sixty when he took the role in 1920 and

Eille Norwood, the first great screen Holmes, in a still from *The Hound of the Baskervilles* made in 1921 by the Stoll film company.

John Barrymore starring in *Sherlock Holmes* (released as *Moriarty* in the UK), a Goldwyn Pictures movie released in 1922. Its plot owed much to Gillette's stage play.

was best known as a stage actor. Over the next three years he reprised the role of Holmes a remarkable forty-seven times in a series of twenty-minute silent films. Hubert Willis was his Watson for the vast majority, although Arthur Cullin took over towards the end of the run. Norwood was particularly skilled in the art of disguise, which made for plenty of extravagant flourishes in the series. He was also a respected crossword setter for the *Daily Express*, so it is likely he felt a natural affinity for the analytical Holmes. Conan Doyle was a firm fan, as were the critics and the public at large. The films stand up well today, despite some overly long intertitles explaining plot twists. Norwood also played Holmes on stage in London in 1923. His relationship with Holmes was brief and came late in life but ultimately defined his career.

John Barrymore, widely regarded as the greatest actor of his generation, starred in 1922's *Sherlock Holmes*, based in large part on Gillette's stage play. With Roland Young as his Watson, Barrymore was a particularly noble-looking Holmes but the relationship was to be fleeting. The first 'soundie' version came in 1929, with Clive Brook starring in *The Return of Sherlock Holmes* for Paramount, the first of three outings. H. Reeves-Smith was his first Watson, and played a part in the dumbing-down of the good doctor. In 1932's *Sherlock Holmes*, Reginald Owen replaced him as Watson, a year before being promoted to the starring role in *A Study in Scarlet*. He was a likeable and effective Holmes but his lack of physical resemblance to the detective of Conan Doyle's stories was unfortunate.

RIGHT: A rather superior Holmes (Raymond Massey) seen besting a menacing Grimesby Rylott (Lyn Harding) in 1931's *The Speckled Band*. Harding appeared as Professor Moriarty in two other films.

BELOW: *The Man Who Was Sherlock Holmes* was made by the German UFA studios in 1937. Starring Hans Albers as Holmes and Heinz Rühmann as Watson, the plot was 'off-canon'.

Raymond Massey and Athole Stewart played Holmes and Watson in *The Speckled Band* in 1931. The first attempt at a Holmes soundie by a British company, it was not entirely satisfying and its efforts to place the crime-fighting duo in a high-tech 1930s setting were jarring. Arthur Wontner made his debut as Holmes in *The Sleeping Cardinal* in 1931, the first of five films he would make in a seven-year period. Noted for his resemblance to Paget's *Strand* illustrations, he brought much needed compassion to the role and won instant popular and critical acclaim. He looked set to win long-term fame but the imminent arrival of Basil Rathbone on the scene rather cruelly left him as a largely forgotten figure. Wontner's Watson was Ian Fleming (no relation to the creator of James Bond) and he took Watson ever closer to the territory of the buffoon. It should be noted that the great British icon intriguingly found a place in the heart of Nazi Germany, which produced several versions in the 1930s. These included the still much lauded *The Man Who Was Sherlock Holmes*, with its light comic treatment, and 1939's *Der Hund von Baskerville* (a favourite of Adolf Hitler).

1939 saw 20th Century Fox produce *The Hound of the Baskervilles*, with Basil Rathbone as Holmes and Nigel Bruce as Watson. It was to mark the start of a landmark series of films that – for many – still defines the Great Detective and his sidekick. The production was remarkably faithful to Conan Doyle's original story and was the first film to keep Holmes in his native period, rather than transporting him forward in time. With the luxury of a tight script, Rathbone remoulded the character. Born in Africa, Rathbone was public school-educated in England before serving with distinction in the First World War. He became a highly acclaimed theatre actor before achieving success in a string of silent movies. However, it was the talkies that best showcased his abilities. Everyone who had preceded him as Holmes suddenly seemed not quite right. Rathbone with his angular good looks, pristine vocalisation and ability to imbue Holmes with both arrogance and humanity seemed to lift the character from the pages of the books and convincingly breathe life into him.

While Rathbone has remained a much complimented Holmes, Bruce's performance has been derided over the years as rather one-dimensional. Indeed, he must squarely shoulder the blame for turning Watson from the empathetic and honourable man of medicine into an incorrigible bumbling fool. Bruce did not play the Watson of Conan Doyle's creation at all but he gave a beautifully executed comic turn that no doubt leavened the series at a time when the world had little to laugh about. Crucially, he elevated Watson from the bit-part player he had been in most of his prior celluloid excursions into a key element. These were decidedly the films of Rathbone *and* Bruce.

Basil Rathbone as Holmes and Nigel Bruce as Watson bookend Evelyn Ankers' Kitty in *The Voice of Terror*. Released in 1942, it was the first Rathbone Holmes movie produced by Universal Pictures.

Rathbone debuted as Holmes in 1939's *The Hound of the Baskervilles*, which was an instant box-office success and remains perhaps the most admired cinema adaptation of the classic tale.

Fox followed up *The Hound* with the equally successful and well-received *The Adventures of Sherlock Holmes* but, prematurely, chose to end the franchise there. So it was that Universal took up the reins, transferring Holmes to the present and making far scanter use of Conan Doyle's original texts. They factory-farmed the series throughout the Second World War, often using them as rather clumsy propaganda tools. It is difficult to watch Rathbone's *Henry V*-inspired speech at the end of *The Secret Weapon* without feeling a pang of embarrassment for all involved. Nonetheless, Rathbone and Bruce were never less than watchable and there were some delights to emerge from Universal, notably *Sherlock Holmes Faces Death*, *Spider Woman*, *The Scarlet Claw* and *The Pearl of Death*.

Rathbone, like Conan Doyle himself and many others before and since, found that the more his professional fortunes became entwined with those of Holmes, the less he liked the character. He would eventually describe Holmes as a man who could not 'know loneliness or love or sorrow' – rather a flaw for any actor wishing to show his range. He was afraid of becoming so associated with Holmes that other doors would close to him so decided to leave the series, much to Bruce's chagrin, in 1946. It was already too late and Rathbone would never escape the deerstalker-shaped shadow that hung over him. Indeed, Holmes would ensnare him again, with Rathbone reprising the role sporadically on stage, TV and radio, but it is the movie output that remains longest and most cherished in the memory.

In the 1950s Carleton Hobbs established himself as the pre-eminent Holmes on radio, starring in a series for the BBC and continuing in the role until 1969. Norman Shelley was his erstwhile Watson. Incidentally, Hobbs had himself taken the role of Watson in a series of radio broadcasts of the 1940s opposite Arthur Wontner's Holmes. Though by no means a faultless partnership, perhaps the starriest radio Holmes and Watson was assembled by the BBC in a joint venture with the American Broadcasting Company. In these productions John Gielgud played Holmes with Ralph Richardson as Watson. Famously, the role of Moriarty was taken by Orson Welles. Welles had played Holmes himself in a one-off production on American radio in 1938.

It is estimated that there have been over 750 English-language radio adaptations of the Holmes stories. Of these, few have come near to the quality of the BBC

Sir John Gielgud (left) as Holmes, Sir Ralph Richardson (right) as Watson and Orson Welles (centre) playing Moriarty for a 1954 BBC radio production.

series that ran from 1989 to 1998. Scripted predominantly by Bert Coules, they initially starred Clive Merrison as Holmes and Michael Williams as Watson. When Williams sadly passed away in 1991, his role was taken on admirably by Andrew Sachs. Not only did the series include versions of every single canonical story (completed before Williams's death), they even found time to develop new stories based on passing references to other cases. As a body of work, they are as evocative as virtually any of the great TV and screen productions.

American television bosses made an attempt to bring Holmes to the small screen in 1937, with Louis Hector in the title role, but there were no fireworks. A similar fate befell the BBC's attempts in the early 1950s, when Alan Wheatley played Holmes alongside Raymond Francis as Watson. However, Ron Howard took on the role on American TV in 1953 and Holmes on the box at last came of age. With Howard Marion-Crawford playing his trusty sidekick, Howard filmed 39 episodes over two years, pleasing audiences despite low budgets and production values.

The BBC got in on the action again in 1964, producing thirteen fifty-minute-long episodes that, unlike the Howard series, returned to the canonical stories. Douglas Wilmer as Holmes and Nigel Stock as Watson made a fine pairing, highlighting the humanity behind the characters. Wilmer hinted at Holmes's darker side while Stock did excellent work in chipping away at the buffoonish image of Watson. Unfortunately, the BBC used a mishmash of directors and writers who presented the cast with material of varying quality. Indeed, Wilmer himself was responsible for much rewriting to whip scripts into shape, and by the time the first series had run its course, he had little urge to continue the experience.

With a ratings winner on their hands, the BBC were unwilling to turn their back on the series. They persuaded Stock to stay and turned to Peter Cushing to replace Wilmer. Cushing had starred in Hammer's *Hound of the Baskervilles* in 1959 (the first Holmes to be made in colour), doing a sterling job alongside André Morell's Watson in a film that received a lukewarm reaction at the time but is now viewed as one of the better adaptations. Cushing did a decent job for the BBC but met many of the same challenges that had confronted Wilmer. Cushing would again play Holmes, but not until the mid-1980s when he

Ron Howard, the son of screen star Leslie, starred in a series of half-hour television adaptations for Guild Films which were an enormous success.

Despite initial reservations, the Holmes–Watson partnership of Peter Cushing and André Morell first visited in *The Hound of the Baskervilles* in 1959 has weathered well.

John Neville, pictured with Robert Morley playing Mycroft and Donald Houston as Watson in *A Study in Terror,* was one of several Holmeses to take on Jack the Ripper.

Robert Stephens endured a torrid time playing Holmes in *The Private Life of Sherlock Holmes.* He attempted to talk Jeremy Brett out of taking on the role several years later.

cut a rather ageing figure opposite John Mills's Watson in *The Masks of Death.* Similarly, Sir Christopher Lee, who had played Sir Henry for Hammer, would later have a go as an older Holmes, alongside Patrick Macnee in *Sherlock Holmes: The Golden Years* in 1992.

Several cinema productions of the 1960s and '70s played up the horror element. The Conan Doyle estate was a driving force behind the production of 1965's *A Study in Terror,* which pitted Holmes against Jack the Ripper in a film clearly influenced by the Hammer studios. John Neville played a nicely nuanced Holmes, although Donald Houston as Watson was a little on the wishy-washy side. Much more unsettling was *Murder by Decree,* which appeared in 1979 and again saw Jack the Ripper as Holmes's nemesis. The storyline was based on a then popular trend in Ripper research that suggested involvement in the murders at the highest levels of society. Christopher Plummer was a fine Holmes (admired by Jeremy Brett) and James Mason a good Watson. The film created a rich air of tension and David Hemmings as Lestrade was particularly haunting.

The 1970s also saw a move towards intimately probing the personality of Holmes. The decade started with Billy Wilder's landmark *The Private Life of Sherlock Holmes,* most notable for the extraordinarily fragile performance of Robert Stephens in the lead role. The film almost did for Stephens, whose relationship with Wilder was at best strained. Stephens's marriage to Maggie Smith was also in freefall and at one stage during shooting he was taken to hospital after consuming a volume of sleeping pills with whisky. The implicit suggestion of a physical relationship between Holmes and Watson (played by Colin Blakely) caused inevitable outrage but the film provides a generally affectionate portrait of the two men. It has stood up well against the tides of time, despite an overreliance on sideshow attractions including a group of itinerant midgets and a faked-up Loch Ness monster. 1974 saw the release of *The Seven-Per-Cent Solution*, based on Nicholas Meyer's mega-selling novel that provided a (literally) Freudian analysis of Holmes's drug dependency. The film had a stellar cast, with Nicol Williamson as Holmes, Robert Duvall doing a preposterous English accent as Watson, Laurence Olivier as Moriarty, Alan Arkin playing an understated Freud and Vanessa Redgrave as an Irene Adler-inspired character. Never before had Holmes been seen in quite such a state of collapse but the film helped pave the way for Holmes to be regarded as more than simply a deerstalker and pipe.

For all his leading man credentials, Stewart Granger's turn as Holmes in a 1972 TV movie version of *The Hound* did not capture the popular imagination.

In 1978 Peter Cook reimagined Holmes as a bumbling fool of Jewish extraction while Dudley Moore played Watson as a crazed Welshman. For their version of *The Hound of the Baskervilles*, they gathered together some of the finest comedy actors Britain had ever produced. The roll-call included Denholm Elliott, Joan Greenwood, Irene Handl, Terry Thomas, Max Wall, Kenneth Williams, Roy Kinnear, Penelope Keith and Prunella Scales. The result was cringeworthy. Kenneth Williams summed things up succinctly in his diaries when he wrote that the script was a 'hotch-potch of rubbish'. If this film was the nadir, it followed in a long line of failed comedy takes on Holmes, who seems to have inspired some of the world's greatest comic minds to some of their worst work. The likes of Buster Keaton, Laurel and Hardy, the Marx Brothers, the Three Stooges, and Abbott and Costello had all attempted to release the humour, with varying degrees of success.

Though not a comedy, *Sherlock Holmes in New York* had a few unintentional laughs in 1976, with the arch Roger Moore playing Holmes and Patrick Macnee doing little for the cause of Dr Watson. John Cleese and Arthur Lowe sent up the crime-fighting duo in 1977's *The Strange Case of the End of Civilization as We Know It*, which did somewhat redeem itself with a scene in which Watson reads a series of crossword clues to Holmes. '1 Across. A simple source of citrus fruit, 1, 5, 4,' says Watson, to which Holmes replies, 'A lemon tree, my dear Watson.' 1988's *Without a Clue* made a better stab at the comic side of Holmes, with Michael Caine starring as an actor employed to play the Great Detective, who is actually a creation of Ben Kingsley's Watson, the brains behind the operation. While not universally loved and at times a little laboured, it at least had a promising premise.

The 1980s began with one of Britain's finest actors, Ian Richardson, taking on the role of Holmes for the American producer Sy Weintraub. Though perhaps on the short side, Richardson was physically well suited to the part and displayed the precision and charisma he brought to all his roles. Yet the two films he made (*The Sign*

Brett's close study of Conan Doyle's original stories and Sidney Paget's illustrations helped him create a performance that defined Holmes for a generation.

of Four and *The Hound of the Baskervilles*) lacked dynamism as a whole and were somewhat hamstrung by the 'deerstalker and curved pipe' feel that the American market demanded. Nor were things improved by swapping the Watson of David Healy for that of Donald Churchill, with whom Richardson did not get on. The death knell for the project was the news that Granada Television, taking advantage of the expiration of copyright on the stories, was planning to film the whole lot. In different circumstances it is quite possible that Richardson might have been a great Sherlock Holmes, had he chosen to devote such a hefty chunk of his prestigious career to the role. As it was, he went on to play Joseph Bell in the BBC's *Murder Rooms* series of the early 2000s. In it we saw Bell crime-solving with the able assistance of his student, Arthur Conan Doyle. The idea was an interesting one and well executed, with Richardson giving yet another bravura performance in films that were ultimately more satisfying than his outings as Holmes. Meanwhile in the Soviet

Union Vassily Livanov starred in a much respected series of Holmes films from 1979 to 1986 that proved the Detective could transcend even the Iron Curtain.

Back in the UK, the Granada series that usurped Weintraub's project would be – for many – the definitive take on Sherlock Holmes, blessed with stunning performances, (mostly) faithful and credible writing and an unsurpassed evocation of Holmes's England. The series, the brainchild of producer Michael Cox, ran for forty-one episodes between 1984 and 1994 with inevitable lows as well as highs. The original fifty-minute format which so suited the stories was seriously overstretched to twice the length in a number of specials. Equally, production responsibility moved between Michael Cox and June Wyndham Davies (and their very different visions) with too much regularity, while the vagaries of television saw initially lavish budgets sliced over time. For instance, the Swiss setting for 'The Disappearance of Lady Frances Carfax' was swapped for the cheaper option of the Lake District. Some of the later episodes were so distant from the series' early fidelity to Conan Doyle that they seemed hardly to belong to the same stable. The Gothic horror fluff of 'The Last Vampyre' and the utterly bewildering expressionism of 'The Eligible Bachelor' particularly spring to mind.

Nonetheless, the highs far outweighed the lows. And the highest highs were the performances of Jeremy Brett and of both of his Watsons. Brett was Eton-educated and his diction was honed by exercises he practised to overcome a childhood speech impediment. Blessed with dashing good looks, he was a familiar face on TV from the 1960s. In 1980 he appeared on stage as Watson opposite Charlton Heston's Holmes in *The Crucifer of Blood*. But it was Holmes he was born to play. No one else has come close to the seamless transitions from moroseness to ecstatic glee and back again that he perfected. His performance is full of nervous energy, fragility, strength and humour. Such was his commitment to faithfully echoing the Sherlock Holmes of the *Strand Magazine* that great effort was put into framing specific scenes so that they accurately recreated Sidney Paget's classic illustrations.

His Watson for the first thirteen episodes was played by David Burke, who redefined the character. No longer was the good doctor to be simply a buffoonish foil for Holmes. Instead he was a fully rounded, faithful, sturdy, insightful and amusing companion. When Burke quit, it was difficult to see how the loss could be overcome. Then, on Burke's personal recommendation, in stepped Edward Hardwicke who brought yet more layers of characterisation, even in productions of some of the weaker stories. The two of them laid to rest the ghost of Nigel Bruce that had for so long stifled Watson.

Brett, Burke and Hardwicke were supported by a remarkable cast of recurring actors, including Rosalie Williams as Mrs Hudson, Colin Jeavons as Lestrade, Charles Gray as Mycroft Holmes (a role he had already played in *The Seven-*

Per-Cent Solution) and Eric Porter as Moriarty. Such were the series' production values that the cream of the British acting scene were eager to appear. The roll-call included the likes of Cheryl Campbell, Robert Hardy, Roy Hudd, Jenny Seagrove, John Thaw and even a young, dragged-up Jude Law, to name but a handful.

It has been well documented that Brett was very unwell for a large part of the series. Suffering from bipolar disorder (which surely informed his understanding of Holmes's own wild mood swings), he lost his wife in 1985 and descended into a spiral of depression. He would also develop serious heart problems and the combination of drugs he was prescribed for both his physical and mental ailments often conflicted. One very visible side effect, which Brett particularly hated, was the puffiness and bloating which took him away from his ideal of Holmes, particularly in later episodes.

As time went on, Brett appeared to be drowning under the responsibility of playing Holmes. His friend Robert Stephens, who himself had had such a torrid time in *The Private Life of Sherlock Holmes*, once tried to talk Brett out of ever taking the part. Shortly before his death from heart failure in September 1995, Brett would describe Holmes as the hardest role of his life, harder even than Hamlet or Macbeth. 'Holmes has become the dark side of the moon for me,' he would say. 'It has all got too dangerous.' What remains is a landmark body of work that may never be bettered.

The 1980s and 1990s saw an increasingly wide array of television series bringing Holmes in for cameo appearances. Everything from *Star Trek* to the 'Muppets' to *Magnum, P.I.* got in on the act. Several productions looked to give the Detective more child-appeal. In 1982 (the year Tom Baker acted in an unsatisfying *Hound of the Baskervilles*), Granada ran a gentle series called *Young Sherlock*, while the following year the Irregulars accompanied Sunday teatimes in *The Baker Street Boys*. Then in 1985 Steven Spielberg produced *Young Sherlock Holmes*, with Nicholas Rowe a sterling teenage Holmes. Going 'off-canon', the plot has Holmes and Watson meeting as schoolchildren but the screenwriters had clearly read their Conan Doyle and inserted plenty of knowing jokes. Despite a few jolting Hollywoodisms and a bike-riding scene lifted clean out of *E.T.*, it is overall an enjoyable romp. The kids were to get a further look-in with 2007's *Baker Street Irregulars*, in which Jonathan Pryce appeared as Holmes. There was also an animated series, *Sherlock Holmes in the 22nd Century*, which ran from 1999 to 2001.

Perhaps unsurprisingly, in the wake of the Granada series other actors struggled to make the role of Holmes their own. In 1990 Edward Woodward and John Hillerman teamed up as Holmes and Watson in *Hands of a Murderer*, but the chemistry wasn't there and Woodward looks too much like a bruiser to convincingly pull the role off. The following year Charlton Heston played the lead role in a film version of Paul Giovanni's successful stage play *The Crucifer in the Blood*. Then, in the early 2000s, Matt Frewer took on the mantle for a series of Canadian films. They never quite hit the mark and it was difficult for the viewer to fully dislocate Holmes from one of Frewer's earlier creations, Max Headroom.

In 2002, *Sherlock – Case of Evil* saw James D'Arcy and Roger Morlidge in the lead roles, a rare occurrence of young twenty-something actors being given the opportunity. They were supported by a glamorous Gabrielle Anwar, while Richard E. Grant stepped in as Mycroft. Also in 2002 Grant appeared as Stapleton in a BBC version of *The Hound of the Baskervilles*. Richard Roxburgh was Holmes and in the early scenes hinted at a punchy and witty portrayal but there was a lack of development during the course of the film. Ian Hart offered an unusually spiky and angry Watson, a role he reprised in *The Case of the Silk Stocking* in 2004. Roxburgh's role did not attract great praise and he was unwilling to go through the process again, so Rupert Everett came in as Holmes. He did a reasonable job but is intrinsically too pretty for the role. Of Holmes and Watson, it was the latter who seemed to have most about him, which is not the way it should be. For many the question remains why Richard E. Grant is yet to be promoted from supporting player to the main man.

Then towards the end of the first decade of the twenty-first century, something quite remarkable and unexpected happened: Sherlock Holmes suddenly became cool. A series of Hollywood films plus two new television interpretations (one each from the UK and US) introduced the Great Detective to a new generation.

First to market in 2009 was the Guy Ritchie-directed *Sherlock Holmes* movie, starring Robert Downey Jr as Holmes and Jude Law as Watson. For those versed in Ritchie's back catalogue of violent, lary, Mockney dramas, there were some initial alarm bells. In fact, the film was not only the biggest commercial success of his career thus far, it was arguably his most impressive artistic achievement.

Downey Jr was nothing short of a revelation in the lead. Having previously played Charlie Chaplin, there were no worries about his handling the accent but no one could have predicted how completely he would inhabit the character. But perhaps it should not have been such a surprise for, as the actor himself noted, Holmes is 'quirky and kind of nuts – it could be a description of me'. Law was an admirable Watson too, exploring the too-often ignored depths of the good doctor and steering well clear of the 'bumbling sidekick' act that it would have been so easy to produce. Few of those who remember seeing the young Law playing opposite Jeremy Brett could have predicted that this lay ahead.

Downey Jr's Holmes stares down Jared Harris's Professor James Moriarty in Guy Ritchie's 2011 movie, *Sherlock Holmes: A Game of Shadows* (the follow up to 2009's *Sherlock Holmes*).

Jude Law as Watson (left) and Robert Downey Jr as Holmes (right) have so far appeared in two Guy Ritchie-directed movies. But even the greatest crime-fighting duo in history sometimes need to stop for a cup of tea and a biscuit.

There was much else to admire, including clever use of slow-motion action sequences accompanied by an artful interior monologue, plus a liberal sprinkling of genuine comedy (the movie received several award nominations in comedy categories). Ritchie did a great job of evoking 1890s London too, while the casting also deserves mention. A great supporting cast included Rachel McAdams as a feisty Irene Adler, Kelly Reilly as a luminous Mary Morstan, Eddie Marsan giving one of the most memorable Lestrade performances, and Mark Strong as the menacing Lord Henry Blackwood.

There were imperfections – notably a slightly overblown plot that owed a little too much to James Bond for this writer, and some wilful misrepresentation of London geography. But overall this was a fine Hollywood return for Holmes. It was backed up two years later with the release of *Sherlock Holmes: A Game of Shadows*, with all of the principals still in place. Critical judgement was split as to whether this was an improvement on the first film. The element of surprise was, naturally, less but the story was arguably stronger. Regardless, it did good enough business that a third film in the series remains on the cards.

Hot on the heels of the first Ritchie movie came a TV series, *Sherlock*, from the BBC. Created by Mark Gatiss and Steven Moffat, both of whom had built reputations for devising (and in Gatiss's case, performing in) unmissable and idiosyncratic television shows, it was nothing short of a revelation. If Jeremy Brett's Holmes provided the last word in reproducing the character as he was created by Conan Doyle, *Sherlock* is unmatched in reinventing him.

Following the tradition started in earnest by the Rathbone films, the action is moved to the present day. Nor are the writers afraid to play fast and loose with the characters we thought we knew. This Sherlock wears nicotine patches instead of smoking a pipe, for instance, and embraces modern-world technology – but then, as Gatiss has argued, Conan Doyle's Holmes utilised cutting-edge scientific developments too. And for all the bold invention of *Sherlock*, the writers are always respectful of the heritage, which they clearly know inside-out. Every episode is jammed full of witty references. Consider some of the episode titles: 'A Study in Pink', 'A Scandal in Belgravia', 'The Empty Hearse'. Indeed, if there is a criticism to be levelled at the production, it is that sometimes the *homage*-ing can occasionally get in the way of the action.

But the clever writing would be for nothing if it were not accompanied by extraordinary performances. Take the eponymous star, Benedict Cumberbatch, who took the role as a respected young actor and quickly found himself a global superstar. All brooding moodiness one moment and manic energy the next, he has become the poster boy of geek-sexiness. Meanwhile, Martin Freeman (so lovable as Tim in the era-defining comedy, *The Office*) cements his place as Britain's favourite everyman. His depiction of Watson – as a troubled Afghan war vet who is simultaneously infuriated by and bound to Holmes – is pitch-perfect.

All of which is to mention nothing of the beautiful performances from Mark Gatiss as Mycroft Holmes (breathing deserved life into a character never quite given his wings by Conan Doyle), Una Stubbs as the demure Mrs Hudson with a colourful past (her husband was executed by the State of Florida!), Andrew Scott as quite the most captivating Moriarty I can remember and Rupert Graves as the enjoyably nuanced DI Greg Lestrade.

The result was nothing short of a phenomenon. The series attracted gigantic audiences and sold around the world. More notably, it caught the public imagination and had armies of people exploring the world of Holmes for the first time. At the start of Series 3,

Although bringing Holmes definitively into the twenty-first century, the BBC's *Sherlock* never forgets its roots. Here Sherlock and John are seen in their somewhat chaotic rooms on Baker Street.

Benedict Cumberbatch as Sherlock (left) and Martin Freeman as John Watson (right) have shone a light on to the Great Detective that has helped draw a brand new generation of fans to Conan Doyle's greatest hero.

speculation as to how Sherlock had survived his apparent death at the end of the previous series not only drove conversation around the fabled 'water cooler' but even featured on current affairs programmes.

Next came *Elementary* from America, a series created by Robert Doherty and first shown in late 2012 on the CBS channel. When news of the production emerged, it seemed designed to shock and appal fans of classical Holmes everywhere. Like the BBC version, *Elementary* is set in the present day but in addition, the action had been moved out of London and into New York. Gasp! And if all that were not enough, Dr John Watson had been reconfigured as Dr Joan Watson, played by the glamorous Lucy Liu. An actor less like Nigel Bruce would be hard to imagine. In a further twisting of the original tales, Liu's Watson has been employed by Holmes's father to serve as a paid companion to the post-rehab Sherlock, played by Johnny Lee Miller. (There is also some interesting adaptation of the roles of Moriarty, Irene Adler and Mrs Hudson to get to grips with!)

For the purists, there was yet more insult to add to the injury – *Elementary* turned out to be really quite good. Miller and Liu have undeniable chemistry and give us an edgy lead pairing. Before long, you even forget that Watson is a *woman*. Instead, she is simply Holmes's foil. If the series lacks some of the flamboyance of *Sherlock*, it has plenty of clever plot twists and feeds into a grand tradition of American detective dramas, offering a darkness and gritiness that its British counterpart perhaps lacks. At the time of writing in 2014, there were already 42 episodes to delight an audience that surely includes a few who enjoy it despite themselves.

It is official then – Sherlock Holmes lives.

THE ADVENTURE OF
THE THREE GARRIDEBS

FIRST PUBLISHED: The *Strand Magazine*, January 1925, UK; *Collier's*, October 1924, USA
SETTING DATE: 1902

ONE OF THE more intriguing titles in the canon. One Nathan Garrideb has made contact with Holmes concerning some very specific business proposed to him by a Mr John Garrideb. The latter is rather put out that a detective has become involved in the affair, though he does decide he might be able to make use of Holmes. So it is that we first meet John, an American dwelling in London.

It seems that back in Kansas a property magnate by the name of Alexander Hamilton Garrideb has died and left a rather playful will. Aware of the rarity of his name, he has provided for his estate to be divided three ways to three men called Garrideb, should three such people be traced. John has tracked down one other Garrideb, Holmes's client Nathan who lives in London. But they cannot muster another male relative between them. Holmes at once smells a rat. It does not require his fullest intellectual reasoning to suspect that all is not as it seems in such an outlandish story.

It appears the case will come to a sudden close when John reports that he has received notification from an agent in Birmingham about a builder of agricultural machinery called Howard Garrideb. Convinced a fellow Englishman will receive a better reception than an itinerant American, John persuades Nathan to make the trip to the Midlands on their behalf. Yet events in London take a dramatic turn in Nathan's absence. Dr Watson suffers a gunshot wound (an affliction to which he is rather prone) and Holmes endearingly expresses deep concern for his companion.

In this story it is noted that Holmes has rejected a knighthood for unspecified reasons. At around the time that the story is set, Conan Doyle was reluctantly accepting one. Additionally, Holmes's first documented use of the phone gives the tale a distinctly 'twentieth-century' feel.

HORACE HOVAN,
ALIAS LITTLE HORACE,
BANK SNEAK.

AUGUSTUS RAYMOND,
ALIAS GUS RAYMOND,
SNEAK AND FORGER.

FRANK BUCK,
ALIAS BUCKY TAYLOR,
BANK SNEAK.

Holmes consulted Scotland Yard's rogues' gallery, a collection of mug shots of wanted men. Allan Pinkerton, the famous American detective, is credited with devising the rogues' gallery.

THE ADVENTURE OF THE ILLUSTRIOUS CLIENT

FIRST PUBLISHED: The *Strand Magazine*, February–March 1925, UK; *Collier's*, November 1924, USA

SETTING DATE: 1902

A STORY WITH no mystery but nonetheless a true test of Holmes's skills. The tale opens with Holmes and Watson spending some quality time together in a Turkish bath (though Holmes has inexplicably kept his coat with him). The Detective is soon approached by Sir James Damery, who is representing an unnamed third party (the 'illustrious client' of the title). He wants Holmes to somehow extricate one Violet de Merville from her proposed marriage to Baron Gruner, a truly devilish cad.

Holmes dislikes his client's secrecy but the chance to lock horns with a dangerous Continental lothario from the higher orders is too much to resist. In a heated stand-off, he fails to persuade the Baron to do the decent thing and break off the engagement so instead he attempts to make his fiancée see sense. Holmes is accompanied by Kitty Winter, who has known first-hand the Baron's cruelty and is determined to save another from the same fate. Violet proves to be a rather silly young thing, blinded to the truth by love and generally unsympathetic.

The Baron's pledge to take action should Holmes insist on interfering in his private matters turns out to be no empty promise. Watson is distraught to see the newspapers reporting a murderous attack on Holmes, who it seems is unlikely to see out the week. Yet driven by his desire to defeat an enemy, Holmes sets Watson off on a project to master the history of Chinese ceramics. But while Holmes has in mind one particular conclusion to the drama, Kitty Winter is cooking up a finale all of her own.

The horse-drawn hansom cab came into use during the 1830s and has become one of the enduring symbols of Sherlock Holmes's London. Their popularity was in terminal decline by the 1920s, though.

THE ADVENTURE OF THE THREE GABLES

FIRST PUBLISHED: The *Strand Magazine*, October 1926, UK; *Liberty*, September 1926, USA

SETTING DATE: 1902

STEVE DIXIE, A none-too-bright thug in the pay of one Barney Stockdale, bursts into 221B and throws his weight around as he warns Holmes against interfering in some business in Harrow. Holmes wrong-foots him by revealing that he knows of Dixie's involvement in the death of a certain Perkins outside the Holborn Bar.

Prior to the interruption, Holmes had received a missive from a Mary Maberley of the Three Gables, Harrow Weald. So it is that Holmes knows Stockdale must somehow be involved. He heads to Harrow Weald where he discovers that Mrs Maberley's son, Douglas – an attaché in Rome – has recently died of pneumonia. His *joie de vivre* had been replaced by a dark cynicism before he died, apparently the result of a broken heart.

Mrs Maberley has lived a quiet life at the Three Gables for over a year. Then recently a man offered to buy the property, despite several similar houses being on the market. Asked to name her price, she hit upon a rather inflated £500. The man agreed on condition that he have the entire contents too. Legally forbidden to remove anything, she got cold feet and pulled out of the deal.

Holmes discovers that a maid, Susan, has been eavesdropping on their conversation. It

Holmes as featured on a silk cigarette card from John Player & Son's 1933 Characters from Fiction series.

emerges that she is in league with Stockdale and she reveals that he has been employed by a rich woman. Realising that this woman is interested in the contents of the house and not the property itself, Holmes hits upon the theory that Douglas's recently returned belongings must hold the key.

Holmes leaves to consult Langdale Pike, a famous society gossip. He returns to the house the following day after hearing it has been burgled, the thieves stealing a manuscript from Douglas's baggage. As his mother tried to stop them, she was chloroformed but managed to grab a page of the document. Upon inspection it appears to be the end of a sensationalist novel, which strangely turns from the third person to the first. Holmes realises this is a classic case of *cherchez la femme* and soon seizes upon the culprit, as well as winning some hefty compensation for the put-upon Mrs Maberley.

The unflattering and rather patronising depiction of Steve Dixie, a black man, has seen charges of racism levelled at this tale.

THE ADVENTURE OF THE BLANCHED SOLDIER

FIRST PUBLISHED: The *Strand Magazine*, November 1926, UK; *Liberty*, October 1926, USA
SETTING DATE: 1903

SOMETHING OF A curiosity. The story is one of only two narrated by Holmes, who bemoans the absence of his biographer Watson and at last acknowledges that Watson's dramatic flair rather adds something to the tales. 'The Blanched Soldier' counts among the small collection of mysteries in which there is no criminal activity.

Holmes is approached by James Dodd, a fine fellow recently returned from the Boer War. He wants help in tracing Godfrey Emsworth, his former companion with whom he has lost contact since leaving South Africa. Dodd is concerned some ill has befallen Emsworth and his suspicions are fuelled by the evasive and unfriendly responses he has received from Emsworth's parents (and particularly his father, the Colonel) when enquiring as to their son's well-being. Then, while staying at the Emsworth residence in Bedfordshire, Dodd is sure he has seen the spectral figure of his old friend peering through his window late at night. Dodd's further investigations prompt the Colonel to throw him off the property.

Holmes and an esteemed colleague, Sir James Saunders, accompany Dodd back to Bedfordshire. A quick sniff of a pair of gloves owned by Ralph the butler assures Holmes that he has unravelled the case. He hands the Colonel a piece of paper on which is written a single word and the Colonel is forced to confirm Holmes's hypothesis. The potentially tragic narrative finishes with a happy twist.

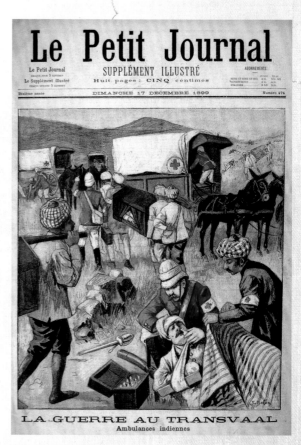

This 1899 edition of *Le Petit Journal*, a Parisian newspaper, gave its readership a hint of the horrors to be found on the frontline of the Boer War.

HOLMES AND ME 🔍 MARK GATISS

A performer, writer and producer, Mark Gatiss rose to fame in the late 1990s as part of the macabre comedy troupe, The League of Gentlemen. *He has appeared extensively on stage, screen and radio in an array of roles, has written a series of novels starring his spy creation, Lucifer Box, and realised a childhood dream by joining the* Doctor Who *team in 2005. In 2010 the BBC premiered* Sherlock, *the smash-hit series starring Benedict Cumberbatch and Martin Freeman that Gatiss co-created with Steven Moffat. Gatiss also appears in the series as Sherlock's brother, Mycroft.*

When did Holmes first come into your life?

I was thinking about this only recently. My sister-in-law has started working in my old primary school and asked me if I would come and talk to the kids. It was a lovely experience but so weird to be back in the same classroom. I suddenly remembered that I did a painting of Sherlock Holmes that was put up on the wall there and labelled 'The Great Detective'! I must have been about seven I think. Because I'd just seen *The Hound of the Baskervilles* with Rathbone. It was the first Holmes I ever saw.

I have vivid memories of first seeing *The Private Life of Sherlock Holmes* [Billy Wilder's 1970 movie], which was an immediate favourite and still my favourite Holmes movie. After that, I mopped up any Sherlock Holmes I could get hold of. I very much remember the Christopher Plummer and Thorley Walters version of *Silver Blaze* [1977] and John Cleese in *The Strange Case of the End of Civilisation as We Know It* [also 1977]. I was just mad about it! But I didn't actually read the stories until I was off school with German measles and I got the *Adventures*. The edition with the Eric Ambler introductions, which I still have. He said, 'I wish I were reading these stories for the first time,' and I was so excited by the fact that I was.

And then a little bit later I bought the *Complete Sherlock Holmes*. I was possessed by this idea that it

Mark Gatiss makes for a considerably more svelte Mycroft than the one Conan Doyle depicted in his original pen-portraits of Sherlock's brother.

would be really cool to say I had read all of them! So I read them all over a summer holiday. I just loved the whole creation. The characters, the atmosphere, the weirdness of the stories, the fun of it all. And then the Brett series arrived and I was at that sort of age where fidelity to the original stories seemed very important. For some reason I had it in my head that Nigel Havers had been cast as Holmes so when I saw the first trailer and saw Jeremy Brett in *The Speckled Band* wearing that pale blue, close-fitting clothe cap and he turned round – I thought 'My God! So exciting'. So it's been a lifelong love affair in all its permutations.

Do you have any particular favourite stories?

The Red-Headed League. The Blue Carbuncle. The Yellow Face. Oh so many. But particularly *The Bruce-Partington Plans.* It's just the most wonderful story. In Christopher Morley's introduction to the Penguin *Complete* edition, he talks about the later stories not being in the same league. But he says about *The Bruce-Partington Plans,* 'does not the light shine brightly again' or something like that. And it does.

I always had a fondness for the slightly more obscure stories, ones where Holmes got things wrong and so on. Like most Sherlock fans, you end up re-reading bits of them. *The Adventures* are still my favourites not just because they were the first ones I read but because they seem to be one brilliant idea after another. Just bursting with invention. It's not too much to say Doyle was a genius. As a short story writer, possibly the best we've ever produced. He was amazingly economical, deft, funny and thrilling. There's that wonderful bit in *The Yellow Face* when Grant Munro says: 'I am not a very good man, Effie, but I think that I am a better one than you have given me credit for being.' That still makes me cry. And he was quick! The fact that there aren't more of those amusing continuity errors is astonishing.

Did Holmes influence your work pre-Sherlock.

Yes. I've always prided myself on a certain facility for pastiching periods. Particularly the Victorians. I adore Dickens. I learned my moral code from Jon Pertwee but my sense of adventure comes from Sherlock Holmes! Of course, the Victorian Chinnery story in the *The League of Gentlemen Christmas Special* is totally Doyle, with perhaps a bit of Saki thrown in. That idea of Eastern mysticism – the curse of the monkey's bollocks! – all that stuff is very Doyle. And on the DVD I did a *Jackanory* style retelling of the original story which I wrote for the League book and that was entirely meant as a *Strand Magazine* pastiche, complete with a deduction that's entirely wrong.

With *Sherlock*, we've resisted any attempts to do novelizations. It's vital that people go back to Doyle. I'd love to do a pastiche story though. Maybe one day. What I need is a magazine to commission me! If *Colliers* still exists… Or the

New Strand… It would be quite daunting but I'd love to have a go.

Was it always the plan to update Sherlock *to the present day?*

I've known Steven Moffat for 20 years and when we were working on the first series of *Doctor Who* together, we always ended up on the same trains back and forth to Cardiff. In my mind now, it's like the famous Paget illustration! We often talked about Sherlock Holmes and at some point we had a very careful exploratory conversation about the fact that we loved Rathbone and Bruce the best. And actually the ones we really liked were the heretical ones that brought it all up to date.

A film like *The Spider Woman* is outrageous. Fifty-nine minutes of the most fun you'll ever have watching a film. But it's only as outrageous as Doyle would have been. It's films like that, precisely because they're B Movies and they're written by people who love the subject that seem to have more of the brio and the real sense of adventure and fun of the original stories than a lot of more 'careful' adaptations.

In a light bulb moment I said to Steve, isn't it odd that Dr Watson was invalided home from the Afghan War and here we are in the middle of it again – essentially the same, unwinnable war? We looked at each other and said 'Someone should do that then talked about it for four years. It seems ridiculous now but we did nothing about it. Eventually, Steve mentioned it to his wife Sue Vertue and she said, 'Why aren't you doing it then?' It was like we didn't work in television or something!

We then had the easiest pitch in TV history. I know I'll never be fortunate enough to have another one like it in my career. We went to see Julie Gardner who was then head of drama at BBC Wales. We sat down and she said, 'Modern Sherlock Holmes? Yes.' That was it!

Of course, the actual process of making it was a little harder but one thing that was useful was the series *House*. There was a modern precedent, if you like. The only real resistance we got once we started working on it was that Sherlock isn't really *very nice*. And we could just say, 'But look at *House*' (which is implicitly Sherlock Holmes). The reason people love it is because he is such a bastard. I think if we hadn't have had that it might have taken a bit more convincing to let us do it our way. But it was really comparatively straightforward.

After the initial excitement ideas just tumbled over each other. Of course, the two principals should still live in a flat in Baker Street but people might now assume that they were a couple. That would be fun (and, again the Wilder film had explored this idea so beautifully). Heretically, they would have to call each other Sherlock and John. Holmes and Watson would be ridiculous-sounding in the 21st century. That took a bit of getting used to. Then it became slightly stickier. Where would Sherlock fit into our world? In the original stories he was essentially the father of forensics but now such things are routine. So what makes him special?

Of course his speciality is omniscience. He's the only one who will ever be able to make those connections. It doesn't matter if the police are routinely handling the stuff he used to do – plaster casts or even DNA – he's the one who can look at someone's shirt collar and say 'I'm sorry your wife left you this morning.' It's like a magic trick. So as long as you ring-fence it, that's what makes him special. It's a super-power. Or an achievable super-power. When you read him as a kid you think, 'Maybe I could do that.' There's that lovely thrill of satisfaction when he explains how absurdly simple it is.

Was the casting a straightforward process?
Benedict was the only person we considered. I knew him a little as we'd done a film together and *Atonement* had come out and Steven and Sue had just watched that. We had a conversation and it was just sort of perfect. OK, he doesn't have the nose! In fact, when he told his mother that he'd got the part, she said, 'You have a little button nose, darling, you can't possibly do it.' But he has the angularity, the cheekbones, a Byronic look. And, of course, he's brilliant.

Finding Dr Watson was a little more involved because we already had Sherlock and it was a question of finding the chemistry. But it's an intangible thing that you know when you see it. Then Martin Freeman came along. His first audition didn't go very well, actually. He'd just had his wallet stolen so he wasn't in the right place mentally, as it were. But he asked to come back and simply knocked it out of the park. Steve lent over to me and said, 'There's the show.' They had immediate chemistry as people and Benedict's game rose straight away.

From the very beginning we tried to give John Watson something to chew on. *Sherlock* is very much a co-lead show. Much as we love Nigel Bruce, one of the marvellous things about the original stories is that there's no sense that Watson is stupid. He's a very good doctor. And Lestrade, too, is the best of the Scotland Yarders. But none of them are Sherlock Holmes. That's the crucial thing. Holmes would be an idiot if he surrounded himself with idiots. But he doesn't. They may not be on the same intellectual plane as him but they're good, bright, dependable people. It was very important to us to make sure that John Watson had a good story and an ongoing one. There needs to be proper development. As Doyle himself found, you can't continue with Watson just being constantly astonished.

And were you always going to be Mycroft?
That came about in a funny way. We were originally going to write six hour-long episodes but when the commission came through it was for three ninety-minute episodes. We had to reimagine much larger stories which could incorporate more. So we had this idea to present Mycroft so the viewers expect him to be Moriarty. And it worked!

I had auditioned for the part of Peter Mandelson in the Mo Mowlam drama [2010's *Mo*, starring Julie Walters]. I came back from that to have a meeting with Steve and Steve Thompson [another writer on the series]. We'd already talked about how much like Mandelson our Mycroft should be and Steve Thompson said, 'You should play him.' And of course I said, 'Oh, I couldn't possibly…' Like Richard III, I refused the crown a few times!

My performance is directly inspired by Christopher Lee's wonderful Mycroft in Billy Wilder's *Private Life*. What they did was what we like to think Doyle might have done if he'd written a third Mycroft story. That is to give the brothers a spiky relationship which was much more interesting than him just being avuncular and lazy and fat. You do get these wonderful hints that he *is* the British government but what Wilder and Diamond [screenwriter I. A. L. Diamond] did was to make him more sinister. There's the wonderful stuff in the film about unrest in the Himalayas and the Diogenes Club suddenly show up looking for the Abominable Snowman! It's very funny but it's sort of plausible. The idea that Mycroft is so Establishment but actually, in a slightly sinister way, pulling the strings. It increasingly resonates in the current climate.

Did the phenomenal response to Sherlock *take you by surprise?*
Very much so. We were extremely proud of it and hoped it would catch on but it's amazing what a phenomenon it's become. It's very flattering but we've still only made nine episodes! It's extraordinary. I've just been to Brazil to promote it and the response was extraordinary. Russia, China, Korea… everywhere.

Of course, it's partly because Benedict's Sherlock has become a sex symbol. In a funny way, the original Sherlock Holmes was. I don't think you can avoid the fact that Paget's illustrations made him more handsome than he was meant to be and those illustrations might have gone a long way to stirring some housemaids' hearts. That's part of it. But the thing I take most pride in is that people who know their Sherlock Holmes know that our series is born of love. There is nothing cynical about it. It's born out of the idea that he is a character who can go on and on and that the Victorian trappings are only that – trappings. Sherlock wasn't some sort of Luddite. He strained against the restrictions of his time. So that became an exciting thing. The idea of what would he be doing now.

Have you encountered any resentment towards the modernisation?
Hardly any. There was an initial disbelief that it would work and I'm always meeting people who start a sentence with 'I heard they were doing a modern Sherlock Holmes I thought I'd hate it…' But everyone was convinced almost immediately. There was a preview in the *Independent* newspaper which very snottily said that you can't have Sherlock Holmes without gas lamps and top

hats, so in protest the reviewer was going to go home and watch one of the Basil Rathbone's. And I thought, 'well you've got a choice of two out of those fourteen movies' because only two of them are set in the Victorian era! But after the show went out they published a retraction, which is very unusual.

The weird thing is that you think that most fan communities are conservative and inward-looking but I find Sherlock Holmes fans incredibly all-embracing. Maybe it's because there are so many Sherlock Holmes that they can't afford to be anything else! But as I said, what I am most proud of is that people know that we love it ourselves so they can enjoy the details the way that you do when you read the stories.

Around 2005 Stephen Fry took me as his guest when he addressed the Sherlock Holmes Society in the House of Commons. They asked me to do it the year after and the body of my speech was essentially Steven and my idea for *Sherlock* because by then we were already having discussions. And everyone told us it was a great idea so that gave us hope. Incidentally, I want to know if they [the Society's members] call themselves ulsters rather than anoraks…

Do you envisage Sherlock *as having a specific lifespan or will you just keep on going?*

We would love to. We're doing more but the dates of the shoots are difficult to plan. But we'd certainly like to continue. I saw Benedict the other day and he said he'd love to still be doing this when he's sixty. The idea of seeing Sherlock and John getting older is so intriguing. Eventually we might see them the way that Holmes and Watson are normally seen – in their 50s. Almost every version starts with them in Baker Street having known each other for years. But we've started right at the beginning of the friendship so there are vast tracts of the original that have never been touched. Beating the bodies in the dissection room which we put into 'A Study in Pink'. When I read that as child I thought it was the most electrifying thing. But has it ever been in a Sherlock Holmes adaptation before? But having the chance to start from the beginning, you regain that excitement. 'What on earth does this man do?' Steven and I are always saying that basically what happens to Dr Watson is that he falls down the rabbit hole. His world is just ordinary and then suddenly he meets this man and his perspectives just shift. Everything is different.

One thing we realised early on is that we couldn't just do a straightforward run of stories. Ninety-minute episodes are essentially movies and they need that scale and higher stakes. We couldn't really now do Sherlock, John and Mary in three nice adventures. It's intimidating but brilliant and we're all aware this is a special time. When it does come to an end we'll be able to look back on it with pride I hope. The reach of it and the massive popularity and the fun of it and think, well, for a time the keys to Baker Street were ours and we did right by Sherlock Holmes.

THE ADVENTURE OF THE LION'S MANE

FIRST PUBLISHED: The *Strand Magazine*, December 1926, UK; *Liberty*, November 1926, USA

SETTING DATE: 1907

THIS STORY IS narrated by Holmes, who has retired to the Sussex coast. Out one morning on a clifftop walk, he bumps into his friend Harold Stackhurst, headmaster of the Gables, and the two men are then confronted by Fitzroy McPherson, a science teacher at the school. Clearly in pain, he is wearing only trousers and a coat and as he collapses, dying, in front of them he mutters the words 'lion's mane' (following in the proud tradition of enigmatic final utterances *à la* 'Speckled Band'). On his body are a series of vicious-looking red welts.

Another member of staff then makes an appearance, the maths teacher Ian Murdoch, who claims not to have seen the attack. The only other people in the area are a couple of strangers, too far away to have perpetrated the wounds on McPherson, and some fishermen out at sea. Suspicion falls on Murdoch, a man with a short fuse who had once thrown McPherson's dog through a window, though the men were latterly friends. It later emerges that McPherson had taken a secret fiancée, Maud Bellamy, the daughter/sister of a pair of local businessmen.

An investigation of the pool where McPherson had been about to swim suggests that the dead man never made it into the water. Holmes and Stackhurst intend to question Bellamy but arrive at her home to discover that Murdoch has already been there. When Stackhurst demands an explanation, Murdoch refuses to cooperate and is instantly sacked. The male Bellamys have only just become aware of Maud's dalliance and are most unhappy.

It also emerges that Murdoch was once a rival for Maud, intensifying the suspicion upon him.

Later, McPherson's dog is found to have met a similarly grisly end to its owner and at the same spot too. Inspector Bardle, a local police officer, is preparing to arrest Murdoch but Holmes is less sure. Perhaps there is a clue in McPherson's final words? If only Watson were on hand, he might have helped Holmes seize upon the truth a little more rapidly.

An Edwardian gent in cutting-edge swimming gear, far removed from the modesty-preserving garb associated with the Victorians.

THE ADVENTURE OF
THE RETIRED COLOURMAN

FIRST PUBLISHED: The *Strand Magazine*, January 1927, UK; *Liberty*, December 1926, USA

SETTING DATE: 1889

Josiah Amberley is the sixty-one-year-old retired former employee of an artists' materials manufacturer. He engages Holmes to investigate the disappearance of his wife, twenty years his junior, who he claims has run off from their Lewisham home not only with the local doctor but also Amberley's life savings. And to think, Amberley only befriended the doctor to satisfy his need for a chess companion!

Is this simply 'the old story . . . a treacherous friend and a fickle wife', as Holmes initially suggests? Watson is sent off to Lewisham where he finds the Amberley house in a decrepit state, though Josiah was at least giving the place a new lick of paint. He also has a seemingly cast-iron alibi for the night of the disappearance, as he shows Watson a ticket stub for a seat at the theatre.

Then out of the blue a note arrives at 221B from a vicar in Essex who suggests he holds the key to the mystery. Despite initial reluctance, Amberley and Watson set off to investigate. Yet the real answer lies back in Lewisham as Holmes considers the question of the colourman and his paint. Though inevitably MacKinnon of the Yard gets all the credit.

The story also introduces us to a professional rival of Holmes, a private detective called Barker who is working for the family of the missing young doctor.

A humorous, and even slightly saucy, overview of the classic Holmes story structure that appeared in *Punch Magazine* in 1910.

THE ADVENTURE OF THE VEILED LODGER

FIRST PUBLISHED: The *Strand Magazine*, February 1927, UK; *Liberty*, January 1927, USA

SETTING DATE: 1896

AT THE START of this story Watson takes the opportunity to warn off those parties attempting to destroy documentation relating to 'the politician, the lighthouse, and the trained cormorant'. He then explains that the tale of the veiled lodger is an example of a human tragedy rather than an exposition of Holmes's powers of detection.

It begins with a visit from a buxom landlady of South Brixton called Mrs Merrilow. She is concerned about her lodger, Mrs Ronder, a woman who keeps her face permanently hidden and whose history is unknown. On the one occasion that Mrs Merrilow glimpsed her face, she saw it was horrifically mutilated. The landlady is increasingly worried about her for she is wasting away and has been heard crying out in the night. Her outbursts include 'Murder, murder!' and 'You cruel beast! You monster!'

At Mrs Merrilow's behest, Mrs Ronder agrees to tell her story to Holmes before she dies. She tells Merrilow to explain that she was the wife of Ronder (of the wild beast show) and to mention the name Abbas Parva. As she had predicted, Holmes understands the reference. It concerns an incident at Abbas Parva, a small Berkshire

A lion-tamer in an 1891 scene painted by Henri Meyer. The dare-devil performers were a firm favourite in travelling circuses and fairs.

village. Ronder was a great showman (and reputedly something of a drunk) and he or his wife would often put on performances in the cage of a North African lion. One night the lion apparently turned on its handlers. Ronder was killed, the back of his head crushed and his scalp clawed. Mrs Ronder was discovered with the lion over her, her face torn to pieces. Leonardo the strong man and Griggs the clown managed to force the beast back into its cage. Mrs Ronder screamed 'Coward!' as she was led back to her lodgings.

An inquest ruled misadventure but there were some curious features. What had caused the lion to suddenly turn? Why did it not make a bid for freedom? And what of the terrified shouts of a man heard when Ronder was already dead? Holmes and Watson set off to see Mrs Ronder. She reveals to them a marriage that was far from happy and tells a tale of illicit love and betrayal beneath the Big Top. Holmes does all he can to prevent another death.

THE ADVENTURE OF SHOSCOMBE OLD PLACE

FIRST PUBLISHED: The *Strand Magazine*, April 1927, UK; *Liberty*, March 1927, USA
SETTING DATE: 1902

HAVING HELPED MERIVALE of the Yard clear up a problem, Holmes turns his attentions to a case brought by John Mason, the trainer at Shoscombe Old Place racing stables in Berkshire. Its star act, Shoscombe Prince, is fancied for the Derby.

Holmes mines Watson's knowledge of the turf. The stables are owned by Lady Beatrice Falder and belonged to her husband, Sir James. On her death they will revert to his brother. She lives on the estate with her brother, Sir Robert Norberton, who has a reputation as an excellent jockey but a dangerous man with money worries. Watson recalls he once almost killed a moneylender at Newmarket. And now Mason suspects he is going mad.

Mason describes how Sir Robert spends vast amounts of time at the stables, wide-eyed from lack of sleep. There seems to have been a terrible bust-up with Lady Beatrice. She no longer shows any interest in her beloved Shoscombe Prince and he has shipped off the pet spaniel she adored to a local publican. The siblings no longer spend time together and she has taken to drink. He spends nights in the old crypt, where he has been spotted meeting a mysterious man. Mason and Stephens the butler have discovered the remains of an ancient mummified body in the crypt and some charred bone fragments beneath a furnace in the house. Things are further complicated by an apparent affair between Sir Robert and Carrie Evans, his sister's maid.

Holmes and Watson take up the investigation, arriving in Berkshire as keen anglers. They stay at the inn which is now home to the spaniel and take it for a walk to Shoscombe. There it enthusiastically meets its ex-mistress's carriage before fleeing in terror. An unexpected voice is heard from the carriage urging the driver on.

Holmes and Watson then discover the ancient human remains are missing from the crypt before an aggressive Sir Robert interrupts them. Holmes tells him that he largely knows what has occurred and Robert is left to fill in the gaps. Despite some unpalatable goings-on, a happy ending is close at hand.

Holmes and Watson crossing a particularly vibrant Baker Street, drawn by Danish illustrator Nis Jessen.

INDEX

The Adventure of the Missing Three Quarter.

We were fairly accustomed to receive weird telegrams at Baker Street but I have a particular recollection of ~~can remember~~ one which reached us on a gloomy February morning some seven or eight years ago and gave Mr. Sherlock Holmes a puzzled quarter of an hour. It was addressed to him and ran thus

"Please await me, Terrible misfortune, ~~Uncertain how to act~~. Right wing three quarter, ~~indispensable~~ missing, indispen tomorrow. Overton"

"Strand post mark and dispatched 10.36" said Holmes, reading it over and over. "Mr. Overton was evident considerably excited when he ~~dispatched~~ sent it and somewhat incoherent in consequence. Well, well, he will be here I dare say by ~~the time that the table is cleared~~ the time I have looked through the Times and then we shall know all about it. Even the most insignificant problem would be welcome in these stagnant times."

Things had indeed been very slow with us, and I had learned to dread such periods of inaction for I knew by experience that my companion's brain was so abnormally active that it was dangerous to leave it without material upon which to work. For years I had gradually weaned him from that drug mania which had threatened once to ~~destroy~~ check his remarkable nature. Now I knew that under ordinary conditions he no longer craved for this artificial stimulus but I was well aware that the fiend was not dead but sleeping, and I have known that the sleep was a light one and the waking near when in periods of